LAND ROVER

The Unbeatable 4x4

Fourth Edition

K & J Slavin with
G N Mackie and D McDine

Foulis

Haynes

®

..

First published, by Gentry Books Ltd, 1981
Second edition published 1984
Reprinted 1986, 1987 and 1988
Third edition published 1989
Reprinted 1991 and 1993
This edition published 1994
Reprinted 1996 and 1997

G. T. Foulis & Company is an imprint of Haynes Publishing,
Sparkford, Nr. Yeovil, Somerset BA22 7JJ

Tel: 01963 440635   Fax: 01963 440001
Int. tel: +44 1963 440635   Fax: +44 1963 440001

E-mail: sales@haynes-manuals.co.uk
Web site: http://www.haynes.com

Haynes Publications Inc.
861 Lawrence Drive, Newbury Park
California 91320 USA

British Library Cataloguing in Publication Data
A catalogue record for this book is
available from the British Library

ISBN 0 85429 950 5

Library of Congress catalog card number 93 80184

Printed and bound in Great Britain by
Butler & Tanner Ltd, Frome and London

Contents

Foreword
to the 4th Edition

By
John Towers
Chief Executive
Rover Group Limited

Over the last six years, since the end of the 1980s, all the major economies of the developed world have suffered from the worst recession since the Second World War. However, while most manufacturing industries in the UK and elsewhere were languishing in difficult trading conditions, Land Rover bucked the trend by increasing production and sales, and by recruiting additional employees.

Land Rover's success has been the result of carrying out proper market research, manufacturing the right products with the right quality, and by exploiting business opportunities in a variety of markets worldwide. At the heart of Land Rover's improved business performance has been the Land Rover Discovery in the fast-growing leisure sector of the four-wheel drive markets. In the latest edition of this book, Ken and Julie Slavin, both steeped in the Land Rover tradition, have dedicated a whole new chapter, 'The Discovery Story', to the development and success of this remarkable product that now accounts for half of all Land Rover's production. They have also taken a new look at our operations in North America where our subsidiary company, established in 1986, has vigorously promoted the Range Rover and is now enjoying even more success with the launch of the Discovery earlier this year.

This edition also includes a detailed new appraisal of Land Rover's military heritage in Chapter 3, 'Land Rover Conscripted'. Defender vehicles are in service with over 150 armies and military organisations around the world and have played major profile roles in the Gulf War and Bosnia.

The progress of the Range Rover, a legend since its launch in 1970, has not been forgotten and the all-new Range Rover, launched at Paris in October 1994, is also included in 'The Range Rover Story', Chapter 4. This new vehicle, packed with 4x4 pioneering innovations like its unique H-gate automatic transmission and its revolutionary rear suspension, is now spearheading a new world-wide drive to bring even greater success to Land Rover.

I have no doubt that Ken and Julie will be charting our progress for some years to come.

Foreword
to the 3rd Edition

By
J A Gilroy
Managing Director
Land Rover Group
1982 – 1988

The Land Rover is now firmly established as a part of British History. Time and time again it has shown beyond doubt to be the most durable 4 x 4 vehicle ever produced. The fact that 70 per cent of all Land Rovers ever built are still in use is evidence enough of the vehicle's longevity.

To some people the Land Rover is not just a vehicle – it's a way of life. And Ken and Julie Slavin fit into that category. In this edition they have painstakingly built on their previous works to bring their Land Rover story up to date in its 40th year. This meticulous research now tells the stories behind the Royal Land Rovers and they also record how the Company is rapidly accelerating product improvements on both Land Rovers and Range Rovers.

Ken and Julie have also recounted how we spent four years not only thoroughly researching the North American market but also improving the Range Rover product to meet the high expectation of potential American customers. For us the launch into the US market, a key export market for us, was a milestone in the Company's history.

Land Rover Limited is now a very different Company from the one it was a few years ago.

We rationalised our manufacturing facilities. This has involved closing down a dozen satellite component plants in the Midlands and transferring to the Solihull site 3,500 people carrying out 22,000 process operations. This major development has made us more efficient and has been carried out at the same time as we have invested in new technologies.

Solihull is now one of the most advanced vehicle manufacturing factories of its type. It is in good shape for the future and will enable us to further improve Land Rovers for the most important people in our business – the customers.

We believe we have a sound future and that the remarkable Land Rover will continue to play a key role in making our Company even more successful than in the past.

Introduction

For hundreds of miles around the terrain is scorched and unrelenting desert — volcanic mountains, immense slabs of cracked rock interspersed with scattered patches of sand, a lunar landscape in monotones of brown and grey. The only sound as we wait beside the deserted airstrip is the unfailing wind, until eventually the throb of an engine can dimly be sensed, and we know the aircraft is arriving. Then gleaming and shimmering through the haze of heat, it is bouncing gently towards us along the runway which is a glaring band of brightness in the harsh drabness all about.

It is 1969, in West Africa, and we are taking delivery of two prototypes of a 'revolutionary' new 4 x 4 design from the Land Rover factory – for a month's field testing in the toughest conditions we can find ...

No other freight or passengers are unloaded, just two vehicles veiled in paper, ungainly packages with only their wheels visible. Once they are unmasked, we are looking, of course, at the earliest Range Rovers. The murmurs of cautious confidence in the factory before its release hardly anticipated the enormous impact this vehicle was to make both nationally and internationally, nor that it was to mark the dawning of an era in the 4 x 4 market: here was a cunning combination of style and strength, comfort and ruggedness that had evolved as an inspired development from the Land Rover stable, while incorporating a V8 engine for greater power, and permanent 4-wheel drive, thus producing one of the world's most versatile vehicles – a Go-Anywhere car that was quickly to join the élite in motoring circles, and which, without the workaday Land Rover, could never have been.

So let's go back to the real beginning ...

Authors' note to the second edition
Recently we drove across to Solihull, in our 1950 Series I 80-inch Land Rover, to pick up a brand new automatic Range Rover from the factory to evaluate its performance. No one could fail to be struck by the extraordinary contrast in vehicles! Land Rover Ltd. has come a very long way in 35 years. Up-dating this book has been an interesting exercise as, since its first publication in 1981 and the materialization of the £200 million investment programme, Land Rover has evolved more than during the entire previous decade, and cataloguing the evolution has been a pleasure for all three of us.

Authors' note to the third edition
Since publication of the second edition of this book in 1984 time has by no means stood still for Land Rover. For this, the third, edition we have the opportunity to include a Foreword by the man who was Managing Director of Land Rover Limited from 1983 to 1988, Tony Gilroy.

This coincides – as aficionados cannot fail to be aware – with the 40th anniversary of the Land Rover, out of which the media has made plenty of mileage, comparing the original, post-Second World War vehicle with that of the late eighties and marvelling at the fact that, while practically every inch of the old Land Rover has been redesigned and modified, today it is still recognizable at once as belonging to the same family. In 1990 the Range Rover will be 20 years old and it, too, has been evolving with the times. In November 1986 it was finally ready to receive its American visa, and a UK launch was orchestrated by Land Rover's PR department for key American Press people (and their partners) which kicked off in the imposing Royal Geographical Society's building in Kensington. We were there, to show them the Range Rover's worth on expeditions, with the help of photographs of its earliest days, and then there was a guided tour of the RGS before the Americans disappeared in a cavalcade of new Range Rovers for America, to Eastnor in the West Country, then Scotland for a spot of shooting courtesy of Land Rover.

At the end of Chapter 4 Bill Baker, of Range Rover North America Inc, has contributed some observations of his own on the sort of reception the vehicle has had over there, and Geof Miller (Range Rover Project Engineer at Land Rover) has enlarged on several aspects of the Range Rover, pre- and post-launch (1970), as well as producing some rarely published photographs of prototypes for us.

At the end of The Special Projects Department (Chapter 2) we have included a description of its modern equivalent, Special Vehicles Operations, which came into being in 1985; this section is followed by a description of the 'Royal Land Rovers', contributed by Roger McCahey.

The threatened General Motors buy-out of the company earlier in 1986 led to heated debate, and a lively campaign to 'Keep Land Rover British'. There were demonstrations in Downing Street with Land Rovers sporting the Union Jack, and much talk of a management and workers buy-out as a preferable option. An impressive array of Land Rovers and Range Rovers of all ages foregathered in Battersea Park on a Sunday morning in March to protest at an American take-over and duly appeared on the TV news. Rumours were rife. Maybe Lonrho would buy it instead, renaming the vehicle the Lonrhover, but at the end of the day, ownership of the company remained unchanged until two years later, when British Aerospace made their bid and agreement was reached. As things turned out, shortly before this edition of the book went to press, the Rover Group announced a complete revision of senior management.

In the intervening years sales figures and markets have fluctuated –

Land Rovers selling best in 1985 – while Range Rover sales have progressively risen, culminating in over 20,000 units in 1987, breaking all previous records by an impressive margin.

The One Ten has of course become a very familiar sight during the last five years, as has the Ninety, while the old 109-inch and 88-inch models have been phased out of production entirely (though we know people who will still go to great lengths to track down a trusty 109-inch, rather than succumb to the power and speed inherent in the new range of vehicles). Development milestones of all the Land-Rovers have been included at the end of Chapter I, (Chapter 4 for Range Rover) together with revised standard specification. The Turbo D engine has since become available across the range, adding a powerful new dimension, and broadening the appeal of the Range Rover in particular, with the improvement in running costs.

Updating this edition was mainly undertaken in 1988 but immediately prior to going to press (1989) there were dramatic changes to report at Land-Rover. Tony Gilroy, who worked so hard through the eighties to transform Land-Rover into a viable concern ready for its inevitable denationalisation, was no longer captaining the ship. His decision to leave in the New Year was followed by a streamlining of the Rover Group management structure. Effectively his seat has been filled by Chris Woodwark, as Land-Rover's Commercial Director.

Authors' note to the fourth edition
There have been significant changes to the 4th Edition in that there are two completely new chapters, both written by experts in their field. David McDine has contributed Chapter 3 Land Rover Conscripted, and James Taylor, well known in Land Rover circles as writer/historian, has updated Chapter 4 The Range Rover Story and written Chapter 5 The Discovery Story. The technical specification at the end of Chapter 1 has been revised by Vince Davis and – hot from the Press Office – details of the 'new' Range Rover are included at the end of Chapter 4.

Mr Woodwark left the Rover Group in 1993 and the post of MD of Rover International was temporarily covered by Group MD John Towers, until it was taken up by John Russell in 1994.

Acknowledgements

For the 4th Edition, we are grateful for the excellent contributions of David McDine, James Taylor and Vince Davis, and from Rover: John Towers, John Russell and Colin Walkey. We also thank Land Rover North America Inc for the co-operation, Land Rover Canada Inc and Richard Thomas, editor of *Land Rover Owner International*. For their photographic contributions, we would like to thank Jonathan Slavin FRGS, who also took all the photographs used on the jacket, Donald Miller FRGS (USA), Col David McDine, Vince Davis FRGS, CAFOD, FZS, MOD, Norwegian Church Aid, WWF, ODA, Short Bros, Evers and Wall, Land Rover Canada Inc and the Rover Group.

Chapter 1
The Land Rover Story

The Land-Rover has been so big for so long that it is hard to visualize life without it. There it is, daily, on the screen: a fire-engine copes with a blazing emergency, a convoy heads doggedly for some trouble-spot loaded with soldiers, an ambulance roars off bearing the wounded to hospital, the police arrive with blue lights flashing; and there it is again, pulling trapped cars out of the snow, moving a farmer's sheep to safety; now it's full of camping gear as an expedition gets under way, and – would you believe? – there's one disguised as a zebra, in an African Game Reserve.

The uses of the Land Rover are so diverse as to be impossible to enumerate, which in itself is a good enough excuse to write a book about it, but now, after leading the world in the 4 x 4 market ever since the Second World War, its supremacy is being challenged as a host of competitors jostle for position: so let's look not only at what Land Rover has meant in the past, but at what place it can hold in the future ...

The prime factor in the conception of the Land Rover was, indirectly, the Second World War, although the idea emerged well after peace had been declared, and – at that stage – no military connection had even been imagined. To sketch in the background from which the Land Rover was born, we shall have to go back a bit further, however, to Victorian England, when Coventry was best known as a centre for watch-making and ribbon-weaving.

Coventry's first-ever 'car' – a machine called the Rover Electric Carriage – was built in 1888 by JK Starley who founded the Rover company. Unfortunately this extraordinary vehicle, a battery-operated, electrically driven hybrid tricycle, was destined to die at the prototype stage, and the company did not start serious car production until after the turn of the century, in 1904. By then, the age of mechanization was dawning, and beginning to gain respectability, when even the King himself purchased a car (King Edward VII's example was to be followed, nearly 50 years later, by King George VI, who ordered his own

Land Rover when it was still regarded as a very new phenomenon on the market).

Rover's first cars were a development from building motor cycles, which were a development from building bicycles, which were a development from building sewing machines, way back in the early 1860s. The designation 'Rover' emerged in 1884 with the advent of 'The Safety' – a tricycle produced that year which was considered to be ideally suited to 'roving' around the countryside. This machine was rapidly followed a year later by a 'Safety' bicycle – the forerunner of the present-day pedal bicycle, and successor to the acclaimed Compressus Ordinary, or Penny Farthing. The company officially became known as the Rover Cycle Company Limited in 1896, but this title was to be changed less than 10 years later to the Rover Company Limited, when production of motor cycles ceased.

The Rover Company experienced fluctuating fortunes through the first three decades of the century – firmly establishing itself as one of Britain's important car manufacturers in the years prior to the First World War, levelling out by the start of the 1920s, and in grave trouble by the time the Depression hit the world.

This then was the background of the business to which Mr Spencer Wilks was to harness his considerable talents when he made the decision to leave Hillman, where he had been Managing Director since 1919, and join the Rover Company in 1929. Mr A B Smith, who was Managing Director of the Rover Company from 1969 till 1973, recalls those distant days with clarity:

'I now know exactly how hard times were for Rover in those days. There were, of course, no labour problems as we know them today. Everyone's ambition was first to get a job and second to hold on to it. The people in authority were the foremen and the time-keepers who looked after the clock cards. It was difficult to find the money to pay the suppliers and the question arose of pleading with them for further extended credit. I have a recollection of Ted Commander – our Chief Buyer – offering to guarantee some supplier's account with his own pension fund! Spencer Wilks, Managing Director of Rover from 1933 to 1957, has often spoken of the drama that surrounded almost every weekly pay day in those early days. The appointment of Spencer Wilks was the first major step that saved Rover and even today his philosophy of building only quality cars has been adhered to strictly – to our very obvious benefit ... Spencer Wilks' brother Maurice joined Rover in 1931 and together with Robert Boyle assumed responsibility for engineering and design, and on the production side Spencer Wilks brought Geoffrey Savage from Hillman to become Works Director. This was really the team that put Rover back on their feet ...'

From 1933, when he was promoted to Managing Director, Spencer Wilks' consistent policy was to eliminate mediocrity from the firm and specialize in the production of prestigious vehicles. Very soon after his appointment, the name of Rover began to denote the respectability that its cars have retained to this day. One of his first actions when he took over the reins at the Rover Company was to form a new department for material control, the object of which was to time material flow precisely, in order to minimize work in progress and match production. This could well be regarded as a fore-runner of the computerized control systems of today, and thereby gives an idea of the breadth of Spencer Wilks' competence as the man in charge.

The outbreak of the Second World War, however, put an abrupt end to the steadily increasing sale of Rover cars, and for the time being Mr Wilks had to shelve his elaborate plans for expansion. As a result of his impact on the firm, the Rover Company had been invited to join the Government's 'Shadow Factories' scheme, to build aeroplane engines at two different sites – at Acocks Green as early as 1937, and at Solihull in 1939. All through the war years the company was stretched to capacity, fulfilling its commitment to the production of aircraft engines and a whole range of other military equipment which included, in the latter stages of the war, the Rolls-Royce V12 Meteor tank engine. Of this period, A B Smith recalls:

'At the end of the war we had a reservoir of highly skilled people, and pre-emptive rights on the buildings and plant from the Shadow Factories. Since our Coventry works (Helen Street) had been bombed in 1940, Spencer Wilks decided to come to Solihull, although I well remember him saying in despair to his brother, "We shall never be able to use a million square feet in all our lives! We shall have to let it out ..." '

So Helen Street was sold and the two new plants taken on at a 'peppercorn' rent, Acocks Green to continue with the production of the Meteor tank engine – the demand for which continued even after the end of the war– and Solihull as Rover's headquarters, where Spencer Wilks began to prepare for the renewed manufacture of his cars.

These preparations were on the ambitious scale of an annual output of 20,000 vehicles – 15,000 to the old Rover design, and 5,000 of a new design (the 700cc 6 hp 'M'-type) that his younger brother Maurice, by now Chief Designer for the Rover Company, was already working on. But all these plans were to be thwarted by the Government, which was hamstrung by the war-crippled economy. The great cry in these times was, not unlike today, Export! –but then it was to recuperate some of the monumental losses suffered during the preceding years. This in itself was made extremely difficult by the gross lack of raw materials, and of sheet steel in particular, without which cars such as Rover had hitherto produced simply could not be made. Government allocations of necessary materials including steel were made to those industries whose plans included a high level of export, but the new design that Maurice Wilks was developing, the 'M'-type, was considered unsuitable for the export market because of its relatively high cost; since nearly all its parts were brand new, the tooling costs were prohibitive. After building a number of prototypes, the reality of the necessary capital outlay finally sunk in, and the 'M'-type had to be cast aside. Until this period the Rover Company had never in its whole history designed or built a left-hand-drive vehicle, which serves to illustrate how un-export-minded they had always been (their own Export Department was not created until 1945).

Their application to build 15,000 of the old pre-war models per year was then squashed by the Government response that it could only allocate steel for the production of 1,100 vehicles. This was so far short of their target that Spencer and Maurice Wilks now came to realize that a compromise born of desperation must be achieved if the company was to have any hope at all of survival. Although their problems were pretty immense, they were not regarded as anything other than short-term. Once the country was 'back on its feet', production of motor cars could be stepped up again and the labour force usefully employed. But what, in the meantime, could they possible do with their factories and their men, and with all the restrictions of the age to contend with? Without question, a 'stop-gap' was vital – and one that met the essential requirement of export potential, without demanding the usual quantities of sheet steel for the body manufacture, or too much additional expenditure for its assembly. It had to be something that would utilize only what was already there. One way and another, a very tall order!

Maurice Wilks had a fairly big farm in Anglesey on which he found, in his spare time, that an old, beaten-up ex-WD Willys Jeep – one of the many that had become so familiar in Britain during the war – was a very useful thing to own, for many different practical purposes. Legend now has it that when this old vehicle was nearing the end of its usefulness, Spencer Wilks asked his brother what he intended to replace it with. Maurice answered that he would have to get hold of the same again as no alternative existed – though for such patriotic motor manufacturers as the Wilks, it went powerfully against the grain to buy any vehicle that wasn't British. Another factor not in the Jeep's favour at that time was the unavailability of spare parts; they could only be obtained in bulk, at sales of United States surplus stock – for instance, to get a replacement set of four spark plugs, a hundred had to purchased!

And so it was from this bald fact, that the American Jeep had no equivalent, that the original notion to design and build a purely agricultural vehicle is said to have sprung. All of a sudden, the Wilks brothers became conscious of a glaring gap in the market: a machine for the farmer that was not a tractor but something much more versatile, rugged without being too cumbersome, thus keeping pace with the increasing trend in the years after the war towards mechanized farming. As A B Smith told us,

'It is difficult today, to imagine the size of the gamble that was taken then. It all started when the Wilks brothers bought a war-time Jeep. It was constantly in trouble and they were forever having to bring it into the factory for some repair job or other, and I well remember Maurice saying to Spencer that if he couldn't make a better, more reliable vehicle he shouldn't be in the business!'

The governess to Maurice Wilks' three sons at that time was Kathleen Griffiths and she remembers, with affection, 'the insatiable boyish enthusiasm' with which Maurice tackled this (and every other) new venture. She recalls being bounced over sand dunes, bogged down on wet beaches and hurtled through the shallows in one of the first Land Rover prototypes to be built.

The Rover Company was about to design a vehicle for the land – a 'Land-Rover', as Maurice Wilks had already christened the project. According to the minutes of the Board Meeting held in September 1947, Spencer Wilks recommended 'that the all-purpose vehicle on the lines of the Willys-Overland post-war Jeep was the most desirable,' and for some of the following reasons: 'The P3 engine, gearbox and back axle could be used almost in their entirety; little additional jigging and tooling would be necessary, and body dies would not be required ...' But by this time the first prototypes were already running, for Maurice Wilks had wasted no time in deciding the brief, in the spring of that same year. This was unusually broad:

'...to design a vehicle rather similar to a Jeep ...even more useful to the farmer ... a proper farm machine, not just another Jeep...Much more versatile, much more use as a power source ... able to drive things, to have power take-offs *everywhere,* and to have all sorts of bolt-on accessories, to be used instead of a tractor at times ... to be able to do everything ...!'

This was the outline he gave to Tom Barton, the man who over the years has earned himself the title of 'Mr Land Rover' but who at that time was one of five section leaders to whom the job of designing and building the Land Rover was handed. Maurice Wilks could afford to be confident in passing the project over to his team, which included Robert Boyle as Chief Engineer, Gordon Bashford as Research Engineer, Arthur Goddard as Assistant Chief Engineer, and John Cullen as Project Engineer for the Land Rover, and to turn his own energies back towards the car market. All that Tom Barton and Co had to do now was to get their heads down and get on with it.

One of the most remarkable elements in the development of the Land-Rover was the speed with which plans and drawings became realities. Great urgency was imposed upon the project from the moment the Wilks brothers decided to make this the stop-gap vehicle they so badly needed: there was a work force to employ and the Rover Company simply had to have the export potential that this machine might provide. Even so, it is still quite amazing (especially by contrast with the standards of today) that while the concept was not thought up until early in 1947, prototypes were running by the end of the summer, and the first Land Rover was shown to the public in April 1948! This is all the more impressive considering the traditional conservatism and cautiousness of Rover as a company – hardly known for making snap decisions and then implementing them!

Using the Willys Jeep as the jumping-off point, the design team had to scrutinize every detail of the American product and drive it about in all possible conditions to learn its limitations. Two Jeeps were acquired early on, solely for dissection purposes, but although certain of its stronger points were without doubt copied in the Land Rover, the Rover team maintained vehemently that there was nothing on the Land Rover that corresponded exactly to the Jeep. For one thing, the Land Rover project was severely restricted by the conditions of its manufacture, which imposed a very strict discipline upon the designers: wherever remotely feasible, existing Rover car components had to be used; the budget for alternative machine tools was meagre, and for press tools for the bodywork, non-existent. If the body panels, which were to be made almost exclusively of aluminium alloy, could not be formed by the simple bending method they were no use, and any form to be incorporated in the skin could only be achieved by using such machinery as they already had. With the earliest prototypes, bits of Jeep were certainly in evidence but these were used only to save time – for instance a Jeep chassis was 'borrowed' for the original vehicle, though most of its fittings were Rover's. When Rover started to build the Land-Rover its own chassis, there were more innovations as a result of the low-expenditure policy: the chassis frame side members were of box-section, built up from four plates of flat steel sheet, instead of U-section pressings. Olaf Poppe (whose Norwegian father Peter Poppe, engine designer, had joined the Rover Company in 1924, bringing with him his designs for the 14/45 engine that Rover used through the 1920s) devised this 'four-plate' concept which was, after much deliberation, taken up by Gordon Bashford – with surprising and lasting success, as is proved by the fact that it has endured to the present day on all the short wheelbase models.

One way in which even the earliest prototype Land Rovers differed dramatically from the Jeep was in the engine: the Land Rover engine was considerably smaller, allowing more carrying space. After a fair bit of trial and error, which determined the 1,389cc Rover 10 engine as lacking the necessary power and torque, the new 1.6-litre engine was fitted.

Always bearing in mind Maurice Wilks' original instructions 'to have power take-offs *everywhere!*', the first Land Rover chassis to be built already incorporated the central power take-off, and, by the time that a number of pre-production vehicles were completed, the versatility that this afforded was being fully explored. Prototype 80-inch Land Rovers with 4-wheel drive and power take-offs could be harnessed to a whole range of machinery, which made innumerable jobs a lot simpler and quicker to carry out, and their cross-

Side view of the first Land Rover: the first appearance of the now familiar profile

Everything about the first Land Rover was purely functional.

A typical 1948 80-inch model in L.H.D. guise. Right from the start the export market was vital to the sales of the Land Rover. Up to the present, over 70% of all Land Rovers produced have been sold overseas.

country ability – from fording streams, crossing ploughed fields, to climbing steep hill-faces – was improving by the week. But the timing was becoming crucial. Spencer and Maurice Wilks were quite determined that the Land Rover should be 'unveiled' at the Amsterdam Motor Show which opened on 30 April 1948, regardless of whether or not it was finished. The Show, which was of international interest, was far too good a promotional opportunity to miss for the launching of their new machine, and so this was the target to which the Land Rover project team was committed. At this stage they envisaged building up to 50 Land Rovers per week, but theoretically the state of the nation could hardly have been worse for new vehicle prospects: even if the interest was there and orders flowed in, without adequate materials to supply them, Rover would as quickly lose custom as they obtained it.

During the initial stages of construction, progress was disconcertingly slow. Because of the very complicated casting and machining operations to transmission casings, the first prototype took about six weeks to complete, and the second emerged several weeks after that. During this phase, however, the chassis jig had been designed and proved workable, so that the Land Rover

Peter Wilks with his young son, Andrew, in 1964. Andrew is standing beside a miniature Land Rover that was built as a gift for the King of Jordan's children.

team were then able to proceed with the production of their pilot-run vehicles, of which the intention was to build 50 – though finally only 47 or 48 were finished, probably because the components for the last few were 'sabotaged' to keep the existing vehicles running. These pilot-run or pre-production Land Rovers varied in many particulars, as was required by the experimental and developmental purpose of their production – to the extent that the very first completed prototype had a central steering wheel, steering column and centrally positioned driving seat, with no doors! The common denominator, though, was always the galvanized steel chassis frame.

Of the pilot-run vehicles, only 25 had been finished before the official launching, which was in fact somewhat premature in that the company was hardly geared to forge ahead with production, but on the other hand they were deliberately awaiting the general public reaction before finalizing certain design details, since it was the first-ever 4-wheel-drive vehicle of this sort to have been produced in Great Britain.

It was decided that for the Amsterdam Motor Show, two of the 80-inch Land Rovers would be exhibited, one right-hand drive for display, and a left-

Farmers were quick to recognize the Land Rover's potential.

hand drive demonstration model. Now, at last, the Wilks brothers were to see whether or not they had backed the right hunch in creating this unusual machine ...

At its initial launching in Amsterdam, the Land Rover was received with universal enthusiasm and very serious interest. The Land Rover archives at Solihull bulge with press comment of the day, but *The Autocar* and *The Motor* magazines reported in depth, dwelling on the innovative aspects of the vehicle. 'An All-Purpose Rover', said *The Autocar* (30 April 1948), and proceded to describe it in the following terms:

> 'There is now something to describe which can either be regarded as a private car able to perform many most valuable duties other than sheer transport, or as a general purpose countryside worker which is also capable of providing comfortable and efficient transport. This dual role of the new Land Rover, regardless of which range of duty is of the greater value to the owner, cannot be too highly stressed, because it opens up possibilities of the greatest value to those who live in the country, whether under cultivation or in the wild state. So much has been said and written in the past about the so-called People's Car, much of it nonsense, that the advent of a really practical British vehicle which goes far beyond that over-publicised proposal should be hailed with genuine acclamation ... It has been designed and built by the Rover Company, and that in itself is a guarantee of quality which will be instantly accepted by any British

motorist. Its appearance is starkly practical; there is nothing of the luxury vehicle about its looks. Nevertheless it is not ugly and has a distinctly attractive appearance all its own ... The Land Rover can go through floods up to its wheel centres or deeper without trouble. The operative word about the whole car is "substantial". All these features alone make one think. If the world has to be strictly economical for years to come, is not this the sort of car that most of us need, one that is entirely practical and essentially usable? Washing is reduced to a minimum, and maintenance is easy; there is no carrying about of weight more or less uselessly devoted to fashionable appearance and not really essential luxury. And it is a car usable in open form or completely enclosed. These points alone proclaim themselves. But they only tell half the story. The Land Rover is a mobile power station as well, and will tow or do a variety of useful work on the land over rough ground. It can drive a large circular saw and cut up timber for firewood. It can be used with trailers to transport heavy loads over ploughed fields or other hard going. As a mobile power unit it takes the power to the job. Through the power take-off it can be harnessed to drive a threshing machine, an elevator, or a chaff-cutter. It can draw a plough, and most other farm implements. It can perform all these tasks because it is specifically provided with a four-wheel drive, and a power take-off ... Provision is also made for a power-driven winch of the capstan type mounted at the front of the vehicle, which can be used for a variety of jobs from moving machinery in a factory to grubbing out old tree roots on the farm. It is a vehicle of almost unlimited uses ...'

The Motor presented a similar glowing account, over a full four-page report, calling it 'a go-anywhere vehicle with a plain utility-type body, a portable source of power, and an alternative to the light tractor' but finished by saying:

'In launching this new vehicle the Rover Company has displayed an enterprise which should be well rewarded, and there is no doubt that a big market, both at home and abroad, exists for a machine such as the Land Rover. There is no doubt also that in its design the Rover Co has applied a wide knowledge and experience not only of vehicle manufacture, but of agricultural and industrial requirements.'

So, from the outset, it was established that here was something much more versatile than a mere agricultural machine. And the public pounced on it! Apart from its appeal on the grounds described in the above-quoted press comments, another favourable factor was its price – only £450 for the basic vehicle (though 'extras' such as passenger seat cushions, doors, heater, sidescreens, spare tyre – and even starting handle! – were additional):

Soon after its release, the Rover Company submitted two Land Rovers to the National Institute of Agricultural Engineering and Scottish Machinery Testing

Station for thorough test-work to be carried out over a period of about nine months. Their impartial report on the two vehicles was published in 1949, and the following extracts, while rather long-winded by today's standards, give an idea of the extent of their probe, and their findings:

Report on test of PROTOTYPE LAND ROVER

Manufactured by: The Rover Company Ltd., Meteor Works, Solihull, Birmingham.

Test requested by: The manufacturers.

Brief Specification: The Land Rover is a light 4-wheel drive vehicle designed to transport goods and/or personnel by road or across country and for general use in farming operations. Two models were supplied for test purposes: one right-hand drive vehicle (Chassis No R.32, Engine No 33) and one left-hand drive vehicle (Chassis No L.31, Engine No 32).

Engine	
Fuel	Pool petrol
Arrangement and number of cylinders	4 cylinders in line. 2.736 in bore x 4.134 in stroke. Aluminium alloy pistons.
Compression ratio	6.8 : 1
Valves	Overhead inlet, side exhaust
Engine speeds	Governed 3,000 ± 100 rpm. Maximum 4,500 rpm.
Carburetter	Solex 32 PBI down-draught including economiser and accelerator pump. Supplied by electric SU pump from tank via AC sediment bowl filter.
Air cleaner	AC Sphinx oil bath heavy duty type fitted with pre-cleaner.
Ignition	Lucas coil. Centrifugal and vacuum automatic advance and retard.
Lubrication	Forced feed from gear type oil pump delivering 160 gals/hour at 2,000 engine rpm. Filters on pump inlet and by-pass.
Cooling system	Centrifugal pump, pressurised radiator and fan with cowling. Thermostat control. (Fine mesh radiator screen available as extra.)
Electrical equipment	12v Lucas 51 amp/hour lead acid battery. Headlamps, side-lights, rear-lights, horn, instrument panel, windscreen wiper, socket for trailer light. Starter motor and dynamo.
Governor	Iso-Speedic. Driven by V-belt from crank-shaft.
Capacities	Fuel – 10 gallons Cooling water – 17 pints Oil – 10 pints

Chassis and Body

The chassis is made up of two longitudinal and five lateral members of 14 gauge steel box-section, welded throughout and galvanised. The fuel tank is underslung on the chassis and is provided with a double bottom carried up to form the mounting and guard. Suspension is by semi-elliptic leaf springs controlled by Monroe hydraulic dampers.

The scuttle and dash are of steel and the floor, seats, and rear section are of high tensile light alloy. The wings and bonnet are also of light alloy. The windscreen can be folded down on to the bonnet if required and a detachable fabric hood with Perspex side windows can be fitted for weather protection. Provision is made for carrying a spare wheel in the rear section of the body or extra fittings can be obtained for clamping it on the bonnet.

Overall dimensions of vehicle
(on 6.00 x 16 tyres at inflation pressure 24 lb/sq in).

Length	128½ in.
Width	62½ in.
Height	Without hood and windscreen folded down: 53½ in.
	Without hood and windscreen upright: 65¼ in.
	With hood: 72 in.
Ground clearance	To bottom of differential housing: 7½ in.
(on hard surface)	To bottom of spring clamp bolts: 7¾ in.

Overall dimensions of rear section

Length	42 in.
Width	60 in.
Depth	Centre portion: 14½ in x 34 in wide.
	Side portions (forming seats if required): each 5½ in x 13 in wide.
Capacity (to top of sides)	15½ cu ft (including spare wheel space)
Recommended payload	10 cwt.
Dimensions of tailboard	14½ in deep x 34 in wide

Transmission

Clutch	Single plate, dry. 9 in diameter. Foot operated.
Gearbox	A normal gearbox giving four forward speeds and reverse (synchro-mesh on 3rd and 4th gears) transmits power to a transfer box having

21

two ratios – high and low. From the transfer box output two Hardy-Spicer open propeller shafts drive the front and rear axles: a free wheel on the front axle drive is incorporated in the transfer box.

Oil capacity	Main gearbox: 4 pints
	Transfer box: 6 pints
Wheels	16 in rim fitted with Avon 6-ply 6.00 x 16 Traction or 7.00 x 16 Super-Traction tyres.
Brakes	Girling Hydrostatic on all wheels: foot operated. Girling mechanical handbrake on transfer box output shaft for parking.
Wheelbase	80 in.
Track (fixed)	50 in (on 6.00 x 16 tyres)
Drawbar	The drawbar consists of a lateral plate 29½ in long x 3 in wide welded to the rear chassis cross-member. Ten ⅞in diameter holes are drilled at 3 in centres. A cranked drawbar extension plate 16 in long is also provided for bolting to the drawbar when the pto unit is fitted. One ¾ in and one ⅞ in bolt holes are drilled at 4 in centres. The extension cannot be fitted centrally.
Height of drawbar above ground	(a) on hard surface with 7.00 x 16 tyres at inflation pressure 22 lb/sq in Body empty – 14 in. 1,200 lb in body – 10½ in.
	(b) on hard surface with 6.00 x 16 tyres at inflation pressure 24 lb/sq in Body empty – 13¼ in.
	(c) height of extension plate, conditions as (b) Four positions giving 10½, 11½, 13½ and 14½ in.

Total weight (on 7.00 x 16 tyres without fuel, operator, or pto assembly but including oil, cooling water, hood, doors, and spare wheel on bonnet):

	Body empty – 2,780 lb.
	1,200 lb evenly distributed in body 3,980 lb.
Weight on rear wheels (conditions as above)	Body empty – 1,205 lb. 1,200 lb evenly distributed in body 2,465 lb.
Weight on front wheels (conditions as above)	Body empty – 1,575 lb. 1,200 lb evenly distributed in body 1,515 lb.
Power take-off and belt pulley assembly	The power take-off is driven through a Hardy-Spicer propeller shaft from the main gearbox

output and two interchangeable pinions giving two ratios. The pto gearbox casing is bolted to the rear chassis cross-member and an 8 in x 8 in belt pulley driven from the pto shaft through two bevel gears can be bolted to the pto gear-box casing.

The test-work carried out by the National Institute of Agricultural Engineering and Scottish Machinery Testing Station included comprehensive testing of the belt power and drawbar performance, road trials, and farm and field trials, applied to both the prototype Land Rovers. The field trials involved ploughing, disc harrowing, drag harrowing, rolling and chain harrowing grassland, hauling a reaper and binder, rolling on a hillside, hauling a pto-driven muck-spreader, and potato harvesting and cultivation. At the conclusion of all these tests, the left-hand drive Land Rover was dismantled at the manufacturers, and the component parts were inspected for wear and damage. Here is what the report had to say:

Engine

Cylinder block and crankcase:	Good condition
Cylinder bores:	Maximum wear 0.0015 inches above production limits
Pistons:	Very little carbon on crowns or in control rings. Dimensions within production limits
Piston rings:	No damage. No increase in side clearance. Maximum increase in compression ring gap 0.001 inch above production limits.
Gudgeon pins:	Good condition.
Crankshaft:	Some score marks on all journals particularly centre one which had one deep mark. No ovality on journals or crankpins. Maximum wear on crankpins 0.0005 inch.
Bearings:	Main: some score marks on all three, particularly centre (thrust). Maximum wear 0.004 inch (on centre bearing). No ovality. Big ends: within production limits. No ovality. Piece of metal broken out of No 3. Small ends: good condition.
Camshaft:	Very little wear on cams.
Cylinder head and gasket:	Good condition.

23

Valves:	Exhaust valves in need of regrinding. Inlet valves in good condition. Some play between stems and guides on all valves but new guides not required.
Tappet and push-rods:	Good condition.
Valve springs:	Within production limits.
Flywheel:	Starter ring in good condition. Score marks on clutch side.
Chain drives and sprockets:	No wear. Chain tensioning device in original position.
Carburettor:	Good condition. Fine dust present in float chamber.
Water Pump:	Good condition.
Oil Pump:	Good condition.
Oil filters:	Primary: clean and intact. Secondary: dirty and intact.

Transmission

Clutch:	Score marks on flywheel. Score marks on pressure plate and slight blueing. Clutch plate not very badly worn. Dirt and dust in clutch housing.
Gearboxes:	Gears in good condition except 1st in main gearbox on which leading edge of teeth broken. Some corrosion on springs and roller bearing housings.
Propeller shafts:	Good condition.
Front axle free-wheel:	Good condition.
Power Take-Off drive shaft:	Play in end coupling to pto giving rise to noise.
Front axle:	Shafts and Tracta joints in good condition. Some corrosion and score marks on swivel pin roller bearing housings. Differential not stripped (almost new).
Power Take-Off:	Good condition.

Steering

Steering box:	Good condition. Mounting on dash panel –bolts loose.
Steering relay box:	Good condition.
Linkages and pins:	Good condition.
Front wheel castor:	2°20′ (originally 3°).
Front wheel camber and toe in:	Within production limits.

Chassis and Suspension

Chassis frame:	Good condition except plates pulled out on rear cross-member. No corrosion.
Engine and gearbox mountings:	No appreciable deterioration. No distortion.
Exhaust pipe and mountings:	No appreciable deterioration.
Springs:	Rear offside set 3.69 in at 720 lb Rear nearside set 3.75 in at 710 lb (when new were 4.13 in at 750 lb) Both front 2.5 in at 520 lb (were 2.65 at 530 lb). No obvious wear on shackles, pins or Silentbloc pushes.
Shock absorbers:	Good condition.
Body:	Generally in good condition (this applies to both models) with no rusting or corrosion. Hood badly out of shape at rear and fasteners broken. Rear window gauze broken. Door catches no longer positive. Sidescreen steady arms broken and peg sockets strained.

Electrical System

Wiring:	Good condition.
Components:	All serviceable, no damage. One rear lamp missing (broken off). Mixture strength warning light fickle.

Wheels and Brakes

Brakes:	Hydraulic system in good condition. New brake linings were fitted during the tests.
Tyres:	Three badly worn but not completely unserviceable. One rear tyre worn down to canvas and replaced at 8,500 miles.

At the end of this report, the conclusions of the testers are listed as follows:

'The results of the test show that the Land Rover is an excellent transport vehicle which can be used instead of a tractor for some agricultural operations including belt work. It is capable of carrying a load of up to 10 cwt across difficult conditions and of hauling trailer loads of the order of 4 tons. The fuel consumption on road work ranged from 30 mpg when driven unladen at an average speed of about 30 mph, to 21 mpg when fully laden and engaged on a long journey interspersed with some short runs. It is very suitable for the transport of livestock in trailers since the choice of gear ratios in the four-speed gearbox has been such that a constant rate of acceleration and deceleration can be maintained in traffic and when negotiating difficult corners. When not heavily laden and without a trailer, it can be driven at a cruising speed of 45-50 mph with a maximum slightly in excess of 60 mph. On one test run an average speed of 42.9 mph was maintained over a 162 mile journey. At the higher speeds necessary to maintain such an average, however, the vehicle was too noisy for comfortable travelling.

'One particular advantage of the Land Rover for farm transport is its ability to go practically anywhere since its cross-country and hill-climbing performances are very good. It is very stable and has an obvious usefulness both for carrying small items of equipment across terrain which would otherwise require the use of a tractor and trailer and for internal and external farm transport. Its capacity for draught work is shown by the results of the drawbar tests in which maximum sustained pulls obtained when unladen and equipped with 7.00 × 16 tyres ranged from 2,200 lb on tarmac to 1,700 lb on rough cultivated loam.

An Evers & Wall conversion of a forward-control Land Rover 250 Fertiliquid Sprayer, with boom in spraying position.

'The results of the belt test show that the Land Rover develops sufficient power for many farm operations such as driving threshing drums or medium-sized hammermills although improvement to engine governing is desirable. The maximum power obtained was 27.3 belt hp at a belt linear speed of 3,840 ft/min and maximum equivalent crankshaft torque was developed at a belt speed of 2,525 ft/min. It is possible that a Land Rover being used for agricultural purposes may spend an appreciable part of its time on stationary work and attention is therefore drawn to the need for some simple means, such as a locking device on the foot-brake pedal for securing the vehicle and to the necessity of advising operators on how to eliminate the rear axle springing for anything but light belt work.

'The vehicle, as tested, could be employed on many jobs where good manoeuvrability and row-crop wheel spacing are not required but its usefulness for farming operations would be improved by lower gear ratios. The results of the drawbar tests show that the factor limiting maximum sustained pull on all three types of land was engine stall and it is recommended that the practicability should be considered of modifying the transfer box low ratio so that the forward speeds of the vehicle on a hard surface are about 2.5 mph in L_1, 4 mph in L_2, and 5.5 mph in L_3, (ie about twice the ratio of the vehicle as tested). A modification of this nature would not only increase the usefulness of the Land Rover for farm work but would also increase the maximum pull. The transmission differs from that of a tractor in that the pto drive passes through the gearbox so that, irrespective of the gear being used, the ratio of pto speed to vehicle wheel speed remains the same. Thus the normal tractor pto speed of 540 rpm is only obtained at one forward speed – about 4 mph – with new 6.00 x 16 tyres, dropping to 3.7 mph with the same tyres well worn. (The manufacturers have pointed out that, if required, their agents could interchange the gears in the pto assembly on any individual vehicle and the machine would then give 540 rpm of the pto shaft at about 2.7 mph.) This method of driving the pto would be a disadvantage on a general purpose tractor but is not expected to lead to difficulties with the range of pto driven machines likely to be used with the Land Rover; it has the noteworthy advantage that, as the belt pulley attaches to the pto shaft, a wide range of belt speeds is readily obtainable for stationary work.

'The field trials showed that many farm operations other than heavy cultivations and row-crop work could be satisfactorily carried out with the Land Rover. Disc and drag harrowing, rolling and reaping were successfully attempted and ploughing – except for the headlands – with a two-furrow mouldboard plough was found to be possible. The fuel consumption of the vehicle on drawbar work on conditions giving good adhesion was found to be good. The specific fuel consumption curves obtained during the drawbar tests on grassland were flat over a wide range of pulls and the optimum consumption was more than 10 drawbar hp-hours per gallon. The fuel consumption when disc-harrowing and drag-harrowing in L₁ gear was 14.7 and 12.1 gallons per 8-hour day respectively, the average drawbar pulls being 950 lb and 730 lb respectively and the speeds approximately 3¾ and 3½ mph.

'The extensive and arduous nature of the tests to which the two models were subjected showed them to be very robust vehicles capable of heavy work with low maintenance requirements. The total mileage of the two vehicles during the test was 23,000 of which a considerable proportion was low gear work and the inspection of the left-hand drive model at the end of the performance tests and field trials showed it to be in very good condition. The use of light alloys and the heavy galvanizing of the steel components of the body and chassis had prevented any rusting or corrosion. The test showed the need for certain modifications and refinements, many of which are already being incorporated in production models. It is suggested that modifications to the drawbar, gear ratios, driving position and parking brake system are particularly worthwhile.'

Report No RT.1/49034: 27 August 1949

This very positive reaction to the Land Rover was to be echoed by many other professional motor-vehicle assessors, but even apart from that, it seemed that the time was ripe for the general public to latch on to this new land-roving machine. Its reception both at home and overseas was immediately more enthusiastic than its makers had even dared to hope: after all, it was intended only as a hand-to-mouth emergency measure, and never as anything lasting or substantial in terms of Rover products. In Britain, the fact that during the post-war years the public was restricted to the purchase of not more than one new car every two years, and that Land Rovers were classified as exempt from this ruling, gave the vehicle an unquestionable advantage which was at once reflected in the sales figures. In its first full year of production, it was to exceed the sales target of 5,000 vehicles by as much as 3,000, a figure way beyond everyone's expectations. In the second full year of production sales doubled, and by 1951 Land Rovers were out-selling Rover cars at the rate of two to one. Once the dazed and delighted Rover people had grasped the implications of this success, plans were rapidly adapted in an endeavour to meet the orders that came pouring in.

Production got off to a very slow start. The launching at the Amsterdam Motor Show had been premature in that the company were far from geared to produce Land Rovers in any quantity at that stage, but it served its purpose: while it attracted international attention, Rover got the feedback it needed, and production was able to begin, albeit haltingly. From that day to this, Land Rover has never been able to match its production to demand.

A Land Rover fitted with a 'Fortemist' kerb unit in travelling position, converted by Evers & Wall.

Every Land Rover built has found an eager customer waiting to buy it – and customer reaction has played a vital part in the vehicle's evolution. It became clear from the outset that it would be expected to function in widely differing spheres of operation, which was perhaps the least anticipated selling factor during the period of initial development. The clue to its unpredicted success lay in this breadth of its appeal – not just to farmers, but to police forces, armed services, building contractors, expeditions, rescue services, electricity boards, and private estates, to name just a few.

Later, another enormous bonus which further helped to indoctrinate the public into the everyday use of 4-wheel drive vehicles for road-going purposes, was the successful application to have Purchase Tax removed on those Land Rovers that could be categorized in the commercial class as opposed to the private car class. Every motor vehicle had to be slotted into a category for the imposition of appropriate legislation, but the versatility of the Land Rover made this an issue of extreme complexity, affecting not only its eligibility for Purchase Tax exemption, but the type of fuel on which it could be run (in the days of petrol rationing after the war, commercial vehicles could be run on the cheaper 'pink' petrol), and the maximum speed up to which it could be driven on the road (the speed limit for commercial vehicles was then 30 mph, which meant an unacceptably slow journey for the relatively spry Land Rover). It was not until the mid-1950s that the position was eventually clarified, when it was pronouced a 'dual-purpose' vehicle: if it was used for carrying freight, it was a commercial vehicle and free of purchase tax, while if it was used in place of an estate car, it was liable. After the introduction of the 12-seater Station Wagon in 1962, the authorities had to exempt this one because it was officially tagged a bus – which meant of course that this model became immensely popular, whatever its intended purpose, to the virtual exclusion of the 10-seater which didn't qualify.

One year earlier, nobody could have foreseen that by October 1948 a second type of Land Rover would have been produced: a hard-top version of the 80-inch with a new light alloy body, new doors, horizontally split tailgate hinged top and bottom, and two inward-facing seats on each side of the rear, giving a seating capacity for seven passengers. In theory, this was an excellent first step in providing an alternative to the basic machine already in existence, but there was the problem of pricing. Because it had to include Purchase Tax of over £200, the final price was about £960 – compared to £450 for the open model. The latter was now extremely good value, especially as within a very short time Rover had included such 'extras' as the doors and sidescreens, passenger seat and seat cushions, spare tyre, spare wheel carrier, starting handle and driver's hood, without raising the overall cost of the vehicle. This first estate model effectively priced itself out of the market and by 1951 it was discontinued. Here was a lesson learnt, and no subsequent Land Rover development has proved to be such an expensive and inglorious failure, thanks to much improved market research.

Having accepted that the Land Rover was here to stay, and had indeed become a well-established part of the rural, industrial and military scene, the Wilks brothers realized that development was inescapable. They had simply got off on the wrong foot with their first attempt. Before the original Land Rover was four years old, a different variation on the theme was available, and proving very popular this time. This sister model was a revised, cheaper version of the 7-seater Station Wagon in a much more basic form, with a hard-top and side windows – all built on the same 80-inch chassis and using the same 1,595 cc Rover P-3 engine. The only mechanical alteration to have taken place since the introduction of the Land Rover was to the transmission in the front power line: with a more powerful engine in the offing, it was felt advisable to protect the transmission by making 4-wheel drive automatic in low transfer gear and splitting the torque. To do this, the free-wheel was dropped in favour of the system in use today, using a simple dog clutch. In 1952 the engine itself was changed to the larger, more powerful 1,997 cc unit because the physical demands being made of the vehicle were in excess of its capability. Once in possession of the innovatory machine, owners expected it to balk at nothing, and the company decided that, rather than trying to re-educate them, it would be justified in providing more power. This was only the start of the public dictating the direction in which Land Rover was to evolve – but Tom Barton's engineering team were united behind the Wilks in their decision only to implement such modifications as would improve the vehicle's versatility, durability and saleability. This most definitely did not include any refinements conducive to driver or passenger comfort.

Predictably enough, the 1950s were to prove the most dramatic decade for Land Rover development, the era when it matured into the go-anywhere/do-anything transport for which it has become so famous. For several years the designers, engineers and planners scarcely had time to draw breath at Solihull – where by then the Land Rover had become the principal product. The next customer quibble that had to be quietened was that there was insufficient length in the rear loading area. Initially, the solution to this problem was found to be in extending the wheelbase dimensions of the chassis, from the well-known 80 inches to 86 inches – technically a more exacting and costly development than it would seem – but this was accompanied by a far more daring and ambitious development: the long wheelbase Land Rover. This model was born in 1954, simultaneously with the 86-inch short wheelbase. The extension of the short wheelbase model was effected by the addition of 6 inches between the bulkhead and back axle, with a further 3 inches of floor behind the axle, so that in practice the load space behind the seats was increased by 9 inches; the new long wheelbase model enlarged the load space by 21 inches more than that. The customers' complaint had been heeded, and most efficiently silenced, but at no small cost. Apart from the obvious requirement of new chassis members, the 86-inch version demanded a new propeller shaft, new springs (rear), new body panelling and a new exhaust system, not to mention a host of more minor modifications, which all added up to a high percentage of new components. The 107-inch long wheelbase, however, was a far larger undertaking. It shared common components with the 86-inch vehicle in the frame construction but the main side members had to be completely retooled, and in many other respects it was like producing an entirely new vehicle – though the end product was the familiar Land Rover, only longer.

Both these extended versions were destined to be manufactured in this form for little more than two years, when further changes took place, this time partly to quell a totally different customer grumble. A demand had rapidly grown up for a diesel-powered Land Rover. Many fleet-users were having to purchase petrol just for their Land Rovers, and commonization of fuel was soon to be regarded as both practical and logical. The Rover Company had so far had neither use for nor experience of diesel engines, but with typical thoroughness it embarked on the arduous business of researching and developing its own design of light diesel engine, unique to the Land Rover and very different from the existing petrol engine. During its development it became apparent that it was too big to drop into the existing engine housing, whatever they contrived to do with it: so the vehicle had to be enlarged yet again. Both 86-inch and 107-inch models had to have an extra 2 inches inserted in the chassis behind the front axle and in front of the toeboard, though for a year or so this mystified the public because the transfer of engine did not take place concurrently with the puzzlingly slight chassis extension. The new dimensions, of 88 inches and 109 inches, have existed ever since, for both petrol and diesel powered Land Rovers.

With the implementation of all these developments, the range of options increased dramatically. Alternative power units and a choice of body styles ensured Land Rover of ever expanding trade – but after 10 years it could not count on holding the centre of this particular 4 x 4 stage forever, and neither could it afford to rest on its laurels. The Series I model needed reappraisal. The challenge was given to the Rover's styling department: to do something with the vehicle's appearance, which had never before been under serious scrutiny at any time of its life. The subtlety lay in improving its style without damaging its rugged efficiency and without adding any superfluous trim for the sake of mere appearances; in other words, changes had to be discreet, and very carefully considered.

As the Rover diesel engine was introduced, a new Rover petrol unit was already in the pipeline, sharing many common features, engineering and production tooling with the diesel to replace the original P4-based engine. By now Land Rover exploitation was rife, and everybody who owned one tended to expect more from it than it had been designed to provide: an increase in power was unavoidable. The power of the new 2,286 cc petrol engine compared with Rover's first diesel was as follows:

Maximum power:	*Maximum torque:*
Petrol: 52 bhp at 4,000 rpm	101 lb/ft at 1,500 rpm
Diesel: 52 bhp at 3,500 rpm	87 lb/ft at 2,000 rpm

This new unit provided the most significant technical difference in the revised Land Rover, Series II. Evolved from the same basic layout as the Rover diesel engine, the 2,286 cc petrol unit had a bore and stroke of 90.47 x 88.9 mm (compared to 85.7 x 88.9 mm for the diesel), and it was bigger and stronger than its predecessor. The latter was by no means insubstantial, but it had been around for a long time – 10 years powering Land Rovers and 10 years before that. Land Rovers were ready to take on something more impressive, and the Series II was to provide the shell in which it would be accommodated.

In styling terms, the differences between the new Series II and the Series I which it was to supersede, were practical and in no way extreme: gentle reshaping of doors, wings (front and rear) and bonnet panel; sill panels fitted to conceal the exhaust system and chassis frame from view in profile (the designers felt that the vehicle was improperly dressed without this skirting below wings and doors); glass to replace the perspex of the sliding side windows; and several unseen improvements such as increase in wheel move-ment caused by relocation of rear springs, improved lock (reducing the turning circle by over 3 feet in the case of the short wheelbase model, and 5 feet on the 109-inch), and better ventilation through manually adjusted air-intakes along the base of the windscreen. From £450 for the 1948 80-inch Series I model, the 88-inch petrol Series II was introduced at £640, while the long wheelbase equivalent was £730. It is no coincidence that the Austin Gipsy appeared on the open market at about the same time as the Series II, but neither would it be fair to say that the threat posed by the Gipsy's appearance on the scene caused the Series II to be produced. Sales of the Series I were going well and a change of model was bound to cut back supply temporarily, but Land Rover were in need of a competitor, and this product provided a necessary and healthy fillip to maintain Land Rover's standards and keep its customers happy. Two years later the Home Sales Manager claimed that the changeover to Series II had caused home sales to double, so this policy was clearly the right one.

By the time its tenth birthday came around, the old 80-inch canvas-topped petrol Land Rover had been replaced by two 88-inch Land-Rovers (petrol or diesel powered), and four 109-inch Land Rovers (basic or de-luxe, petrol or diesel). However, by then the price the company was having to pay for its famous product was in having every other 4 x 4 machine ever invented being referred to as a land-rover. This caused the Rover Company to come up with the telling advertisement, 'When better land rovers are made, the Rover company will make them'. For the BBC, the problem had been reversed: because of their commitment not to advertise, they would not use the term Land-Rover, but – illogically – spoke freely of the 'Jeep', until the Rover

This Series II Land Rover was specially customized for HM Queen Elizabeth II.

Company pointed out that in so doing they were inadvertently promoting an American product over a British one. Thereafter Land Rover was given its rightful name.

The Series II Land Rover sold over 28,000 in its first full year, and over 34,000 the year after. Just over three years after its introduction, the Series II was to be replaced by the Series IIA, but the only appreciable difference in this applied to the diesel engined version. In 1958 the Series II had introduced the up-graded petrol engine to increase commonization of tooling with the diesel unit, but now in 1961 it was the turn of the diesel 2,052 cc engine to be up-graded to match the bore and stroke of the petrol 2,286 cc unit. By the end of that year Series IIA Land Rovers were rapidly replacing the original Series II off the production line. The following year, 1962, saw the introduction of the first 12-seater Land Rovers seating three people in the front, three in the back on a forward-facing bench seat, and three on each of the two inward-facing seats accessible from the rear door. This meant that the vehicle fell conveniently into the category of a bus, as far as the authorities were concerned, and hence could be sold free of Purchase Tax. This ploy soon virtually killed any demand for the 10-seater on the home market as, naturally enough, the public opted for the cheaper vehicle which was otherwise identical – but it is doubtful (to say the least!) that these 12-seaters have always been used to transport twelve people at a time. Anyone who has tried being one of twelve passengers in a Land Rover will confirm that it is far from ideal, especially for the six in the rear where the lack of headroom is only eclipsed by the lack of legroom. However, as a device to cut the purchase price for home market Land Rover Station Wagons, it has continued to work very well for over 20 years.

The 12-seater was not the only new model to emerge from the Solihull plant in 1962. It was accompanied by an entirely different-looking Land Rover – one that seemed at first glance to be more related to a truck than to the regular Land Rover. This was the forward-control unit that grew out of the demand for a far more robust load-carrier, one that was capable of bearing up to 30 cwt in reasonable conditions and 25 cwt cross-country, with a much enlarged load-space. Basing such a requirement on the Land Rover 109-inch chassis and engine meant total revision of layout, body style and transmission – the obvious first amendment being to the basic structure. In order to achieve the flat platform for additional load-space, a new frame was built to marry on to the existing 109-inch chassis. This proved to be much more economical than developing a completely new chassis for the purpose but resulted in a relatively heavy unit, given that the normal Land Rover 2,286 cc petrol engine was to be used. This possibly explains the comparatively short production period of the vehicle in this form, from its announcement in 1962 at the Commercial Vehicle Show until 1966, when it was redesigned to offer the option of the diesel 2,286 cc engine and also a 6-cylinder engine. Because of the drastic changes in layout from the conventional Land Rover plan, forward-control was incorporated at the outset, as well as heavy duty axles and much bigger tyres, but the majority of components were, surprisingly, the same as those used on the regular Land Rover. The appearance was altered as much by the repositioning of the cab as by the increase in ground clearance and load-space area. The forward-control Land Rover's cab was placed much further forward to allow load-space behind, and provided the only seating arrangements. Adapted from the existing cab, it could be either open or of the truck variety. Gear change linkage and the layout of the steering had to be redesigned among all the other more minor details, but the end result was still unmistakably a Land Rover. When, four years later, it was altered to accommodate the 2,286 cc diesel engine option, it also became available with a 6-cylinder, 2,625 cc petrol engine that had been developed from the earlier Rover car P4/P5, noted for its reliability. The wheelbase was extended by 1 inch, and the wheel tracks by 4 inches for improved handling and stability. This model was to endure in its revised form until just before the introduction of the specialized forward-control military Land Rover built on the 101-inch wheelbase, with the V8 3,528 cc engine, and constant 4-wheel drive – a far more sophisticated machine. Although a prototype was to be seen at the Commercial Vehicle Show in 1972, production didn't start until 1974/5. The new light-weight military 88-inch Land Rover was introduced concurrently, and full descriptions of both these units are included in the Military chapter.

This same 6-cylinder 2,625 cc engine also became available in the 109-inch wheelbase of the conventional Land Rover in 1967, to give it greater refinement. Being longer, it was a tight squeeze to fit it in but by allowing the space for bellhousing and clutch to be pared down to the barest minimum it was achieved without extending any existing dimensions. At the same time, both 88-inch and 109-inch models were treated to an internal facelift in the driving compartment, encompassing windscreen wiper, handbrake, controls, instruments, switches and dials, as well as vastly improved front seat cushioning which became available as an optional extra on all Series IIA models. None of these adjustments affected the external appearance of the Land Rover which had remained basically unchanged since its initial restyling. In 1968, however, the headlamps on export models were to change their position, which noticeably altered the front view: having been mounted close together, deep-set between the wings and protected by the radiator grille, they were moved out to the wing position that they have held ever since. This was induced by specific legislation in certain overseas territories relating to motor vehicle lighting. A year later home market models were to follow suit and have wing-mounted headlamps as well.

The advent of the Range Rover in 1970 and its subsequent development is dealt with in detail in its own chapter, so we shall skip on to 1971 when the Series IIA Land Rovers were replaced by the Series III, with the exception of the forward-control 109-inch vehicles. These continued to be produced in the Series IIA form until they were finally superseded by the 101-inch 1-tonne Land Rovers.

Land Rover 1947 prototype.

The Series III came about for reasons which were very similar to those behind the introduction of the Series II. While there was nothing in particular wrong with the current model, it was not noticeably moving with the times, had not undergone drastic changes or improvements since its beginnings, and was facing increasing competition with every passing year. This time, had the capital been available, perhaps a totally revamped version could have resulted from all the probing and questioning that took place behind the scenes at Solihull, but – as always – despite its success as an exportable commodity as well as on the home front, the cash to expand and develop was limited. Additionally, Land Rovers buyers were not clamouring for radical change, because the old-style workhorse was still proving very popular. Thus, what eventually came about was not a remarkably restyled machine, but the Land Rover as we know it today, which is still being assembled in ever greater quantities each year. It differs from its predecessor in many details, but the chassis, wheelbase dimensions, body styles, suspensions and general layout remained unchanged. One crucial difference was in the transmission: the original basic gearbox was finally discarded in favour of a new all-synchromesh design which was unique to the Series III Land Rover within the Rover stable. With synchromesh on all forward gears, it had revised internal ratios (first and reverse ratios were much reduced), and a reduced low-range step-down ratio, which combined to uphold stoically the Land Rover's climbing capability, while facilitating a smoother and quieter gear change, helped by the inclusion at this stage of a diaphragm spring clutch. Other mechanical alterations to the basic specification of the vehicle included the replacement of dynamos by alternators, improved brakes, and heavy-duty rear axles (and strengthened stub axles) fitted as standard on all long wheelbase models, while vacuum-servos were also standardized on all 6-cylinder models. Visually, there was little alteration externally, the principal difference being in the new radiator grille, but internally it was another story: the dashboard was completely redesigned, incorporating an open stowage locker, and the new steering-column switchgear and steering wheel (as well as steering lock) were prominent features. There was also a much better fresh-air heater. Land Rover was beginning to recognize that its customers did not necessarily have to be penalized by undergoing a constant endurance test, but were quite entitled to their creature comforts, especially considering the hardships to be suffered in some areas of Land Rover operations. The Series III even had provision for a radio to be fitted, which would have been laughable in 1948.

Before moving on to the 1970s, there is one other model to mention, dating from 1968. This is the heavy duty 1-ton Land Rover, built on the Series IIA 109 inch chassis (and physically resembling this model on completion) but with much reduced overall gearing to allow for the loading and towing of increased weights. The '1-ton' description refers to the official maximum total payload, but like all official limits it has to err on the side of conservatism because it is bound to be exceeded – as Land Rover manufacturers were to discover from the word go. The 1-ton took the wise precaution of bracing itself against such abuse: equipped with the heavy duty transmission components of the forward-control Land Rover, it achieved overall ratios of 15.40:1, 23.10:1, 34.10:1, 55.3:1, and 46.4:1 in reverse when in low range, which effectively widened the potential of Land Rover accomplishments. Although it never became a great seller, this unit held a much-valued place in the more specialized and rarified sector of the market, until it was replaced by the Series III equivalent model when these became standard in 1971.

In 1976 an auspicious occasion was celebrated at Solihull, with the production of Land Rover Number One-Million. This was a short wheelbase 7-seater which was destined to join the very first Land Rover, RO.1, in the Leyland Historic Vehicles Collection. The quarter-million mark had been reached in 1959, the half-million mark in 1966, and the three-quarter million mark in 1971.

From the point of view of product development, the next highly significant milestone was the introduction of the 109 inch V8 engined Land Rover in 1979. The total 4 x 4 market had been growing rapidly and consistently and, accordingly, the product requirements had also been evolving. Interest

Note the redesigned front of the V8 Land Rover.

stimulated by increased ecological awareness, and by increased leisure-use of 4-wheel-drive vehicles, coupled with the improved road networks in many overseas territories, imposed higher standards of performance and comfort both on and off the road. The Range Rover proved beyond all doubt that luxury and ruggedness could be successfully united, and that a market existed for this combination. What the V8 Land Rover presented was the dependability, the load-space and the indestructability of the Land Rover, combined with the proven power unit and drive-line of the Range Rover. Although the power output of the V8 was reduced to suit customer application of the new Land Rover, it is still one-third up on the 4-cylinder model. The 3,528cc 8-cylinder light alloy petrol unit entailed under-the-bonnet enlargement of the standard 109 inch model (the V8 engine was not made available on the 88 inch chassis) which explains the frontal re-styling that distinguishes it so glaringly from all other Land Rovers. The bonnet, fitted with a broad metal radiator grille, extends to fit flush with the wings, and the radiator is no longer recessed between the wings as has been the case on all former models.

The smoother, more powerful V8 engine enhances on-road performance and produces peak torque and power at exceptionally low engine speeds,

1962 109-inch Series IIA station wagon.

First production Land Rover ('HUE'), with Series II 88-inch full-length soft top.

Early V8 Land Rovers fording a stream.

improving towing capability as well as the cross-country performance (this is dealt with in detail in the Expedition chapter). Like the Range Rover, the V8 Land Rover offers permanent 4-wheel drive, and when the going gets really tough the centre differential can be locked for even greater traction. The engine gives a top speed of over 80 mph, and the ability to climb gradients as steep as 45° or 1 in 1. The introduction of the V8 Land Rover was marked by new dazzling colour options – Java green, Masai red, Inca yellow, and Pageant blue – as well as the more sober selection of colours current on existing Series III models.

At this stage it should be pointed out that one great advantage of the 'meccano'-style design of the Land Rover is that it can be exported in kit form and assembled overseas. A total of nearly 50,000 Land Rovers are sold in this way every year, and about 2,300 Range Rovers. The following countries have their own Land Rover assembly plants: Angola, Australia, Iran, Kenya, Malagasy, Malaysia, Indonesia, Morocco, New Zealand, Nigeria, Phillipines, Spain, Portugal, South Africa, Tanzania, Thailand, Trinidad, Zaire, Zambia, Zimbabwe, and most recently of all, Sudan. This is an aspect of Land Rover exports which is constantly developing and growing – though it means that model changes are not always greeted with enthusiasm by the overseas factories: changes at home entail equivalent changes abroad, and the wisdom of it all is not always appreciated by those assembling Land Rovers at long range!

Santana

In 1956 The Rover Company reached an agreement with a company in Spain called Metalurgica de Santa Ana, S.A., manufacturers of 4-wheel drive vehicles. Though BL is still today the largest single share-holder in the company that was formed then, 'Santana' Land Rovers have evolved rather differently from their British-made equivalent models, mainly because of the markets into which they sell. The Spanish factories produce their Land Rovers under licence, selling throughout the Spanish territories and exporting to 25 countries, predominantly in South America, Central America and North Africa. They also manufacture Land Rovers in knock-down form for export to Morocco, Iran and Costa Rica, where they are assembled on arrival.

The original company was founded with a total capital of 3 million pesetas, but there are now four major Santana bases in Spain: two important manufacturing sites, a technical service centre, and the head offices in Madrid. Their output of Land Rovers has steadily risen over the years, topping 18,000 by 1980, and the firm also makes gear boxes, over 93,000 of which were sold in that year.

Most Santana Land Rovers are based on the Series III A unit, but are adapted to suit local market requirements and conditions. Nearly all their vehicles are diesel-engined as their order books always show a heavy bias in favour of diesel, so they haven't become involved with the manufacture of V8s, and they don't manufacture Range Rovers at all. Although there is an infinite

The Spanish-built Santana S-2000.

number of variations on the theme, there are five basic variations of the 88-inch, four of the 109-inch (with either 4-or 6-cylinder engine option) and two of their own model S-2000 which is an extremely tough and versatile forward control truck, not unlike the 101-inch 1-tonne Land Rover that used to be produced for the military market at Solihull. For fans of the 101-inch, it is comforting that there is still a comparably resilient and powerful vehicle being manufactured by Santana, although production of the 101-inch itself has ceased, and their product is sold for use as anything from a tipper to a cattle- or vehicle-transporter, and – unlike the 101-inch – is also available with an extended cab incorporating a second row of seats.

There are instances where Santana has developed in areas that the British parent company has not, for example in taper leaf suspension, and their own turbo charged $2\frac{1}{4}$ litre diesel engine. If you come across a Land Rover when you are abroad that has real leather upholstery and much more comfortable seats, or a polished wooden handle on the gear lever, you can be pretty sure that it originates from the Santana stable.

* * * * *

After publication of the above in June 1990 Land Rover released the following statement:

'Rover Group has announced that it has sold its 23 per cent shareholding in the Spanish Company, Land Rover Santana.

Over 30 years ago Land Rover Limited and Santana manufactured similar Land Rover vehicles. But in recent years the relationship has changed as Land Rover in the UK have launched new vehicles and Santana have developed their own range of four-wheel drive vehicles.

Rover Group's shareholding in the Spanish Company has decreased in recent years as the Spanish operation has become less important to Land Rover's worldwide business strategies.'

The £200 million investment programme, embarked on relatively soon after Land Rover Limited was established as a self-governing company, was geared to encompass a series of new developments. Stage 1 gave us the V8; then came the 4-door Range Rover, which was followed by the up-market 'County' Land Rover, and the High-Capacity Pick-Up, or HCPU as it quickly became known. This was followed, early in 1983, by the 110-inch model, a dramatically different vehicle planned to eventually replace all 109-inch Series III Land Rovers, then, in 1984, the final stage of the investment programe was marked by the launch of the completely new model, the 90-inch, but let us first deal with the 1982 innovations.

The 'County' was introduced to bridge the 'comfort gap' between existing Land Rovers and the Range Rover, focusing mainly on seating, upholstery, trim and noise reduction. The end result is certainly a Land-Rover with a difference, decidedly up-grading it, while only increasing the price by four-to five-hundred pounds above standard models.

The 'County' is easily distinguished from its sister-models by full-length side stripes running horizontally along the body, and also by such refinements as tinted glass windows, reversing light, rear mud flaps, side flashers and spare wheel cover, all of which are standard items. The seats in front are a new de-luxe design for far greater comfort, and all seats are upholstered in a grey-black tweed which is a very pleasant change from the cold black vinyl of the usual Land Rover seating (though we were a bit worried about keeping the fabric clean and looking good: most attractive when brand new but perhaps less of an assett when grubby and stained). Instead of a centre front seat, a

44

Land Rover enthusiasts meet to view the new 110-inch in 1983.

The 110 Station Wagon.

lockable box can be fitted, as in Range Rovers, and the position of both front seats can be adjusted forwards and backwards as well as having a reclining back: very good news for those of us who have suffered from 'Land Rover Back' over the years, owing to the seat's hitherto uncompromising rigidity. It might look a bit gimmicky on such a work-horse of a vehicle, but, particularly on long slow towing journeys, the additional comfort makes for a much more relaxed driver (and passenger) at the end of the day. Engine noise reduction also contributes to the sense of well-being when driving this vehicle, and when 'County' trim is coupled to the 110-inch Station Wagon body and power-assisted steering (as was the case with the first one we drove), it is almost possible to forget you are in a Land Rover at all! On all Station Wagons in the 'County' range, a Boge Hydromat self-levelling unit is a standard fitting, improving the ride still further. For power, lightness and classy detail this model seemed at once to be a sure winner.

As might be expected, the main feature of the High-Capacity Pick-Up is its increased and improved load space. The load bed is completely new, and there is an additional 7 inches behind the rear chassis member. No longer do you see full-length boxes on each side of the load space, the only boxed-in area being over the rear wheels themselves. Effectively the cubic capacity has been increased by 45%, and the tailgate, supported now by coated steel wire instead of the familiar chains, is 18 inches wider than on standard pick-ups. Number plate and light are mounted on the tailgate, and there are now tubular steel protective 'mini-bumpers' below both light panels. Another clever feature is in the load space having a double skin, so that scratching and denting of the interior does not mar the exterior appearance.

Now, what about the 110-inch, the long-awaited 'new' Land Rover? Before its unveiling, rumours abounded about this model, and personally we were quite worried that Land Rover might have gone too far, firmly believing that any vehicle worthy of the name Land Rover must be immediately recognisable as such. Luckily the apprehension was ill-founded, as all the external differences are relatively discreet, like the taller one-piece windscreen, flares over the wheel arches (in flexible polyurethane) and wider plastic, radiator grille and headlamp panel, while the more remarkable differences are concealed from view, like the superb coil suspension, permanent 4-wheel drive, 5-speed gear box on 4-cylinder models, and new disc brakes on the front. The interior, too, has changed. The hand brake has been modified, the dashboard panel updated, the heater improved, the doors lined with new one-piece trim and fitted with new handles and locks (all doors lock externally), and ventilation to the interior is improved by new sliding windows, whose locking device was initially disastrous but quickly remedied. From the driver's seat the windscreen's additional height and uninterrupted expanse can be fully appreciated; it improves visibility much more than the extra 2 inches in height would suggest, and makes older models seem very restricted in comparison. Power-assisted steering is optional on the 110-inch, and engine options are the

One of the most fundamental improvements adopted in the 110 was the coil-spring suspension.

A view of the 110's mechanical components.

4-cylinder, $2\frac{1}{4}$ litre petrol, $2\frac{1}{2}$ litre diesel, and the V8. At the time of its launch, people expressed disappointment that the overall dimensions and form of the 110-inch were not more drastically different, but since the model is intended to elbow the Series III out altogether through time, there are obvious practical and economic reasons why many Series III features should be retained. Gilroy has been quoted as saying, "The element of continuity is very important, because we operate in a conservative market that appreciates evolution rather than revolution ...", which we feel encapsulates Land Rover's philosophy with regard to product development. Even though the approach has clearly been 'evolutionary' rather than 'revolutionary', the resulting model is without question the most important and striking single development from Land-Rover since it became established. Within a year of the 110's appearance on the market in March 1983 its impact was already being felt, not only at home but in Europe, the Middle East and Far East as well, culminating in an unexpected fillip to sales figures with a military order from the Far East for 900 110-inch units, well in advance of anticipated military sales, after what Tony Gilroy described as, "the most extensive testing and trials ever encountered".

For Land Rover's management the other gratifying new area that opened with the 110-inch – especially with the "County" Station Wagon – was that of the large estate car, with which Land Rover had been unable to compete in the past in terms of comfort; the 110-inch broke down those barriers to include a whole new market sector, and in the UK in 1983 Land Rover had its best selling year since 1980 (one third of the units sold were 110-inch models which is not at all bad for a vehicle's first year!).

The 90-inch Pick-Up, new for 1984.

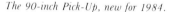

In May 1984 Land Rover was ready to announce the first set of improvements to the vehicle, having evidently quizzed their customers extensively on suggested further refinements. The up-shot was, for the first time ever, wind-up windows on the front doors to replace the sliding type (which greatly improves visibility, and makes putting your head out to reverse, or watch the ground when negotiating 'rough-stuff' off-the-road, a great deal less hazardous); new door trim to smarten up the interior appearance; new sliding windows on the rear section of the Station Wagon which are easier to adjust, and a new wash-wipe system on the rear door window which is also now electrically heated. Keeping the rear window clean is a long overdue refinement in view of the exceptionally wet and muddy conditions through which many Land Rovers travel in the course of a day's work. Added to all this, in the 'County' version you find fitted carpets! When the Range Rover turned up carpeted many years ago there were plenty of raised eyebrows, but whoever would have guessed that this would be the way of the Land Rover as well? In practice, of course, it reduces noise levels still further, is a great deal more comfortable, and looks very good. Gone are the days when Land Rovers were designed essentially for farming, though, of course, you can still get them appropriately equipped just for that. Looking at the new 110-inch though, every indication is that Land Rover knows exactly where it's going, through the eighties and beyond.

If the 110-inch seemed like a breakthrough in 1983, it was certainly rivalled in 1984 by the startling arrival of its little sister, the 90-inch. Here was a vehicle without comparison, a jaunty yet streamlined body sitting lightly on its powerful coil springs, yet as tough and durable as any 4 x 4 anywhere, designed to reach a ripe old age ("where others build in obsolescence, we build in longevity" – Tony Gilroy) without losing any of its work-horse qualities. The ingenuity entailed in conceiving such a vehicle, which combines old attributes with new standards of comfort, efficiency and technology without any evident compromise, in a much more compact package, is a measure of the experience and expertise of the team behind it, who we reckon have earned a standing ovation for this one, though when we said as much at the launch of the new unit, the response of the management was, to a man, "never mind the accolades, as long as we fill the order books!" It is, after all, a ferociously competitive field, and to maintain its forward position Land Rover has not only to create innovative products, but sell them very hard. Nobody could deny that the current models will stand them in excellent stead to combat whatever opposition turns up.

The new 90-inch, or 'Ninety', may be much smaller than the 110-inch, but it is actually nearly $4\frac{1}{2}$-inches longer than the Series III 88-inch and of its class has unsurpassed payload potential with bigger cubic capacity and load length, but one interesting feature of the model is that the rear overhang is $2\frac{1}{2}$ inches *less,* which means the vehicle has an impressive departure angle of up to 52°, as well as better towing ability. The model is manufactured with either a petrol

The interior shared by the 90 and 110, showing how far the Land Rover has come over the years.

or a diesel 4-cylinder engine, the latter being the latest 2.5 litre diesel. The petrol engine develops 74bhp (55kw) and 120 lbf ft (163 Nm) of torque from its 2286cc. The 2495cc diesel engine, introduced only months before the 90-inch itself, gives 67 bhp (50kw) and 114 lbf ft (155Nm) of torque at only 1800 rpm, and is proving to be a very popular development, especially with those who use power take-off equipment, because of the economy and dependability it provides. Throughout the 90-inch range, which includes soft-top, hard-top, pick-up and 6- or 7-seater station wagon in both standard and 'County' versions, as well as chassis-cab for would-be converters, 5-speed transmission with 2-speed transfer box is fitted as standard, plus permanent 4-wheel drive. Power-assisted steering is available as an option for the first time ever on a short wheelbase, (and when combined with the top-of-the-range 'County' Station Wagon makes for phenomenally smooth riding and handling). Externally, the 90-inch has many features in common with the 110-inch: the flexible 'eyebrows' of the wheel arches, the flush black radiator grille, and of course the one-piece windscreen, which is increased in size by 25% over its Series III equivalent. Also in common with the revised 110-inch, there are wind-up windows and new trim on the doors (front passengers might miss the door's arm-rest, however), an improved heating system, decreased noise levels and an up-dated design of instrument panel in the dashboard. Also in common with 110-inch models, 90-inch Station Wagons have heated rear window-glass and a modern wash-wipe system – the water being very effectively squirted from the side of the glass instead of from the base. While on the subject of rear windows it is perhaps worth mentioning a fact that Land Rover is rather pleased about, and that is the introduction of aluminium rear window frames as standard on pick-up cabs and Station Wagons, reducing the rust problem. Aluminium as a material has been a good friend to Land Rover (and a good selling point over the years) so they are always glad to see the percentage of aluminium increased as their vehicles evolve. The 'County'

A Janspeed turbo installation on a 2¼ litre diesel Land Rover engine.

version, as on the 110-inch wheelbase, has its own special refinements: hard-wearing carpet front and rear, tinted glass, a quartz clock, spare wheel cover and radial tyres.

Physically a lot less obvious than all the above modifications, but one of the most significant features of the 90-inch range is the suspension, which is also shared with the 110-inch. The new front and rear long-travel coil springs, with 2-way hydraulic dampers, dramatically improve rider comfort both on-road and off, and make cornering and general handling far surer since the friction inherent in multi-leaf springs is eliminated. Another important innovation is powerful servo-assisted disc-brakes for the front wheels which resist fade, and take less time to dry out after passing through deep water than the Series III brakes. The drums at the rear have improved sealing (like the 110-inch) all of which provides remarkably good and steady stopping power, even when heavily laden, or towing. The discs and drums are supplemented by a 110 inch (254mm) transmission handbrake. The front wheels also have more room to manoeuvre on the new models because the track has been increased to $58\frac{1}{2}$ inches (2360mm), which makes negotiation of awkward spaces or dense traffic much simpler.

The payload of the 90-inch is another of its impressive characteristics (and one which proves that all the 'refining' has not been at the expense of work-horse capability, but rather in support of it). Where such competitors as Daihatsu carry 411 kg, the CJ5 Jeep 531 kg, the Colt Shogun 735 kg and even the Galaendewagen by Mercedes-Benz only 805 kg, the 90-inch exceeds even its own predecessor – the 88-inch Series III – by achieving a payload of 917 kg, and can tow an unbraked trailer of up to 750 kg, or a fully braked unit of up to 4 tonnes. The key to this unprecedented strength lies in the immensely robust separate, box-section ladder-type steel chassis which is in effect just a

Defender 90 county station wagon.

shortened version of the 110's (useful commonality for servicing and spares), and is designed to protect the 12-gallon, side-mounted fuel tank as well as to provide front and rear jacking points.

1988. In the four years since the above was written, sales of Ninety, One Ten and the One Two Seven have fluctuated, peaking in 1984-85 at over 31,000, and bottoming last year at 20,475 which was the lowest figure since 1953-54. The reason is ascribed to the loss of crucial markets due to economic instability, but at Solihull there is confidence that these markets will in due course come back on stream, and Land Rovers have been continuing to be evolved with undiminished enthusiasm. Some variations have ceased to be offered from the factory: the V8 Ninety which had become available in 1985, and will be missed since it was the most powerful short wheelbase ever (and impressively nimble), and the full-length soft top on all models (except for large orders). But a dramatic addition to the range has been the introduction of the Turbo Diesel engine option.

There had been an upgrading of the standard 4-cylinder petrol engine in 1985, from 2286 cc to 2495 cc, whereas the 2.5 litre diesel had already been around since January 1984 when the 2.5 litre turbocharged engine was introduced in 1986, offering a combination of 25% increase in power and 28% more torque. This innovation came after strenuous testing and painstaking development; it was not simply a naturally aspirated engine with a bolt-on kit. The turbocharger is a Garret AiResearch T 2 which underwent Land Rover adaptations until it met with the necessary engineering criteria. The air intake grille, a black rectangle behind the front left hand wheel arch, and a rear end badge are external identifying characteristics of the turbo Land Rover, but from the driver's seat there can be no mistaking its identity: there's never been a diesel Land Rover with such power, and it is there from the outset, no sudden surge as the turbo comes on line. We recently drove a Turbo D Station Wagon from Britain to West Africa (a vehicle loaned by Land Rover to The World Wide Fund for Nature – previously known as The World Wildlife Fund – for a conservation project) and could not fault its performance on or off the road. Including rough piste and deep sand conditions, it still averaged 22 mpg. The only potential snag is unavailability of the special engine oil in remote areas, but for our purposes we had sufficient with us probably to last for the 14 months initial loan period. We also, incidentally, had two 2.5 litre naturally aspirated diesel high capacity pick-ups which were stalwart load carriers, one of which maintained an average consumption of fuel of over 24 mpg.

So now there is a choice of four engines (two petrol and two diesel), two lengths of wheel base, and at least four body options (pick-up, hard top, station wagon and County station wagon). Together with all the options and special adaptations available from the factory, in theory the assembly line could work flat out for 20 years and still not produce exactly the same vehicle twice!

There have been certain refinements to the County, which now has a sunhatch available (with separate accessory pack from Land Rover parts dealers), and a stereo radio/cassette. On the rest of the range, the galvanised steel bumper is no more; along with wheel arch eyebrows, radiator grille and headlamp surrounds, the bumper is now black for an extra touch of distinction. On the County these features are finished in the body colour of the vehicle, which currently, across the range, consists of the following options: Arrow red, Shire blue, Ivory white, Slate grey, Trident or Bronze green; and the body side stripes are in graduated silver. Interior trim has changed as well, to grey, and the steering wheel is leather-trimmed.

TECHNICAL DATA

2,286cc 4-CYLINDER DIESEL ENGINE

Engine, Diesel models

Bore	90.47 mm (3.562 in)
Stroke	88.9 mm (3.500 in)
Number of cylinders	4
Compression ratio	23:1
Cylinder capacity	2,286 cc (139.5 cu in)
BHP } BHP and maximum torque figures are derived	67 (50 Kw) at 4,000 revs/min
Torque } from bench tests and do not allow for installation losses in the vehicle.	14.5 kg m (105 lb ft) at 1,800 revs/min
Firing Order	1, 3, 4, 2
Tappet clearance, inlet	0.25 mm (0.010 in) } Engine at running
Tappet clearance, exhaust	0.25 mm (0.010 in) } temperature
Valve timing (No. 1 exhaust valve peak)	109° BTDC
Oil pressure	2,5 to 4,5 kg/cm² (35 to 65 lb/sq in) at 50 kph (30 mph) in top gear with engine warm
Lubrication	Full pressure
Oil filter, internal	Gauze pump intake filter in sump
Oil filter, external	Full-flow filter

Fuel system, Diesel models

Fuel pump	Mechanical with hand primer (high pressure type)
Air cleaner	Oil bath type with integral centrifugal pre-cleaner
Fuel filters	Paper type element and sedimenter on export models

Injection system, Diesel models

Injector pump	Distributor type, self-governing
Injectors: Type	CAV Pintaux, nozzle size BDNO/SPC 6209
Start of injection	13° BTDC

2,625 cc 6-CYLINDER PETROL ENGINE

Engine, 6-cylinder Petrol models

Bore	77.8 mm (3.063 in)
Stroke	92.075 mm (3.625 in)

Number of cylinders	6
Cylinder capacity	2,625 cc (160.3 cu in)
Compression ratio	7.8:1
	7.0:1 (optional)
BHP } BHP and maximum torque figures are derived from bench tests and do not allow for installation losses in the vehicle	95 (71 Kw) at 4,500 revs/min
Maximum torque	18.5 kg m (134 lb ft) at 1,750 revs/min
Firing order	1, 5, 3, 6, 2, 4
Sparking plugs	
7.8:1 and 7.0:1 compression ratio	Champion N5
Sparking plug point gap	0.75 to 0.80 mm (0.029 to 0.032 in)
Distributor contact breaker gap	0.35 to 0.40 mm (0.014 to 0.016 in)
Ignition timing static and dynamic	
7.8:1 compression ratio	2° ATDC 90 octane fuel United
	6° ADTC 85 octane fuel Kingdom
7.0:1 compression ratio (optional)	2° BTDC 83 octane fuel } use 2 star
7.0:1 compression ratio (optional)	TDC 80 octane fuel } grade fuel
Tappet clearance, inlet	0.15 mm (0.006 in) Engine hot
Tappet clearance, exhaust	0.25 mm (0.010 in) Engine hot or cold
Valve timing (No. 1 exhaust valve peak)	
7.8:1 compression ratio	105° BTDC
7.0:1 compression ratio (optional)	105° BTDC
Oil pressure	2.8 to 3.5 kg/cm² (40 to 50 lb/sq in) at 50 kph (30 mph) in top gear with engine warm
Lubrication	Full pressure
Oil filter, internal	Gauze pum intake filter in sump
Oil filter, external	Full-flow filter

Fuel system, 6-cylinder Petrol models

Petrol pump	Electric, located at chassis side-member
Carburetter	Zenith Type 175 CD 2S single horizontal dust-proof
Air cleaner	Oil bath type with integral centrifugal pre-cleaner

SERIES III SHORT-WHEELBASE LAND ROVER

Engine 2.25-litre (Petrol)

Type	4-cylinder petrol
Bore	90.47 mm (3.56)

Stroke	88.9 mm (3.5 in)	
Capacity	2286 cc	
Compression Ratio	7:1	8:1
Maximum Power	47.8 kW (64 bhp)	51.5 kW (69 bhp)
	at 4000 r/min	
Maximum Torque	154 N m (113.5 lb ft)	159 N m (117.2 lb ft)
	at 2000 r/min	
Firing Order	1, 3, 4, 2	

Engine 2.25-litre (Diesel)

Type	4-cylinder diesel
Bore	90.47 mm (3.56 in)
Stroke	88.9 mm (3.5 in)
Capacity	2286 cc
Compression Ratio	23.1
Maximum Power	41.9 kW (56.2 bhp) at 4000 r/min
Maximum Torque	137.3 N m (101.3 lb ft) at 1800 r/min

Lubrication

Nominal Pressure	Engine warm at 2000 r/min
	2.46–4.57 kg/cm² (35–65 lb/in²)
Oil filters internal	Gauze pump-intake filter
external	Full flow oil filter

Fuel System (Petrol)

Carburettor	Single Zenith 361V
Petrol Pump	Mechanical with priming lever and sediment bowl

Fuel System (Diesel)

Injectors	CAV Pintaux
Fuel Pump	Mechanical with priming lever
Injector Pump	Self-governing D.P.A. distributor type

Cooling System

Type	Pressurised with pump, fan, thermostat and expansion tank
Working Pressure	0.63 kg/cm² (9 lb/in²)
Thermostat	82°C

Transmission

Clutch	Diaphragm spring, single dry plate
Diameter	241 mm (9.5 in)

Main Gearbox	4-speed and reverse
	Synchromesh on forward gears
Transfer Gearbox	2-speed reduction on main gearbox output.
	Two-/four-wheel-drive control on transfer box
	output
Differential Ratios	Both Axles 4.7:1
Front Axle	Hypoid spiral-bevel, with fully-floating shafts
	and enclosed universal joints
Rear Axle	Hypoid spiral-bevel, with full-floating shafts
Propeller Shafts	Open type 50.8 mm (2.0 in)

Steering

Type	Recirculating ball, worm and nut
Lock-to-lock	3.5 turns
Steering Damper	Optional – fitted to drag link (standard for
	certain export markets)
Turning Circle	11.60 m (38 ft)

Wheels

Type	Steel-ventilated disc
Fixing	5 stud
Size	5.00F x 16 in
Tyre Size	6.00 x 16 in

Brakes

Type	Hydraulic drum
Drum Diameter	254 mm (10 in)
Brake Shoe Width	38 mm (1.50 in) front and rear
Handbrake	Mechanical – on transfer box output
Drum Diameter	228.6 mm (9.00 in)
Brake Shoe Width	44.5 mm (1.75 in)

Electrical – Petrol

Type	12-volt negative earth
Battery	58 amps/hour
Ignition	Coil
Alternator	16 ACR – 34 amp output
Starter Motor	Inertia type

Electrical – Diesel

Type	12-volt negative earth
Battery	95 amps/hour
Ignition	Compression ignition
Alternator	16 ACR – 34 amp output
Starter Motor	Pre-engaged type

Capacities

Cooling System (petrol)	8.1 litres (14.25 pt)
(diesel)	7.8 litres (13.75 pt)
Engine Oil (including filter)	6.85 litres (11.5 pt)
Main Gearbox	1.5 litres (2.5 pt)
Transfer Gearbox	2.5 litres (4.5 pt)
Rear Differential }	1.75 litres (3 pt)
Front Differential }	
Fuel Tank	45 litres (10 gal)

SERIES III LONG-WHEELBASE LAND ROVER

Engine 2.25-litre (Petrol)

Type	4-cylinder	
Bore	90.47 mm (3.56 in)	
Stroke	88.9 mm (3.5 in)	
Capacity	2286 cc	
Compression Ratio	7:1	8:1
Maximum Power	47.8 kW (64 bhp)	51.5 kW (69 bhp)
	at 4000 r/min	
Maximum Torque	154 N m (113.5 lb ft)	159 N m (117.2 lb ft)
	at 2000 r/min	
Firing Order	1, 3, 4, 2	

Engine 2.6-litre (Petrol)

Type	6-cylinder	
Bore	77.8 mm (3.06 in)	
Stroke	92.07 mm (3.62 in)	
Capacity	2625 cc	
Compression Ratio	7:1	7.8:1
Maximum Power	53.7kW (72 bhp)	57.4 kW (76.9 bhp)
	at 4200 r/min	at 4500 r/min
Maximum Torque	160.9 N m (118.6 lb ft)	164.8 N m (121.5 lb ft)
	at 2000 r/min	
Firing Order	1, 5, 3, 6, 2, 4	

Engine 2.25-litre (Diesel)

Type	4-cylinder
Bore	90.47 mm (3.56 in)
Stroke	88.9 mm (3.5 in)
Capacity	2286 cc
Compression Ratio	23:1
Maximum Power	41.9 kW (56.2 bhp) at 4000 r/min

Maximum Torque	137.3 N m (101.3 lb ft) at 1800 r/min
Firing Order	1, 3, 4, 2

Lubrication

Nominal Pressure	Engine warm at 2000 r/min
2.25-litre engine	2.46–4.57 kg/cm² (35–65 lb/in²)
2.6-litre engine	2.81–3.51 kg/cm² (40–50 lb/in²)
Oil filters internal	Gauze pump-intake filter
external	Full flow oil filter

Fuel System 2.25-litre (Petrol)

Carburettor	Single Zenith 361V
Petrol Pump	Mechanical with priming lever and sediment bowl

Fuel System 2.25-litre (Diesel)

Injectors	CAV Pintaux
Fuel Pump	Mechanical with priming lever
Injector Pump	Self-governing DPA distributor type

Fuel System 2.6-litre (Petrol)

Carburettor	Single Zenith 175-CD2S
Petrol Pump	Electric dual inlet

Cooling System

Type	Pressurised with pump, fan, thermostat and expansion tank
Working Pressure	0.63 kg/cm² (9 lb/in²)
Thermostat	2.25-litre engine 82°C
	2.6-litre engine 78°C

Transmission

Clutch	Diaphragm spring, single dry plate
Diameter	241 mm (9.5 in)
Main Gearbox	4-speed and reverse – synchromesh on forward gears
Transfer Gearbox	2-speed reduction on main gearbox output Two-/four-wheel-drive control on transfer box output
Differential Ratios	Both Axles 4.7:1
Front Axle	Hypoid spiral-bevel, with fully-floating shafts and enclosed universal joints
Rear Axle	Hypoid spiral-bevel, with fully-floating shafts
Propeller Shafts	Open type 50.8 mm (2.0 in)

Steering

Type	Recirculating ball, worm and nut
Lock-to-lock	3.5 turns
Steering Damper	Optional – fitted to drag link (standard for certain export markets)
Turning Circle	14.3 m (47ft)

Wheels

Type	Steel-ventilated disc
Fixing	5 stud
Size	5.50F x 16 in
Tyre Size	7.50 x 16 in

Brakes

Type	Hydraulic drum
Drum Diameter	279.4 mm (11 in)
Brake Shoe Width	
4-cylinder models	57.15 mm (2.25 in)
6-cylinder models	Front 76.2 mm (3 in)
	Rear 57.15 mm (2.25 in)
Handbrake	Mechanical – on transfer box output
Drum Diameter	228.6 mm (9.00 in)
Brake Shoe Width	44.5 mm (1.75 in)

Electrical – Petrol

Type	12-volt negative earth
Battery	58 amps/hour
Ignition	Coil
Alternator	16 ACR – 34 amp output
Starter Motor	Inertia type

Electrical – Diesel

Type	12-volt negative earth
Battery	95 amps/hour
Ignition	Coil
Alternator	16 ACR – 34 amp output
Starter Motor	Pre-engaged type

Capacities

Cooling System	
(2.25-litre petrol)	8.1 litres (14.25 pt)
(2.25-litre diesel)	7.8 litres (13.75 pt)
(2.6-litre petrol)	11.2 litres (20 pt)
Engine oil 2.25-litre engine	6.85 litres (11.5 pt)

(including filter) 2.6-litre engine 7.3 litres (13 pt)
Main Gearbox   1.5 litres (2.5 pt)
Transfer Gearbox   2.5 litres (4.5 pt)
Rear Differential   2.5 litres (4.5 pt)
Front Differential   1.75 litres (3 pt)
Fuel Tank   68 litres (15 gal)

STAGE 1 V8 109 INCH

Engine

Type	V8, overhead valves, water cooled
No of cylinders	8
Bore	3.5 in (88.9mm)
Stroke	2.8 in (71.1mm)
Cylinder capacity	215³ (3528cm³)
Piston area (total)	77 in² (497cm²)
Compression ratio	8.13:1
Maximum power BHP	90.7
Maximum power PS	92 } @ 3500 rpm
Maximum power KW	67.7
Maximum torque	166.4 lbs/ft. (23 MKg) @ 2000 rpm
Maximum rev/min	5,000
Firing order	1,8,4,3,6,5,7,2
Crankshaft	Spheroidal graphite – iron; number bearings – 5.
Main and connecting rod bearing	Lead bronze, lead indium overlay.
Pistons	Aluminium alloy.
No of compression rings	2, top ring chromium plated.
No of scraper rings	1
Cylinder head	Aluminium alloy
Cylinder block	Aluminium alloy, with dry liners.
Camshaft	Position central, five bearings steel shells with white metal.
Valves	Overhead operation by hydraulic lifters and rockers.
Seat angle	45° inlet and exhaust.
Valve timing inlet opens	30° BTDC
closes	75° ABDC
Exhaust opens	68° BBDC
closes	37° ATDC
Valve Lift	0.39 in (9.9mm) inlet and exhaust.
Ignition Control	Ballasted Coil.

Ignition Timing	Detox TDC
	Non Detox 6° BTDC
Sparking Plugs type	N12Y
gap	0.025 in (0.65mm)
Distributor contact	Static 0.014 in – 0.016 in (0.35mm – 0.40mm).
breaker gap	or 26 – 28° Dwell meter setting at 550 – 650 rev/min.
Cooling system type	Pressurized with pump, fan, thermostat and expansion tanks and cross flow radiator.
Max working Pressure	15 lb/in² (1.05 Kg/cm²).
Thermostat	Wax type.
Setting	Open at 82°C.
Water pump	Centrifugal, driven by 'V'.
Fan	Detox, Seven blade plastic overall diameter 16 in (406mm) driven through a 5,000 centi-stoke viscous coupling.
	Non-Detox five blade steel overall diameter 16 in (406mm).
Capacity of System	17 pints.
Lubrication system type	Pressure.
Nominal Pressure (@ 2400 rev/min)	30-40 lb/in² (2.1 – 2.8 Kg/cm²).
Warning Light	Red light on instrument panel operates when pressure drops below 10 lb/in². (0.70 kg/cm²).
Oil Filters	Gauze pump-intake strainer, full flow external.
Capacity	10 pints (5.68 litres).
	Including 1 pint (0.568 litres) in filter.

Fuel System

Carburettors	Twin Zenith-Stromberg.
Type	Detox CDSE
	Non-Detox CDS3
Needle	BLEW
Jet Size	0.100 in.
Damper Oil	SAE20
Cold Start Control	Variable jet size with manual control and amber warning light on dash.
Air Silencer and Cleaner	Standard Detox AC Delco paper element. ADR27A and non-detox.
	AC Delco cyclone type, metal encapsulated paper element.
Petrol Pump Type	Bendix Electric.
Max. Working Pressure	3.5 – 5.0 lb/in² (0.25 – 0.35 Kg/cm²).

Filters	Tank filter, tank suction pipe, AC Delco paper element.
Petrol Tank Capacity	15 gallons (68.25 litres).
Engine Mountings	Four – Point rubber mountings.
Exhaust System	Single cross-over type with front exhaust pipes, main silencer and tail silencer.

Transmission

Clutch	Single dry plate, diaphragm spring type 10.5 in (267mm) diameter. Operation, hydraulic by pendant pedal (hydrostatic).
Main Gearbox	Four speed and reverse, synchromesh on all forward gears. Control by floor-mounted gear change lever.
Transfer Box	Two-speed reduction on main gearbox ouput. Control is by a heel board located between them. Front and rear drive is permanently engaged with a lockable third differential. Differential locked by vacuum control from a heel board mounted switch.
Capacity	Main gear box oil 4.5 pints (2.6 litres). Transfer box oil 5.5 pints (3.1 litres).
Propeller Shafts	Open type, 2 in diameter, front prop. shaft has a double hookes joint at the gearbox end and gaiter is fitted to the sliding coupling.
Rear Axle type	Hypoid: fully floating shafts
capacity	4.5 pints (2.6 litres)
ratio differential	3.5385:1
Front axle type	Spiral bevel, enclosed constant velocity joints.
capacity	3 pints (1.7 litres)
ratio differential	3.5385:1
Steering lock angle available	26°

Gearbox Ratios: Main Gearbox		
	Top	Direct
	Third	1.5049:1
	Second	2.4480:1
	First	4.0691:1
	Reverse	3.6643:1
Transfer Box	High	1.3362:1
	Low	3.3206:1

Steering

Steering type	Burman Recirculating Ball, worm and nut.

Steering wheel diameter   17 in
Number of turns lock to lock   3.5
Steering damper   Fitted to drag link.

Wheels and Tyres
Type of wheel   Ventilated disc.
Wheel size   5.50 in F x 16 in.
No. of fixing studs   5 per wheel – M16 x 1.5
Tyre size   7.50 x 16 in.
Standard Tread   Avon Ranger HS nylon Mark II.
                           Goodyear Hi-Miler S & G.
Pressures unladen   Front: 25 lb/in² (1.76 Kg/cm²)
                           Rear: 25 lb/in² (1.76 Kg/cm²)
           laden   Front: 32 lb/in² (2.24 Kg/cm²)
                           Rear: 42 lb/in² (2.94 Kg/cm²)

Brakes
Type   Girling
Footbrake   Hydraulic, Servo assisted.
Brake Drum Diameter   11 in (279.4mm).
Brake Shoe width   Front 3 in (76.2mm).
                           Rear 2.25 in (57.1mm).
Frictional Lining area   222 in² (1432cm²).
Hand Brake   Mechanical, Lockheed 7.25 in (184mm) dia-
                           meter, 3 in (76mm) width, duo-servo drum
                           brake on rear of transfer box.

Electrical System
Type   Negative earth.
Voltage   12 volt.
Battery capacity   58 amp hour C9 Lucas.
Ignition System   Ballasted Coil.
Alternator   18 ACR Lucas Model.
Alternator Ouptut   45 amp.
Starter Motor Type   3M100 Lucas pre-engaged.

Capacities
Engine Oil (sump)   10 pints (5.68 litres).
Main Gearbox   4.5 pints (2.6 litres).
Transfer Box   5.5 pints (3.1 litres).
Rear Differential   4.5 pints((2.6 litres).
Front Differential   3 pints (1.7 litres).
Swivel pin housing   1 pint (0.5 litres).

Fuel Tank	15 gallons (68.25 litres).
Cooling System	20 pints (11.37 litres).

Overall Dimensions

Wheelbase	109 in (2770mm).
Track	52.5 in (1334mm).
Ground Clearance	8.25 in (209mm).
Turning Circle	47ft (14.3mm).
Overall Length	177 in (4445mm).
Overall Width	66 in (1690mm).
Overall Height (max)	79 in (2006mm).

Internal Dimensions

Height of body sides	19.5 in (495mm).
Interior width between cappings	57 in (1447mm).
Floor width between wheel boxes	36.25 in (921mm).
Width of wheel boxes	13.75 in (349mm).
Interior length between cappings	72.75 in (1847mm).
Height of wheel boxes	9 in (229mm).
Height of Floor to Roof	48 in (1219mm).

Weights

No. 1 881 Basic rhd Spec. truck cab.

	Front Axle	Rear Axle	Total
Showroom weight	828 kg	712 kg	1555 kg
EEC kerb weight	854 kg	810 kg	1679 kg
Laden GVW	1000 kg	1710 kg	2710 kg

No. 2 886 Basic rhd

	Front Axle	Rear Axle	Total
Showroom weight	820 kg	920 kg	1740 kg
EEC kerb weight	846 kg	1018 kg	1864 kg
Laden GVW	1000 kg	1710 kg	2710 kg

Note List (1) includes the following extras as basic equipment:

E1178/79A	Towing equipment
E6557	Rear mudflaps
E6731	Lifting and towing rings
E1050/1356	Truck cab and fittings
E1072	Rubber pedal pads
E1185	Sun visors
E6773	Interior and exterior mirrors

E6846	Bonnet lock
E6864/5	Deluxe seats
E1550	Astrolan application
E6758/60	Speedo with trip
E6775	Hazard warning system
E6797	Reversing lights

List (2) includes the following extras as basic equipment:
As list (1)

| plus E1015 | front mud flaps |
| less E1050/1356 | truck cab and fittings |

Showroom weight figures do not include driver or fuel.
EEC kerb weight includes driver + full fuel tank.

1994 TECHNICAL SPECIFICATION
by V J Davis

Since the third edition of this book there have been major technical changes in Land Rover vehicles.

ENGINES

2.5 Petrol
This is still basically the same engine as it has been for many years, and is available only in the 90 and 110 Defender range.

2.5 Diesel naturally aspirated
This engine was available in the 90 and 110 Defender until the 1995 model year range was introduced, but is now only available as a fleet order option (of a minimum of 12 units).

2.5 Diesel turbo
This engine ceased production in 1990 and was probably one of the least reliable engines that Land Rover ever produced.

2.5 Diesel 200 Tdi turbo intercooled
This was first introduced in the Discovery in 1989 and immediately became very popular. It is based on the old 2.5 diesel engine, but greatly modified. It was later fitted in the Defender in 1990 and finally fitted in the Range Rover from 1993; but even this engine ceased production at the end of the 1994 model year.

2.5 Diesel 300 Tdi turbo intercooled
This engine was introduced for the 1995 model year range. The same engine is fitted in all three vehicles, Defender, Discovery and Range Rover, and will hopefully be as successful as the 200 Tdi.

67

2.4 Diesel VM turbo intercooled
This was introduced into the Range Rover in 1988.

2.5 Diesel VM turbo intercooled
This replaced the 2.4 VM Diesel in the Range Rover.

3.5 Petrol V8 carburettor
This engine has been around within the Rover/Land Rover company for many years, and is still available with carburettors in the Defender 90, 110 and 130 models.

3.5 Petrol V8 fuel injected
This engine is not currently used in any Land Rover vehicles.

3.9 Petrol V8 fuel injected
This engine is available in the Discovery, Range Rover and the American specification Defender 90.

4.2 Petrol V8 fuel injected
This engine is available only in the Range Rover LSE subject to market territories.

2.0 MPI fuel injected
This engine was adapted from a Rover car engine and fitted in the Discovery in 1993.

GEARBOX

LT77 5-speed
This gearbox was first introduced on the Defender 90 and 110. It has slowly been modified and improved to cope with the increased power output of newly developed engines.

LT77S 5-speed
This gearbox was first introduced into the Discovery at its launch and has been the mainstay of all manual Land Rover vehicles.

LT85 5-speed
This gearbox was used in the Defender range behind the V8 engine, but finally replaced in 1994 by the LT77S box.

R380 5-speed
This is a brand new gearbox, introduced for the 1995 model year range, and is fitted on all Land Rover vehicles.

ZF4HP Automatic 4-speed
This gearbox is fitted in both the Range Rover and Discovery.

TRANSFER BOX

LT230T
This transfer box has been used on all Land Rover vehicles since it replaced the 230S box. On the Defender and Discovery it is fitted with a third differential, and on Range Rover with a viscous coupling.

AXLES

Rover
The Rover axle is fitted in the front of all Land Rover vehicles as well as in the rear of the Defender 90, Discovery and Range Rover.

Salisbury
The Salisbury axle is fitted in the rear of the Defender 110 and 130.

STEERING

Since the introduction of the 1995 model-year range, power steering has been standard on all Land Rover vehicles; however, it can be deleted as a special order on the Defender 2.5 Petrol and Diesel, and the V8 Petrol, (export only).

BRAKES

Since June 1993 all Land Rover vehicles have had disc brakes front and rear with asbestos-free linings. ABS braking has been available as an option on Range Rover since 1990 and as an option on 1995 model year Discovery.

SUSPENSION

All Land Rover vehicles have coil-spring live axle suspension. Range Rover and Defender County have self-levelling rear suspension which is also an option on the rest of the Defender 110 range. Anti-roll bars are fitted as standard on the front and the rear of the Range Rover, Discovery, Defender 130, on the rear only of the Defender 110 County, and are optional on the rear of all other Defender 110 models.

AIR CONDITIONING

With the introduction of the 1995 model year range all air conditioning systems have the ozone-friendlier 134A-type gas.

Chapter 2
The Special Projects Department
by George Mackie

On the outskirts of the Tobruk perimeter, shortly after the siege by the Afrika Corps had been lifted, there came into being a park for unserviceable vehicles of all types, from both sides.

I was advised that it was more than likely there would be one or two Dodge 4 x 4 ¼-ton pick-ups in the collection, from which one might be abstracted and made serviceable. Being at that time officer-in-charge of the workshop unit of a motor transport company, it seemed reasonable to suppose we could make such a vehicle a runner and furthermore, grasp a heaven-sent opportunity to replace my official, not very desert-worthy ³/4-ton Bedford pick-up with a highly mobile 4-wheel drive substitute.

Special vehicle operations gives a new arm to Land Rover's versatility. This vehicle is equipped with video screens and speakers for educational purposes.

All army units have one or two scroungers of varying ability in their midst and in my unit I had a sergeant of considerable merit! He was requested to reconnoitre and report back.

Such correct procedures, however, are somehow lacking in appeal to those of this ilk and my sergeant, exercising a degree of crafty foresight, arranged to be driven to his destination in the unit's breakdown/recovery vehicle. Sure enough, a vehicle of the desired specification was observed on the outer edge of the compound and my sergeant, fearing that he might fail to persuade the officer-in-charge of the compound to release the vehicle, deemed a discreet, unofficial abstraction more likely to be effective. So he directed the recovery vehicle driver to take up station unobtrusively, preparatory to securing a tow rope and purposefully driving away.

But alas, the best laid plans of mice and men . . . Just about to get behind the wheel, my sergeant was horrified to see an officer jump out of the back of the Dodge showing signs of considerable anger. Becoming momentarily entangled in his map case straps and binoculars, a brief respite was created for my party to escape. The slack in the tow rope allowed the recovery vehicle driver to make a fierce enough snatch to break the rope, and rapidly disappear. Our sergeant simply took to his heels in the opposite direction, thus confusing pursuit.

The driver was the first to return to our unit lines and recount the episode to me, the sergeant making a sheepish return a few hours later.

So I didn't get my 4 x 4 then, and had to wait several years before I managed it, but then opportunities came in abundance – and officially!

The idea for a Land Rover Special Projects Department was discussed initially between Peter Wilks, the nephew of Spencer and Maurice Wilks, and myself when we were winding up our Marauder car business in 1952. We both thought such a proposition might work, but on further reflection came to the conclusion that at the time there weren't enough Land Rovers about to justify it. Five years later the advent of the diesel engine and the increased numbers of Land Rovers in circulation made me think again.

The diesel engine was an introduction sparked off by the Sales Director, Alan Botwood, who had been brought in by Spencer Wilks to strengthen the Board on the Sales side. In turn, Botwood brought in Geoffrey Lloyd-Dixon as General Sales Manager, and following him quite a lot of new people were taken on in the Sales Division, which was considerably strengthened up. Increased sales activity resulted in much more work for the Engineering Division, as the new sales people wanted to exploit the Land Rover to the full to justify their existence. It wasn't long before Maurice Wilks began to realize that all the special requests from Sales to the Engineering Department were beginning to interfere with overall development: at the time, cars and Land Rovers were not separated, so that activities for Land Rovers also tended to have an influence on car development and generally slow things up.

This seemed to be a good moment to approach him with a suggestion that this special work should be hived off, and separated from Engineering. Traditionally, the selection of equipment that Rover recommended for use with the Land Rover was handled by the Service Department. This was ill-equipped to undertake the work, and hadn't enough staff anyhow to devote to it, and so would be quite happy to let it go. Added to this was the fact that, since the early days of the Land Rover, we had been trying to market certain special vehicles – a special compressor vehicle, a special welding vehicle, and a special fire appliance. The first two had got nowhere because of the lack of a diesel engine, and the fire appliance was unsuccessful because most fire officers wanted their own particular specification, while our objective was to build one basic vehicle for the lowest possible price. All in all, I think Maurice Wilks felt that he could clear up all these outstanding nuisances by lumping the whole activity into one Special Projects Department.

When I approached him about this, he was kind enough to say he would be perfectly happy to leave it all in my hands, providing that the Sales Department were in agreement – the reason for this being that he intended to form a Technical Sales Department and place all this activity within it. I had to spend about a year lobbying around the Sales Department to get them interested, which I eventually did, but at the eleventh hour Lloyd-Dixon said he didn't want this activity as the responsibility of his Sales Division. This looked like 'curtains' for the whole project, but I decided there was nothing to be lost in appealing to Maurice Wilks again. Rather to my surprise he still supported me and said he would do his best to persuade Lloyd-Dixon and the Sales Division to take the job over. They finally agreed to comply, and in January 1957 Special Projects (or the Technical Sales Department, as it then was) was set up.

It might be helpful here to clarify and define the Special Projects Department, and its activities, because Land Rovers are built to so many specifications that the whole enterprise might almost be described as a special project. Of the Land-Rovers built in the factory, there is a clear division between those built to Rover specifications, and those built to approved specifications on the military and para-military side, for British and foreign governments or para-military fleet-users. But in addition to this, there are many specialist firms who make equipment or undertake vehicle conversions which when applied to the Land-Rover further increase its versatility.

This activity needs feeding with information and advice; liaison between Rover, the outside manufacturer and the sales network is essential; and incoming inquiries must be dealt with without disrupting the overall engineering development programme. It was soon seen to be desirable to exercise some form of control over this work and after studying the manner in which tractor manufacturers faced similar problems, I decided to institute an approval scheme which would evaluate, test and record details of all equipment and conversions which passed our acceptance trials satisfactorily.

Besides protecting the Land Rover warranty in such circumstances and relieving basic vehicle development personnel of these problems, our approval, which came to be known as Special Projects Proprietary Approval, meant that:

1) A conversion or piece of equipment would be sold under the maker's name and warranted, sold and serviced under the maker's arrangement.

2) We in Special Projects would ensure by appropriate tests that the approved item would not be detrimental to the vehicle, in the context of the operation(s) the conversion or equipment enabled it to perform, and so invalidate its warranty.

3) Performance and fitness for purpose of the equipment or conversion would be evaluated to satisfy ourselves that what was to be offered had acceptable marketing quality.

4) An agreement had to be reached between Rover and the approved manufacturer covering these and other aspects. Also it was important to safeguard Rover as far as possible against possible litigation from an approved manufacturer or his customer.

It took a little time for the foregoing to evolve into a satisfactory formula but when they did it was seen that:

1) Such a system was generally well understood and appreciated in the retail trade, and by removing uncertainties over possible warranty claims added to their freedom of action when pursuing business.

2) Adjudication of warranty claims for service department personnel was simplified.

Besides testing items for approval, we also had to respond to many queries from prospective customers concerned with 'work horse' applications for the Land Rover which they had under consideration.

Here is a typical example of such an inquiry:

Typical Enquiry
Customer: Tanzania Water Authority
Requirement: Equipment carried and powered by a Land Rover to pump 600 gallons of water per hour from a well 240ft deep.

Action
A. Search and Find
1) Acknowledge enquiry.
2) Circulate pump manufacturers to find suitable equipment.
3) Tabulate data – power, weight, dimensions, cost, etc.
4) Decide on equipment to be recommended: eg series of 12 pumps electrically driven in series.
B. Prepare Land Rover Basic Specification
1) Basic vehicle: 88-inch or 109-inch
2) Engine type: Petrol or diesel

73

3) Body type: Pick-up, hardtop, or special body
4) Suspension: Standard, heavy duty, extra heavy duty
5) Brakes: Standard or servo
6) Cooling system: Standard, heavy duty, oil cooler

C. Negotiate SID (Special Installations Department) Non-Standard Items
1) Extra fuel tank
2) Split charging circuit for floodlights
3) Blank off spare wheel well
D. Prepare Ancillary Proprietary Equipment Specification
1) Hydraulic winch with shear legs to raise and lower pumps down well.
2) Centre pto to drive generator.
3) Hydraulic lower centre pto to drive winch.
4) 10 kva generator to power pumps.
5) Air conditioning.
E. Compile Draft Specification and Drawings
1) For customer.
2) For Rover Co Ltd.
3) For proprietary equip manufacturers.

To appreciate the vast and varied range of specifications, one should bear in mind that Land Rovers are sold into more overseas territories than almost any other single product. Over the years, they have in fact been sold into 150 overseas territories – and since the total classification of such territories is, I believe, 152, that's a pretty good span of exports! (I can even recall having correspondence about how to fit an independent fuel burning heater to a Land Rover Station Wagon – with Her Majesty's Plenipotentiary for Outer Mongolia! Or maybe it was Inner Mongolia ... Presumably the vehicle was his mobile consulate as well as his means of transport – but we never heard whether our instructions were successful.)

When we started up we discovered that a certain number of firms were already 'approved' in a fashion. Some of them are still with us today, and include British Films, who do mobile cinemas, Pilchers, who do a large range of ambulances and are now known as Pilcher-Greene (whose 109″ 'Popemobile' conversion is illustrated), Evers & Wall, who do crop-sprayers, and Dixon-Bate, who do towing gear. The initial staff consisted of myself, Herbert Topping (who was still there recently), Harry Lenton, Neville Mewse, Stephen Savage (son of the late Sir Geoffrey Savage who had been Personnel Director and Production Manager), and a secretary. We were issued with some new vehicles on which we could start work for special adaptations and equipment, either having the work done ourselves or lending the vehicles out to suitable manufacturers. The diesel vehicle had just been announced and the first ones we were issued with were quite outstanding for noise level – it was fabulous! I recall an occasion when Herbert Topping and I went to visit British Films in a diesel Land Rover: on arrival, we drew up in

The Pilcher-Greene 'Popemobile' built on a 109-in chassis.

their yard between two brick walls and the noise was deafening. As I switched off the engine, I paraphrased the saying which was rife at the time on the BBC 'In Town Tonight' programme: 'No need to halt the mighty roar of Rover's diesel, we can hear who's in town tonight!'

One of the things I wanted to ensure was that we had advertising literature to let everybody know what we were doing, and what was available on our approved list. It seemed to me that the way to do this was to get a clause put in a legal agreement with the manufacturer, once he was approved, stipulating that he would at his own expense print a leaflet to our format, advertising his merchandise and giving pertinent specification data. We would then have the leaflet distributed to all our dealers, fleet-users, etc. This made the agreement rather a cumbersome affair, especially when the Sales people wanted to tack on a whole number of clauses covering the selling conditions, but nevertheless it was a way of getting the scheme started and known about in the widest possible way, and was probably rather more effective than ordinary straight-forward expensive advertising. Apart from this intervention by the Sales Division, we were mercifully left comparatively free to develop our new activity along the lines we thought best.

One of the items that we took over from the Engineering Division when we were formed was the question of a drum winch for the Land Rover. It had not been possible at that time to find anything on the British market, and apart from mechanically driven drum winches available in the States, which were rather expensive, we had no alternative but to develop our own. When Herbert

Topping joined us he brought with him details of a hydraulically operated winch that he had been working on. It was decided that we should go ahead with this, finish the scheme off and make arrangements for it to be marketed as a Land Rover drum winch to give support to the capstan winch we were already marketing. Dowty's were keen to sell their gear-type pumps and motors which were extremely reasonably priced, partly due to the lower efficiency inherent in gear type units. However, in this particular context this was not important as, willy-nilly, the horse-power available from the Land Rover engine was enough to overcome this reduction in efficiency.

The use of winches on Land Rovers has taken up much of our time over the years. It is a fascinating occupation which at first sight appears quite simple; the more involved one becomes, however, the more interesting it turns out to be. There are two simple types of winch which mount on to the front bumper of the Land Rover – the most popular position. The capstan winch is a simple bollard that can be turned mechanically by a pto drive from the engine; if a suitable rope is wrapped round it two or three times, enough friction will be caused for the rotating bollard to pull the rope along with it. The alternative is a drum winch. This again is mechanically driven from the engine of the vehicle, but winds the cable up on to a drum which is all part of the winch assembly. Both have their advantages and disadvantages and a choice between the two really has to be made according to the purpose for which the winch is required. Such purposes often involve what is known as self-recovery. It is slightly ironic that a 4 x 4 vehicle is usually purchased for its ability, when necessary, to leave the tarmac road and go off across country, but however good its traction and ground-clearance may be, there will doubtless come a moment when it loses

The standard capstan bollard is nine-sided. This improves grip on the rope but when the operator releases tension to induce slip the change-over may cause some initial rope snatch.

The smooth surface on this bollard permits more precise control of rope tension by the operator.

Left: Components of the Fairey drum winch hydraulically driven from the centre pto.
Right: Components of the Land Rover drum winch hydraulically driven from the centre pto.

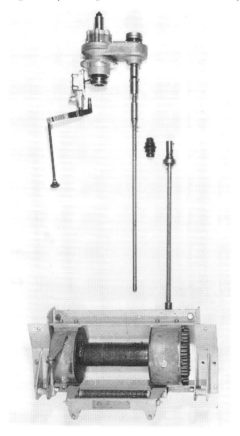

its ability to proceed, due to digging in, bogging down or bellying on the ground. In fact the more efficient and cross-country-worthy an all-wheel drive vehicle is, the further it will go before it comes to a halt, which in turn makes it harder to pull out again. If it is unaccompanied, the driver then has the task of winching himself back on to firmer ground where he can regain traction.

Having said this, it is rather extraordinary that nearly all self-recovery winches are mounted on the front of the vehicle and can only pull it forward, and that the demands for a backwards pull facility are comparatively rare. We thought our hydraulically operated drum winch, with its flexible hydraulic transmission facilitating various mounting positions, would fulfil a much wanted need, but in the event, that need turned out to be a very minor one and the great majority of winches are mounted at the front of the vehicle.

Besides vehicle recovery, much use is made of winches by electricity boards, for instance, to help in the erection of small poles for overhead electricity power lines, and to pull up transformers on to H-poles. I well recall being told by a procurement officer of one of the electricity supply boards that he had heard of our work developing a hydraulic drum winch, but that he couldn't

Hydraulic operation of a separate capstan unit designed to operate below ground level on building estates, for installing electricity supply cables.

Very effective ground anchors. When the winch pulls the vehicle forward, the chains prevent it over-running the anchors and cause their leading edges to dig in. The winch is the Land Rover hydraulically driven drum winch.

understand why we had bothered. He claimed that such a winch would be too expensive for his people and that they would stick to mechanical operation. This rather shook me but we were so near to completing our work that we carried on. Eventually this same supply board became thoroughly converted and used the hydraulic winch in large numbers. In fact they found they could often use just one 109-inch Land Rover for winching on an off-road site as well as for transport for the working party, instead of having to take a tractor-mounted winch in addition to the transport vehicle.

The Post Office also uses winches fairly frequently, for pulling in multi-core telephone lines in underground ducts. In forestry work they are used for hauling the cut timber from the forest to the roadside, where it can be stacked awaiting collection by the timber lorries. Some of these industrial uses call for somewhat more sophisticated winches than the simple drum or capstan, the main problem being the amount of cable required on a particular operation, and a method of storing and handling it. This can be achieved in various ways, one of the most ingenious being that employed by the Swiss Plummet winch. This is virtually a capstan winch but once it is in motion, the rope coming off the capstan is fed straight through to a revolving storage drum on which it is laid. The cable storage drum is coupled to a slipping friction pad which tries to rotate the drum at a slightly faster speed than that imparted by the capstan to

The standard appliance marketed by Rover before the business was handed over to the specialist manufacturers.

the incoming cable. This in turn creates tension to the cable between capstan and drum thereby creating sufficient friction at the capstan to cause the cable to be gripped and hauled in. Secondly, it causes the storage drum to revolve and pay on to itself the incoming cable. With this system the storage drum can accommodate 750 to 900 feet of cable depending on diameter, which is a great advantage, but it does present another problem. When a cable several hundred feet long is being payed out, it becomes extremely heavy. To assist the operator, the capstan is made reversible. A freewheel in the friction pad drive prevents the storage drum rotating but the friction pad itself maintains cable tension between drum and capstan. When he pulls on the cable, he will generate friction at the capstan sufficient for it to pull cable off the storage drum and pay it out. When the operator has gone as far as he wants to and stops pulling, the cable will then slip on the capstan and stop paying out. The Plummet system avoids the use of expensive mechanical storage drum cable-laying attachments and has been used on Land Rovers for many purposes.

Electrically powered and compressed air-driven winches are also available, though the latter are normally used only as a convenient adjunct when compressed air is required in a major role, such as operating paving breakers or underwater tools. The electrically powered drum winch has much to recommend it. It shares with hydraulic operation the flexible choice of mounting positions, installation is often faster, and it has the advantage over hydraulics in that no oil reservoir is required. It does, however, need a robust battery and the number of pulls is limited according to the battery capacity.

As we had decided that we were not well-equipped to sell fire appliances based on Land Rovers, it was a question of selecting a certain number of specialist manufacturers to undertake this work. I had my first slight clash of policy here with the Sales Division, who beat me to it, and made an agreement with Carmichael and Sons, of Worcester, as the exclusive converters of fire appliances for three years. I thought this policy a bad one – no reflection on Carmichael's – simply because fire officers tend to have their favourite manufacturers to whom they go for repeat business, and it is difficult to persuade them to go somewhere else. My intention had been to approve about three or four different manufacturers. However, we were tied to Carmichael's for three years, which at least simplified our work-load as we had to deal with only the one firm to get specifications, overall conversion matters, and any engineering problems sorted out.

Unusual by UK standards was the supply and drive of a front-mounted water pump on the Land Rover. These installations were fairly popular in Scandinavia and America but little known in the UK, and posed the problem of whether we could drive and take full torque from the front of the crankshaft of the Land Rover to drive the pump. With true Rover caution, the engine people would not commit themselves without some rather extensive testing, but in the end we were able to accommodate the demand – not a big one – for such an installation, provided a special torsional vibration damper coupling was inserted between the pump and the engine.

I cannot claim to be an expert on all aspects of fire appliance specifications. Indeed I have always been at pains to make it clear that we regard the specialist manufacturers as the experts in their field, with Special Projects providing engineering support service with the Land Rover. However, in the course of our work we obviously learnt quite a lot about the various specialized activities of these manufacturers, so much so that I sometimes wondered if we weren't in danger of becoming a unit getting to know less and less about more and more!

We also gained insight into many of the problems which apply to the fire prevention field, such as the intricacies of Home Office grants (in simple terms a government subsidy to public authorities who purchase equipment approved by the Home Office), problems created by the development of pedestrian shopping precincts and the difficulty of access for fire appliances to 'incidents', restrictions of movement caused by the ever-increasing traffic density in built-up areas, the arguments for and against the various fire extinguishing chemicals and the introduction of 'light water' – a product of the 3M company which creates about the most effective flame smothering foam available today.

The specialist manufacturers produced many more varieties than Rover would have found economical to handle.

A factory fire appliance.

All these problems seemed to point towards an increase in the use of smaller, more mobile fire appliances, but an important obstacle was that the Land-Rover did not at the time have Home Office approval, their thinking being that it was too small to be effective. Nevertheless several brigades found its usefulness justified purchase without a grant, quite often as a communications centre for the officer in charge.

As a fire appliance for factory complexes the Land Rover was and is very popular and, by the same token, for military depots and air-fields. In the latter case there are two fairly distinct roles, one of protection for plant and equipment, and the other as a first rescue vehicle for crashed aircraft in and beyond the air-field perimeter. When Carmichael's made the 6 x 4 Range Rover available (see page 170) for fire fighting duties, it was immediately seen to be an ideal vehicle for first rescue. It had all the speed, cross-country ability, load capacity and engine power for pumping purposes that such a vehicle required in order to control an incident until the second rescue vehicles – the heavy brigade – arrived on the scene. Indeed it was hoped that the quick action the first rescue vehicles could take might, in many cases, literally take the heat out of the situation, completing rescue and immediate salvage and maybe even making it unnecessary to call out the heavy brigade.

The Carmichael prototype 6 x 4 Range Rover appliance.

At the time this 6 x 4 Range Rover was introduced, airport authorities were becoming increasingly aware, as more and more larger aircraft were being put into service, of the awful consequences awaiting them should there be a major disaster. One scheme that was considered was the possibility that each of the major airports should have anything up to six of these Range Rovers permanently available. If an incoming aircraft signalled that it was in trouble, they could then station themselves at the beginning of the runway, with engines running, ready to pursue it and get into position almost immediately the craft came to rest.

I was presented with what was for me an unusual situation on policy when I was approached by the Ministry of Defence, who wished to purchase a quantity of 6 x 4 Range Rovers for RAF air-field use. I found that it was not sufficient to point them in the direction of Carmichael's to whom we had given our approval for this conversion after our joint, lengthy, cost-sharing development programme. The Ministry insisted that their ground rules made it mandatory that they should purchase the 6 x 4 chassis direct from us, though we could use Carmichael's as our sub-contractor if we wished, and go out to tender for the body and equipment to the specialist fire appliance builders. The fact that Carmichael's were the only specialist builder with our approval at that time and that the vehicles would almost certainly be cheaper if purchased as a single package failed to sway them.

So, contrary to our normal practice with approved conversions, we had to become involved with shipping Range Rover chassis to Carmichael's, together with the additional axles, wheels, suspension units, etc, that they required for the conversion; receive the vehicles back after conversion for the usual Rover and Ministry quality acceptance tests; and then, when a body builder had been

In the end the Ministry got what they wanted.

selected, be concerned with yet another test and approval procedure, as the Ministry insisted that they would require full standard warranty cover from us on the converted chassis component of the complete vehicle. This wouldn't have been so bad if the body specification had been the same as the Carmichael conversion which we had previously tested, but unfortunately it differed sufficiently to come out somewhat heavier, and a period of testing had to be gone through and some compromise reached before all parties were satisfied.

In the end the Ministry got what they wanted at extra cost, Carmichael's had to accept a slowdown in the rate of recovery of their development costs, and Rover suffered a (probably unidentified) rise in their overheads. But Gloster Saro Ltd, the firm who were awarded the contract for the body and equipment, gained an expanded market for their products, and Rover will benefit in the long run by having another reputable firm as a 6 x 4 Range Rover chassis outlet.

It was becoming clear as the years sped by from 1948 that the original idea of using Land Rovers as an alternative to tractors in agriculture wasn't really taking off. As a workhorse, the vehicle was being used far more by public utilities, and by industry. In the farming world, apart from a few dedicated people who insisted on doing everything with their Land Rover, we found that the vehicle was being used for personal transport and for towing horseboxes and trailers, while tillage work, or any farming activity of that nature, was left to the tractors. We looked at various fertilizer spreaders and grass-cutting and

Left: 'Adrolic' 3-point linkage operated by a hand pump situated on the wheel box behind the number plate.
Right: SMOMOT.

Left: Our tests showed a two-furrow plough to be a reasonable limit on medium soil.
Right: A granulated fertilizer spreader which can be effectively operated. A hydraulic pto is required to raise the loading shovel attached to the rear of the trailer.

hay-making equipment, but found that the farming world was becoming much more mechanized in the battle to cut down on labour costs. To this end, tractors were becoming bigger, but the Land Rover stayed the same size, and so from that point of view it was losing the race to become an agricultural tool. The price of tractors and Land Rovers increased over the years, and at one time it looked as if we might find further outlets in the agricultural field when the law requiring tractors to have safety cabs came into effect. But although this put up their price considerably, the demand for Land Rovers didn't seem to increase. Had we been able to produce bigger 4 x 4 vehicles, as I had at one time hoped, the picture might have been a bit different, but even then I think we would have had to pioneer a new system, based on the SMOMOT (see page 139) principle of a good 4 x 4 lorry chassis – very adaptable – and utilizing the swop-body concept in the main.

Another item which had been the subject of much discussion was whether a 3-point lifting linkage, of the type that was then becoming commonly available for tractors, should be made available for the Land Rover. A firm up in Scotland called Adrolic Engineering developed a unit which we had for trial and evaluation. It wasn't terribly successful and – although we weren't convinced at the time – with hindsight one can see that a Land Rover in its present specification isn't really a suitable vehicle on which to fit such a unit. However, having possession of this mechanism did enable us to fit implements to the back, such as ploughs, harrows, etc, and to evaluate the Land Rover's pulling performance when carrying out jobs of this sort.

For a brief period it did look as if a system which encouraged improved grassland husbandry might be particularly adaptable to the Land Rover. Grass grown for fodder has to be cut and partly wilted before it is lifted from the field, the wilting operation being speeded up by crushing parts of the grass stem. A system for economizing and speeding up these two operations was developed by a Mr Murray who farmed in Gloucestershire near a village named Paradise!

We decided to cooperate with Mr Murray.

87

Tooley mobile workshop conversion (Tooley now owned by K. & J. Slavin (Quest) Ltd).

His system was to use a light 4 x 4 chassis, to the driver's side of which he attached a mower cutter bar. Immediately behind this, trailed by means of an offset tow bar attached to the rear cross member of the vehicle, was towed the crimping machine for the wilting process. As his mower, Mr Murray had adapted a cutter bar with two reciprocating knives instead of the single knife and guide fingers used in other mowers. He claimed two advantages for this double knife bar: it could cut at a much faster rate than the single knife mower, and it was available with a hydraulic motor drive which simplified the problem of the side mounting. A chassis with wheel suspension was desirable owing to the higher speed of operation.

We decided to co-operate with Mr Murray, who was also receiving some sponsorship from one of the oil companies, and devised a hydraulic drive and side mounting for the mower. Preliminary tests showed that any significant increase in ground speed for this operation was going to demand extra concentration by the driver on navigation, that there were problems in maintaining an acceptable consistent height above ground for the cutter bar, and that the power required to propel the vehicle, operate the cutter bar and tow the crimper, was going to tax the Land Rover to the limit.

By the time we had got this far, new types of rotary grass mowers were beginning to emerge. These machines were less prone to blockage, simpler to maintain, and, besides cutting, able to windrow the grass for the first drying

The V blade: an effective shape for rural work. The blade shape imparts sufficient momentum at the right speed to cause snow to be deflected several feet on each side.

operation. Although they are generally more costly to buy and use more fuel than the reciprocating knife mower, they have rapidly gained in popularity. Their arrival and popular acceptance prompted new approaches to grassland harvesting, and Mr Murray's scheme had perforce to lapse.

As mentioned earlier, the Land Rover's contribution to operations of a specifically agricultural nature is not as great, after all, as was originally visualized. But in these mechanized times, it is used for several operations performed by non-farmers which have an agricultural flavour, such as semi-mature tree transplanting (see page 153), mobile workshops for repairs in the field, and winching operations. Some counties retain farmers to use their Land Rover with a snow plough attached, to clear country lanes and secondary roads – operations hardly conceived in 1948 but playing an important part in rural activities today.

In the early part of 1958 it was pointed out to us that the Commercial Vehicle Show would be taking place in September and we ought somehow to cash in with our new scheme of approved implements and conversions. Eventually we put up a suggestion to the Sales people that for the period of the Show we should take over part of the service area at Seagrave Road, London, which at that time was a solely Rover-owned establishment. In the event, we took over the workshop for the whole ten days and wrought a transformation. I think even the mechanics there, who were pretty scornful of the whole idea, were rather amazed when they saw the place transformed, with bunting, flags, decorations and an impressive display of the equipment that we had been able to assess and approve in our first two years. We had a gratifying number of visitors, including some fairly senior ones. Spencer Wilks was one who came and had a look round, and seemed suitably impressed. (He was always interested in this activity, and even after his retirement to Islay I continued to have correspondence with him regarding winches and special cross-country tyre equipment for the Land Rover.) A chap called Manby, from Silsoe, also came to have a look at us; it was he who had put his signature on the Report on the first Land Rover, submitted to Silsoe for test purposes in 1948, and which is quoted in Chapter I.

In 1961 it was decided that we should introduce an enlarged version of the diesel engine, up from 2 litres' to 2¼ litres' capacity. The Publicity Department were somewhat at a loss to know how best to put this across and get maximum

This angled blade is very effective for urban snow clearance.

press coverage, because the engines looked pretty much identical externally to the uninitiated. During discussions I pointed out to them that we had for some time been doing tests with another firm who wished to put some equipment on the market to convert Land Rovers to operate on railway lines. What better, said I, than to have a demonstration of Land Rovers pulling rolling stock up and down the railway line, as a means of planting the idea into the heads of the astounded onlookers of what a powerful gain we had made in our diesel engine! It is a fact that with rubber tyres in contact with steel rails the adhesion

factor is relatively much greater than with steel wheels on steel rails, and conventional railway rolling stock has to depend on the massive weight of its engine to make up for this lower adhesion. We found in our experiments that we could start moving 50 or 60 tons dead weight in rolling stock without much trouble. (It wasn't quite so easy to stop it all again, but that's another story!)

Anyhow, my idea was accepted, and over the weeks it snow-balled mightily. Eventually, we ended up with a programme which started with hiring a special train to bring the delegates, Press, fleet-users, overseas distributors and dealers

Operations like these were carried out satisfactorily but the cost of buying and fitting the 3-point lifting linkage and hydraulics was too high.

Left: Powered mowers which are trailed for transport between sites suit the Land Rover well.
Right: In addition to the hydraulic digger, a hydraulically operated concrete breaking hammer was also fitted, making the whole unit useful for construction and repair work.

who happened to be in the country down from London to Knowle & Dorridge Railway Station. The train was drawn by a steam locomotive to which was affixed a rather incongruous notice which said 'Land Rover Diesel'. When they arrived we took them across to a siding and demonstrated 'Land Rover on the Railway Line' operations to them. We also had elevating platforms and mobile workshops mounted as equipment for operating on the railway line, so that we could show them how the workhorse capabilities of the Land Rover could be used for railway maintenance. Once this episode was completed, we took the delegates by bus to a nearby hotel, Chadwick Manor, out in the country, which was fortunate in having fields alongside which sloped gradually down to a lake at the bottom. At this lake we were able to demonstrate all manner of fire pumps and appliances, general purpose pumps, and a certain amount of wading and water-proofing, before we took the delegates back to the hotel for a drink and a meal. After lunch we took them out again to the same field, which was a very effective arena, where we had erected a covered grandstand – not necessary, actually, as the weather was perfect. From here we were able to parade past them all the other wheeled conversions and equipment that we had been able to muster. The finale was provided by the Royal Air Force, who sent a helicopter unit over, giving us one of the earlier demonstrations of how

Demonstration at Knowle & Dorridge station.

Finale at Chadwick Manor.

they could lift Land Rovers with their special lifting gear and transfer them from A to B. In this case they whirled the Land Rover around the arena (narrowly missing some of the super-grid power cables, it seemed to me!) and then neatly deposited it back on the ground in front of the grandstand.

I happened to be talking to our Chief Security Officer sometime during the summer of 1965 when he mentioned the fact that the farmers who farmed all the adjacent land to the Solihull factory were pulling out. He suggested that I make a bid to the management to take over the care and maintenance of this land, amounting to about 100 acres, so that we could have close at hand facilities for field trials, demonstrations and so forth under our own control. I thought this was a good idea and made a bid, without much hope of success. Much to my surprise, I was told that I could go ahead – I think by A B Smith, who was General Manager at the time. He said he would like it kept in 'a park-like condition, with not too much agriculture' as he didn't want to sub-let it again in case we got planning permission to build extensions – agricultural tenancies were so complicated that it could take years to get a tenant farmer off the land. So with this brief I set to work. The place was in a bit of a mess and it was rather difficult trying to visualise quite how it would end up. We looked at various farming possibilities. One chap in the factory was very keen to join me – he was more of a farmer than a car-worker – and he set up a scheme for a mixed farming plan. I wasn't too sure about this, and happened to mention it to Maurice Wilks one day. He replied, 'Oh no, you don't want to get involved in that sort of thing. Your life won't be your own once you start getting animals on the ground. You'll find you'll be called out on a Sunday afternoon to take Daisy to the bull, and then Daisy will have trouble giving birth ... No, don't do that! Keep it all as simple as you possibly can.' This seemed like sound advice to me, so we just started to tidy the place up, verges, hedges and so on.

A high-speed perimeter road had already been built round the farm for testing production cars and Land Rovers. The only problem with this was when slow-speed agriculture cut across the path (quite literally) of high-speed motor cars and Land Rovers. Our Security Officer was a bit worried about this, and one particular incident had occurred to justify his concern. We had been out on one of the fields, looking at a granulated fertilizer spinner attached to the back of a Land Rover, and discussing its merits with the farmer who had his horse and cart with him – his standard equipment! While we talked one of my chaps inadvertently coupled up the spinner to the rotating pto of the Land Rover. It immediately started to discharge pellets of fertilizer over a wide area, and unfortunately caught the faithful old Dobbin of a carthorse right across his arthritic knees. Dobbin didn't like this, and although he had never been known to do other than walk, in a lazy sort of fashion, to our amazement he took off at a loping trot across the field! Before we could gather our wits he was out of reach, heading for a gate that led onto the fastest section of the perimeter track. The fates, however, were kind to us that day and no vehicles bore down on Dobbin as he lumbered across the road – but this incident clearly indicated that we had to become more security-conscious on Foredrove Farm in the future.

During the course of these preparations, I learned from my good friend Peter Pender-Cudlip, who was in charge of Military Sales for Land Rover, that an organization I had never heard of, called Western European Union, was having its annual conference in the United Kingdom in 1966. It seemed probable that during a week's visit by representatives of their members they would give one day to visiting a commercial enterprise. As it seemed probable that the Ministry of Defence would tell them to visit the Rover Company, we decided we ought to make plans to put on a really good show. We had to have some suitable buildings erected for exhibition purposes and prepare some pretty comprehensive demonstrations. It was decided that we would join forces with Alvis who had merged with Rover a few months earlier, and have their armoured cars and other fighting vehicles along as well. So, the stage was set. The location was first class, the audience was of a very high level, with ambassadorial status for the leader of the Western European Union party, and the exhibits were of extreme interest to our visitors, totalling some 80 or 90, of which nearly 50 were mobile.

The weather was absolutely appalling, but fortunately trouble started the previous day at the dress rehearsal and not on the day itself. The static display area was becoming so bogged down that it seemed doubtful whether the exhibits would be able to move from that area to line up for the parade past the grandstand, according to the programme. But the Army came to our rescue, and the ordnance people sent a squad of soldiers along to put down some wire mesh matting to enable the vehicles to keep on the surface, and not dig in. This required a lot of man-power which fortunately the Army was able to provide. We dug trenches in front of the grandstand to enable the Alvis people to show the trench-crossing abilities of their 6-wheel all-wheel-drive vehicles, and we also arranged two items with the RAF: one was that they would fly in the Minister of State for the Army at an appropriate time, to land in front of the grandstand and welcome the visitors; the second was that they would carry out an up-dated helicopter lift of a Land Rover as part of the demonstrations.

On the day in question everything was going like clockwork, and our mobile demonstration was well underway when we got a radio signal from the RAF, reporting that they were ahead of schedule, only 10 minutes flying-time away, and could they bring the Minister in early? 'No!', we said, 'Keep away! Our show's running to time, so we'd like you to land on time too.' This they managed to do, breaking through the cloudbase to land in the arena bang on schedule (which very much impressed our visiting dignitaries). In the afternoon we had arranged for the Alvis people to do their show, which consisted principally of a ditch crossing demonstration. Two ditches had been dug, one 4 foot wide, and the other 5 foot, in front of and at right angles to the spectators. The earlier 6-wheel-drive vehicles were capable of crossing the 4 foot ditch, and the latest vehicles the 5 foot ditch. As soon as the first vehicle started towards its target, it was apparent that something was wrong: it was going far too slowly. It gracefully tilted itself into the ditch, and – sure enough – there it stuck, nose down at a 30° angle in front of the entire audience. It could

A model was made of our exhibition area. The two buildings on the right foreground were permanent, the others to be temporary structures according to the size and scope of the display required.

The RAF delivered the Army Minister precisely on time. He is seen here on the left of the picture being met by Sir George Farmer (Rover Chairman), William Martin-Hurst (Managing Director) (holding umbrella), and the WEU delegation leader, who was later to have his umbrella turned inside out.

not recover, so, unabashed, the Alvis commentator called forward the later vehicle to cross the 5 foot ditch. This approached quite a bit faster, but not fast enough! Its front and middle axles crossed over safely but then it lost momentum, so that its rear axle subsided into the ditch – and we had another Alvis in front of the grandstand, this time with its nose pointing up into the air at a 30° angle! The problem was that while all the tests and practice had been carried out by Alvis drivers, it had been decided that Army personnel should do the driving on the day. They had hardly had enough opportunity to become conversant with how hard the vehicles should be driven, and had simply been too cautious. So there were these two mighty vehicles stuck in front of our distinguished audience, whose attention now had to be distracted at all costs!

In desperation, we called on the RAF to give us a low-flying demonstration of helicopters with Land Rovers dangling from the bottom. They readily rose to the occasion – actually I suspect they must have risen from the beer tent, because by the time they had finished they had swooped down so low that the downward force of the air from the rotors, and consequent up-draught as it bounced off the ground, had lifted the fibre-glass roofs from the mobile latrines we had parked by the grandstand and sent them flying! Had they looked like flying saucers I'm sure the audience would not have been surprised by this time. Most regrettably, that wasn't all: the delegation leader's umbrella was also caught up in the air current and turned neatly inside out as he held on to it ... However, we managed to fix him up with a new umbrella, and by the time the excitement was over, Alvis had recovered themselves and offered the audience rides around the arena. The day finally ended very satisfactorily and to my mind the gefuffle over the Alvis vehicles just helped to make it more memorable without seriously detracting from their obvious ability to perform as per requirement.

In October 1972 we became involved in another military exercise, this time a very interesting and commendable operation named "Helping Hand" which took place at Ash Vale, Aldershot. In his Foreword to the report of this exercise, Lt Gen Sir Norman Talbot, Director General of Army Medical Services, described the objectives as follows:

'During Exercise 'Helping Hand' we studied the role of the medical services of the Armed Forces in disaster relief.

'The theme was provoked by our personal experience of impotence in the face of disaster, impotence arising from the reluctance of a stricken country to see the soldiers of a foreign power on their devastated soil, even to accept material aid which might be represented as demonstrating a political or international bias.

'As medical men it had seemed to us tragic that our affiliation to the Armed Forces, an affiliation itself dictated by humanitarian principles, should prevent our offering a helping hand to those in distress.

'We therefore decided to use the whole of our biennial study period in ventilating this problem; in showing what we had to offer; in drawing upon the lessons of the past; in exploring more effective measures for applying aid quickly where most needed; in identifying the problem areas and considering the means to overcome them.

'We were encouraged and stimulated by the participation of leaders of the medical services of other national Armed Forces, of leading representatives of our own national Voluntary Societies, and of the great international organizations, the United Nations and the League of Red Cross Societies.

'The two main lessons learned were firstly, the importance of co-ordination of relief effort on an international basis and secondly Humanity's need for a formula to enable medical services formed and trained to care for the sick and wounded in war without discrimination, to be used in peace for the benefit of mankind.'

The report included a list of the exhibits and for the Rover Company the entry was as follows:

Land Rover and Range Rover Special Conversions
The Rover Company Ltd., Sales Department,
Solihull, Warwickshire.

The vehicles displayed included emergency, crash and rescue vehicles, and were capable of fulfilling many roles in a disaster, such as aiding and evacuating injured, clearing blocked roadways, clearing of flooded areas, and fire fighting, to name but a few. They were not all manufactured by the Rover Company and the individual exhibitors included:

Pilchers (Merton) Ltd, Victoria Road, Burgess Hill, Sussex.	Ambulance
Herbert Lomas Ltd, Handforth, Wilmslow, Manchester.	Ambulance
Spencer Abbott & Co Ltd, 51 Tyburn Road, Erdington, Birmingham B24 8NN.	Ambulance
Fuller Lucas & Co Ltd, Crowborough Cross, Eridge Road, Crowborough, Sussex.	Plumett Winch
H C B Angus Ltd, Totton, Southampton.	Fire Appliance
Air Drive Ltd, Davenport Vernon Trading Estate, London Road, High Wycombe, Bucks.	Excavator/ Digger
Evers & Wall Ltd, Lambourn Woodlands, Newbury, Berks.	Decontam- ination Sprayer
Cintec Ltd, 1-7 Ernest Ave, West Norwood, London SE27	Video recording and Communic- ation
Carmichael & Sons (Worcester) Ltd, Gregory's Mill Street, Worcester.	Fire appliance
Ledger Equipment Ltd, Airfield Estate, White Waltham, Maidenhead, Berks.	Mobile crane

Our mobile sales team who periodically carried out winter sales tours remember with some fervour the year of the Meat Pie Tour. We had for appraisal a refrigerated box body made specially for the Land Rover, and the tour organizer thought it would be both novel and cost reducing to take this unit along, laden with deeply frozen sustenance for tour personnel. He accordingly made a bulk purchase deal with a local meat pie manufacturer and stocked the container full of pies. He may have been carried away by the large reduction in cost for bulk purchasing, for try though they did, the team were unable to consume all the pies. On occasions, tired and dispirited by bad weather and long hours at the wheel, they came near to lynching the organizer! The pies were going off a bit too, towards the end! We never heard that the makers of the container ever did much good with it either.

It was in 1958 that the Series II Land Rover was introduced. We knew that Austin were thinking of introducing their 4 x 4 vehicle, the Austin Gypsy, in competition with us. Although the Series II design of the Land Rover had been under consideration for some time, there was a reluctance to introduce it and disrupt production, which was then booming and getting in sight of the 1,000-a-week target. However, the advent of a little competiton from Austin proved a marvellous tonic, and the Series II was put into production to counteract any loss of sales that might be incurred because of our rivals' new model. There was some initial opposition from our fleet-users, who didn't like, among other things, the slight tumble-home given to the side of the vehicle to make its styling a little more acceptable. They rather over-looked the fact that the curve at the waist-line went outwards from the original body side so that there was no actual loss of capacity within the vehicle – it was just that much wider overall.

By now the Land Rover's versatility – hitherto unprecedented in the world of 4 x 4s – had really gripped the public's imagination. The many enquiries that were coming in for different conversions and adaptations meant that we were obviously going to have to determine just what sort of a workhorse our vehicle really was, and where it would slot into the general scheme of things. We spent the late 1950s and early 1960s doing this, and also tried out a number of different activities during this period. With the demise of our own marketed

The meat pie job!

Land Rover compressor vehicle, we were soon approached by Alfred Bullows, the paint people, who had developed a new type of compressor, rotary rather than reciprocating as previous ones had been. It was very much smoother, and vibration-free, and because of this capable of being mounted on the rear tail-board of a Land Rover, driven from the rear power take-off. Some quick tests of this installation proved the point that with a special tailboard frame, on to which the compressor was mounted, one could be in operation very fast without making any drastic alterations to the vehicle, other than substituting tailboards and coupling up the belt-drive. This principle of tail-board mounting then led to thoughts of other items which could be similarly attached, such as water pumps, vacuum pumps, welders and generators of various sizes, and it began to look as if we might have a completely new system here which we could develop.

Water pumps were useful for municipal and public service use on maintenance and first aid. The advantages of mobile welders and generators speak for themselves, while the vacuum pump installation was developed to go with a gully-emptying trailer, so that small units could be used in outlying villages for cleaning up foul wells, gullies, and so on.

During the course of our experiments with these installations, we found a need to have what is known as a 'creeper gear'. In other words, we wanted plenty of torque from the Land Rover engine but at a much lower ground speed than was available through the normal transmission. As a quick experiment we obtained a small 8 hp single-cylinder engine, mounted it on one of these special tailboards, fitted it to the back of the vehicle, and then used this engine to drive the Land Rover through the power take-off system. We found we could have a very low speed, ½ mph or something like that, at 8 bhp, with full tractive effort. This was quite a useful experiment which we were to fall back on in the future.

There was also a demand for bigger compressors rather beyond the scope of our tail-board mounted units, and we carried out development work on these with Broom & Wade and Consolidated Pneumatics. An interesting side-line here was that with these bigger compressors permanently mounted in the vehicle, it should have been possible to use rebatable fuel, using the tax paid fuel only for propelling the vehicle along. However, it seemed that the authorities were not going to be sympathetic to this ploy as the basis of the equipment was the well-known Land Rover. It came into effect only at about the third attempt – this time by Broom & Wade – when the tax authorities were approached from a different angle. What Broom & Wade did was to go to the tax people and say, in effect: 'You know our trailer compressors which we tow behind light vans and lorries: we don't have to pay any tax on fuel we use in those trailers; supposing we make the compressor self-propelled, would we have to pay tax on the fuel in this?' 'No', said the authorities, 'You would not'. So, without any mention of the Land Rover name, Broom & Wade got a concession to use rebatable fuel on their Land Rover compressor vehicle. The mistake made by the previous applicant had been to talk about adapting a Land Rover for the job, and this of course introduced the subject from a completely different, and less favourable angle.

We made two special servicing vehicles for Donald Campbell's land-speed record-breaker. They supplied electrical starting requirements for the gas turbine engine, large amounts of air to cool the brakes at the end of each run, and hydraulic jacks to aid wheel changing.

Our representative in the United States, Gordon Munro, appealed to us for help with a problem he was having in what he called the Blue Grass Country in America. It was the fashion there for the horse-riding and breeding fraternities

1

2

3

4

Various pieces of equipment which could be mounted on the tailboard frame: (1) welder; (2) small reciprocating compressor; (3) rotary compressor; (4) vacuum pump. If the compressor at (3) is replaced by a small petrol engine driving the rear pto, the principle of our 'creeper' gear experiment becomes apparent. This principle was used later to achieve creeping speeds for a snow blower conversion.

to have British equipment. Rice trailers and all the tack were of British origin. The trouble was that with the long distances they normally have to cover in America, and the high speeds which are therefore necessary, they found that horse boxes – particularly a two-horse box – were prone to create a rather dangerous swaying effect, something which is not unfamiliar to those who tow caravans in Great Britain. Gordon asked us if we could develop some sort of damper to overcome this problem. After tests with various friction-damping devices, we eventually developed a horizontally positioned telescopic shock absorber, which connected between the A-frame of the trailer, and the rear cross-member of the Land Rover. This was a great improvement – in fact it virtually damped out any swaying tendencies on a normal combination. We didn't feel inclined to market such a device ourselves, and we were eventually successful in selling the patent rights to Girling, who make quite a lot of trailer gear, and they decided to manufacture and market it. I think they paid us £3,000 for the patent rights.

Throughout these activities it was becoming fairly clear that although the Land Rover was adaptable or convertible for a huge variety of uses, some of them would be ruled out on cost. For example, to fit up a Land Rover to compete with tractors – which seemed to be a lingering dream with many – would involve:

1. Modifying the rear end to support a 3-point linkage.
2. Supplying a 3-point linkage.
3. Supplying a hydraulic source for operating 2 above.
4. Transmission modifications to obtain a lower set of gear ratios.
5. Spring lock-outs for the rear axle.

Even then, the vehicle would still be left with only a ground speed rear pto, not so universally useful as a live or engine speed pto, and a relatively large turning circle. (If the pto is engaged when the Land Rover is on the move, the speed of the pto output shaft can only rotate in relation to the vehicle's ground speed. An engine speed pto will rotate in relation to engine speed at all times. Both types can be engaged for stationary operation.) It can easily be realized that the cost of these modifications, carried out in small numbers and after-market, would be sky high.

When we were presented with a prototype Shorland armoured car conversion to test for approval I became rather uneasy. The military scene was not ours and was unlikely to become so in any volume, and the complexity of the conversion, due to the measures necessary to support the much increased axle loads, made me feel that we could become so deeply involved that our other activities would suffer disproportionately. However, a talk to Tom Barton, who fully appreciated my viewpoint, ended with him agreeing that the work should be handled by his military development section.

One of the problems that always intrigued me was how all the advantages of a 4-wheel drive, cross-country vehicle, moving very well across rough terrain, could be virtually nullified when a trailer was attached. The loss of traction always seemed out of all proportion with the fact that there was at least still 4-wheel drive in a 6-wheel unit. We consulted various papers on the subject of supplying power to the trailer wheels as well and came to the conclusion that it was considered to be not a very practical proposition. However, some of the documents were so long we just didn't understand them, and it seemed to me that the easiest thing to do was to build a trailer and find out for ourselves. So simple was it, in fact, that I entrusted the job to our young apprentice, Stephen Savage. He got himself a simple channel-section frame, to which he attached a Land Rover rear axle assembly and a Land Rover rear body, and we were just starting to build the trailer drive when the Commercial Vehicle Show for 1960 turned up.

During this Show, I was introduced to a Major Kitchen who at that time was Sales Manager for Scottorn Trailers Ltd. He had just returned from New Zealand where he had been negotiating a contract for trailers to go behind the New Zealand Army's Land Rovers. The New Zealanders had told him that they wanted a really tough trailer that would be appropriate for the Land Rover, and he wasn't quite sure what he ought to provide them with. The only thing I could suggest was that he should take over our project for a powered-axle trailer, see if the New Zealanders liked the concept, and if so carry on with the development, with all our hardware and our blessing.

This policy was eventually adopted, and Scottorn completed the trailer with the aid of a chap called Rex Sewell – an ex-Chobham man, retired, and a specialist in trailers, who was taken on by Scottorn as a consultant to help them do the final design work on the trailer drive. The unit that Scottorn developed had an effective working angularity of 60° between Land Rover and trailer, and this was felt to be quite adequate for all reasonable cross-country usage; indeed, in tests by the Ministry at Chobham it passed all their requirements satisfactorily. However, when they came to offer it to units in the field, they were informed that the trailer had to be soldier-proof and therefore would have to have a much greater effective operating angularity to its drive, as it was liable to get turned over or jack-knifed, in the hands of the ordinary driver. The Scottorn system could not accommodate these requirements, so Chobham decided that they would have to design something. In due course they did: they produced a very elegant design which catered for 360° angularity, but demanded a specially adapted vehicle for attachment purposes, and a special trailer, neither of which were compatible with other units already in use. This meant, of course, that the trailer Chobham had developed could not be used by any of the other armies throughout the world which were already operating Land-Rovers.

At about this time the Ministry of Defence also wanted a new kind of tractor unit for towing a new gun which they were just bringing into service, and for

The trailer drive came from the centre pto and for the initial tests a Land Rover box was used to synchronize trailer axle speeds with the Land Rover.

The production design had a below floor transmission, a simplified transfer box and a coupling with the trailer permitting articulation of 60° in the drive line.

which no suitable towing unit existed. This eventually led to the development of the 101-inch, 1-tonne Land Rover, which was at the same time adapted for powered-axle trailer operation. As a 6-wheel drive unit for cross-country work this was extremely effective and performed very well – in fact almost too well. In order to get the maximum cross-country performance, the ground clearance was raised, which in turn meant raising the height of the chassis frame and therefore the trailer hitch point. One day, at a demonstration, the inevitable happened. As the outfit proceeded down a steep slope with a sharp turn at the bottom, the extra traction momentarily exerted by the trailer at right angles to the Land Rover had the effect of pushing it at the hitch point, which was rather

Testing with a V8 Land Rover. The extra power available makes this all-wheel-drive combination extremely effective off the road.

high, and therefore turned it over! The realization of this danger point, coupled with the very high cost of the Land Rover as a special vehicle only for the Army, and the even higher relative costs of the trailer as a special trailer only for use with this particular Land Rover, got through to the book-keepers at the Ministry, and the upshot was that the powered-axle trailer concept was abandoned. While all this development had been going on, Scottorns had not been able to make much progress with their own design but now, with the abandonment of the expensive Ministry concept, they were able to come out from under, as it were, and start developing their own powered-axle concept again.

One of the earlier approaches for a special conversion came from a manufacturer of trailers, Ibbett Engineering from Bedford. Ibbett had come across a unit called a TempoWerke made in Germany, which was a light front-wheel-drive truck. The beauty of this was that you could chop the chassis off behind the cab and put on a very low floor. Ibbett provided the rear suspension from one of their trailers, which have the capability of being loaded at ground-level. The complete outfit therefore consisted of a front-wheel-drive cab unit and a very low rear platform, with hydraulically retractable rear suspension allowing the body to be lowered to ground level, the body floor then becoming a shallow grade loading ramp. Ibbett wanted to purchase

Land Rovers from us, and then saw them in half, retaining just the power pack, cab and front-wheel drive. This was an interesting proposition but not quite suitable for our own units. At the time we were just changing over from constant velocity 'Tracta' joints on the front axle of the Land Rover to the ordinary Hooke-type joints. We found that if you put full torque through a normal Hooke-type joint on the front axle, the kick-back on the steering wheel was quite unacceptable, and thus front-wheel drive could only be applied with constant velocity joints. The other problem was that the rear suspension supplied by Ibbett, although adequate for trailers, gave a very firm, limited travel ride which was hardly suitable for a complete vehicle. Added to this, payload space was diminished by the intrusion of the fully bonneted Land Rover layout within the wheel base. The ideal is to get a forward control cab with the maximum weight over the front driving axle, then the pay-load space, and then the rear wheels as far back as you can possibly get them consistent with the turning circle, again to ensure that you have weight transfer on the front driving axle for maximum traction. None of these criteria did we quite meet, and this project was not, alas, a successful one.

I did, however, try to interest the Rover management in looking at a fresh concept of a front-wheel-drive commercial vehicle, utilizing our knowledge of transmissions and front-wheel drive as well as our units and facilities for manufacture. Front-wheel-drive vans are very popular on the Continent, particularly in France where Citroen and Peugeot have made many thousands – in fact, they are almost the standard French light van unit. It seemed to me that we could create a demand in the UK for a front-wheel-drive unit, and quietly put it on the market, rather as we had done with the Land Rover in the

A front-wheel drive, low platform vehicle recovery unit. The vertical quarter-eliptic rear suspension spring is fixed to a pivot on the frame mounting and the rearwards inclined tie bars locate the other end. To retract the wheels the tie bars are hydraulically disengaged from the spring and the forward inclined hydraulic rams contract, causing the spring to rotate on the pivot to which is fixed the link supporting the wheel hub.

beginning. By feeding it in gradually, we could evade expensive market research, and expensive launch programmes. We were certainly getting a demand from other sources for a vehicle of this nature, particularly from public utilities and other similar services which were constantly loading and unloading heavy goods and equipment but didn't necessarily take them off the road. I talked to Maurice Wilks about this but although he could see the sense of it, I don't think he wanted to extend our engineering effort too far beyond what he considered to be our capabilities at that time. He also, light-heartedly, made the comment that if we started sawing our Land Rovers in half and selling the front halves, what were we going to do with all the back-ends lying about the factory? To this I replied that we could use them up by making them into powered-axle trailers! This then became a minor crusade of mine in later years: one of my ambitions was to be so versatile in Special Projects that we could even saw Land Rovers in half and sell the front half for one job and the back half for another. In a way, I suppose we have made it – in that we now sell front halves of Land Rovers for a half-track military vehicle, and a certain number of Land Rover units to be added to a powered-axle trailer. Later on we followed up the front-wheel-drive concept again, even going so far as to ask our distributors in France to purchase a Citroen H-type van on our behalf. This was shipped over to us at Solihull and we kept it for about six months for evaluation, before shipping it back to France for resale. But still no dice: the Sales Department were quite at a loss as to how to consider such a vehicle; they were still very much more motor-car orientated, handling the Land Rover reluctantly, but light vans and commercial vehicles – never!

When the Range Rover was being prepared for production, I realized that several items we hadn't had before were now becoming available, such as constant velocity joints on the front axle, a better turning circle due to the greater angularity through which the front wheels could be turned, and a much improved suspension potential which would make such a vehicle, when finished, something that would meet the criteria of the ambulance world. The Miller Report of 1966, a Government-sponsored investigation into the whole UK ambulance field, came down heavily in favour of a low-platform, front-wheel-drive chassis on which ambulance bodies could be built – as is shown by the following specification, extracted from the Report:

Outline Specification for Type I and Type II Ambulance
1. An ambulance should be a simple and reliable vehicle, easy to drive and maintain. It should have adequate space for the treatment and nursing of patients during the journey and for storage of the equipment necessary for these functions. It should be safe and manoeuvrable in modern traffic conditions and so constructed as to encourage the highest standards of cleanliness.
2. The specific data given below were supported by much of the evidence we received and the answers to the questionnaire which we sent to

ambulance authorities. These answers also contain much information on points of detail (such as ancillary equipment for vehicles, body materials and construction, design of windows, doors, rear steps, etc.) which may be of value as the project we recommend develops. This material is in the possession of the Ministry of Health.

Ambulance (type I chassis)
3. A special chassis for Type I ambulances should include the following:-
(a) *Wheelbase*
This should be long enough to allow a patient to lie entirely between the axles and to minimize pitch. Current experience points to a length of approximately 10'3". Rear wheels should be set as far back to the rear of the chassis frame as possible to minimize inconvenience from wheel arches.
(b) *Turning Circle*
Not more than 40'.
(c) *Engine*
Smooth running and adequate power are highly important and the power output should be related to gross weight of the finished vehicle. It should be a petrol engine since, after many years of experience with both petrol and diesel power units, authorities are almost unanimous in their preference for petrol.
(d) *Drive*
Front wheel drive, by eliminating the transmission to the rear wheels, enables a vehicle to be designed with a lower centre of gravity, thus reducing the effects of pitch and roll, and with a lower floor making for easier loading. There would be a need for trials of front wheel traction.
(e) *Suspension*
Independent on all wheels and designed so as to provide a comfortable ride under all conditions of loading.
(f) *Brakes*
Fitted with pressure limiting device to provide even braking over the whole of the braking distance and to reduce the risk of skidding.
(g) *Fuel tank*
To hold sufficient petrol for 200 miles.
(h) *Road wheels*
14" wheels.
(i) *Driving position and cab*
Forward, or semi-forward, with ease of access of crew.
(j) *Transmission*
Fully automatic or semi-automatic gearbox to reduce driving fatigue and give a smoother ride.

Dual Purpose Ambulance (Type II Chassis)
4. The outline requirements given in paragraph 3 above would be suitable, subject to modifications because of the heavier loads to be carried. A self-levelling device should be incorporated.

Type I An ambulance specially designed for a maximum of two stretcher patients, with seats for a maximum of two escorts, and with sufficient width and height to enable nursing and treatment to be given during the journey; there would thus be a maximum of six persons including crew.

Type II A dual purpose ambulance adaptable for:-
either 2 stretcher patients
or 1 stretcher patient and 4 sitting patients
or 8 sitting patients.
There would thus be a maximum of ten persons including crew.

In so far as vehicles then in use were concerned, the report summarized the position as follows:

Ambulances at present in use for stretcher patients have been widely criticised because:
(a) the centre of gravity is too high and this exaggerates the effects of pitch and roll with consequent sickness, distress and unnecessary suffering for recumbent patients;
(b) the wheel base is too short, resulting in excessive jolting in recumbent patients, who cannot avoid being partly over the rear axle;
(c) the types of suspension and springing used, even when modified, are designed for sitting passengers or inert loads and are not appropriate to the needs of recumbent patients;
(d) heating and ventilation are unsatisfactory.

I rather hoped that with our Range Rover units we would be able to move into this market. The GLC were interested in exploiting this possibility too and we discussed it with them at some length, also constructing various mock-ups of specifications which could be considered. However, in this case, finance put paid to the project. No matter how clever you are, nine times out of ten, if you are only building in small quantities, the price simply has to go way up compared to that offered by more conventional competitors.

When talking to the GLC we mentioned the fact that none of us knew what an ambulance performance – in respect of ride and suspension – was like. We suspected that most of them, being built on commercial vehicle chassis, must have given a very hard ride, beautiful as they looked. The GLC kindly arranged a little demonstration for us and drew together a variety of different makes of ambulance in which we all rode round, both on the stretchers and in the driving seats. Our suspicions were confirmed, and so we went back to our drawing boards. We eventually devised a lay-out which placed the Rover V8 engine ahead of the front axle, with the short prop shaft from the engine passing the side of the off-set differential to an automatic gear box – another thing the ambulance people wanted – with a transfer box behind. There was a bit of a problem here, because the transfer box had to be far enough back to allow for the angularity limits necessary for the propeller shaft driving forward to the live front axle. At this time Rover were developing their next new car, code named P8, which amongst other things was to have a ride-levelling rear suspension. Examination of this suspension led us to believe that we could adapt some of the components for the rear suspension of the ambulance; ride-levelling seemed to be essential, bearing in mind the very low platform and floor that we were going to have with this front-wheel-drive unit. However, no sooner did we begin to see a solution than it was decided to abandon any further development of the P8 Rover car. We now had no hope of obtaining a reasonably priced, off the shelf, rear suspension assembly for our chassis, and this, coupled with the inevitably high cost of small quantity units anyway, made the ambulance authorities with whom we were in contact reluctant to commit themselves to a project of this nature.

When the Land Rover was first launched, the supply of a 2-wheeled, 1-ton or 15 cwt trailer of Land Rover origin for Land Rover and its dealers was something of an innovation. This trailer was actually made to our design by the Brockhouse Corporation, and Rover would buy it in quantity from time to time for Sales stock along with spares for the Parts Department. As time went on, the trailer became rather expensive, and demand was patchy – one would get an order from a fleet user for perhaps a hundred, and then probably nothing for a year or two. The Service Department was fidgeting a bit about having to service this trailer, and the upshot was that it gradually died out, and was deleted from our sales literature as we pulled out of this market. As soon as this became known, we were assailed on all sides by other trailer manufacturers requesting Special Projects' engineering approval for their own units. It soon became apparent that this was not on. A trailer for the Land Rover has to be tested rather more thoroughly than perhaps a normal road-going type. This entails a lot of cross-country work, pavé, wading, and so on, and, as a trailer is not a self-propelled item, I was finding that Land Rover were having to supply the vehicle to tow the trailer along. At the end of the test the cost of the repairs to the damaged Land Rover generally came to several hundred pounds more than the cost of the trailer manufacturer's contribution, so we were really doing development work for them. It seemed sensible to me to rule out all conventional trailers, and confine our approval to trailers specially built for the Land-Rover that couldn't be used with any other vehicles. By so doing we curtailed our activities at that time to two trailers, the powered-axle trailer made by Scottorns, already referred to, and an articulated trailer made by Dixon Bate Ltd of Chester, also a 'special' and made for the Land Rover only.

The articulated trailer attached to a converted 88-inch Land Rover.

Note the trailer's high swan neck attachment to the Land Rover for cross-country articulation clearance, and the rear overhang to minimize excessive nose weight and diminish vehicle front axle traction.

Special pole carrying trailers for off the road use ...

The latter was made possible by the availability of what one might call a mini-sized turn-table coupling which was mounted on to the back of the Land Rover, to which the trailer was attached. Weight distribution was always a tricky problem, as too much weight on the turn-table not only easily overloaded the Land Rover but tended to reduce the traction on the front axle, making it not much better than a conventional vehicle. These trailers were used mostly by electricity boards, who wanted them for off-road, cross-country pole transport when erecting overland, overhead lines. Since the all-up weight wasn't great, load carrying capacity was not an important factor for them, but with a 4-wheel-drive tractor unit they could probably get a bit further a bit faster with a bit less effort than with any other system available.

A unique adaptation of this idea came from the Race-Horse Betting Levy Board. They wanted to use a standardized form of starting gate at horse-race meetings, but couldn't find enough race-courses with enough money to install them. Instead, they made up mobile starting gates which were towed by Land Rovers from race-course to race-course through the medium of a fifth wheel coupling. I don't know whether this system is still in operation today, but it was quite a big thing in its time.

Shortly after the advent of gas-turbine-engined motor-cars, the organizers of the Le Mans 24-Hours Race in France offered a prize for the first gas-turbined car to complete the run. The Rover Company, in conjunction with Rubery-Owen, eventually devised a scheme to get a bit of publicity, whereby Rubery-Owen adapted one of their Grand Prix car chassis to take a Rover-built gas-turbine engine and entered it for the race. The first year it ran, it completed the course satisfactorily but for technical reasons was unable to use the designed heat-exchanger and the fuel consumption was therefore heavy. The following

... and a trailer with a rather special chassis!

year they decided to have another go, and arranged for the car to be tested over the course during the practice period organized by the Le Mans authoritiy in April, preceding the main race in June or July. The Rover gas-turbine BRM was transported to Le Mans by means of a Land Rover and trailer. Unfortunately, on the way back afterwards, the driver experienced a phenomenal avoidance situation. This provoked such a severe swaying action on the part of the trailer that it went off the road and overturned. The major damage was to the gas-turbine car itself and there was no way it could have been made ready for the real race in a month or two. Before the next year's race, when the car had been rebuilt and put back into working order, our gas-turbine people asked me if, through my contacts with the trade, I could find a trailer which was suitable to transport it safely to Le Mans. My reaction was that, since we had already had trouble with a trailer, to try to do the same thing again was perhaps rather mistaken. Instead, I thought they ought to build a transporter to lift the vehicle, preferably a front-wheel-drive ground-level loading job, which I considered to be a great deal safer.

We were able to build this transporter using a spare set of components of similar specification to the splendid 4-wheel-drive, forward-control SMOMOT vehicle. It was built with a special frame to make a front-wheel-drive chassis unit, and used Ibbett trailer ground-level loading suspension units at the rear, which had the capability of retracting the rear wheels when required, thus lowering the rear cross-member down to ground level. It took the Grand Prix car easily and duly set off for France, where I am told (although I didn't attend the race) that it caused more interest in the paddock at Le Mans than almost anything else – almost as much as the exotic racing machinery! Upon its return, after the Rover/BRM's satisfactory completion of the 24 Hours, the

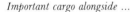

Important cargo alongside ...   *...ready for loading*

transporter was used for a long time for the Engineering Department's general transport duties before it was eventually broken up after wearing itself out in service. Although this vehicle amply demonstrated the potential of front-wheel drive, the message didn't get home that here was a possible extra market for front-wheel-drive vehicles. It now looks as if there has been a hole in this market in the UK for many years, which is at long last about to be exploited by Renault, who have just introduced a new range of front-wheel-drive vans into the British market.

We certainly cannot deny that it is a varied life in Land Rover Special Projects – from boat-builders to mine-vehicles – and at one stage I have to confess that I even ended up in the maternity wing of University College Hospital in London! This came about in the early days of the Range Rover, when we were looking into the ambulance potential. Our Styling Department had come up with a sketch of a possible 12-seater Range Rover, intended as an up-market counterpart to the 12-seater Land Rover, and we were looking at its potential as an ambulance, though it would have to go on an extended wheelbase chassis. One day I was visited by one of our British Leyland representatives from Switzerland. He happened to see this sketch and said he thought it would make a first-class ambulance, especially for the Swiss market. He thought we ought to build one and take it over to Switzerland the following year to an ambulance show that was scheduled to take place in Lausanne. We thought this would be a good introduction to the market as a whole, since with the help of our Swiss people we could try to tap the Swiss market for a start, and so we embarked on building it. It then transpired that the exhibition was a very special one, termed a Peri-Natal Medical Exhibition – in other words it was confined to matters concerning childbirth, before, during and after. It struck me that if we were putting a Range Rover ambulance on the stand it would be better if it were fitted out internally with appropriate equipment, so off I went to seek advice, having obtained an introduction to the Chief Gynaecologist at University College Hospital. I spent about an hour looking at incubators in the maternity unit, as the general idea was that the vehicle should be fitted with an incubator and used to rush premature babies to hospital for further treatment. I can't say I very much enjoyed my hour in the Maternity Unit – it wasn't really my scene – but the doctor did tell me about a firm building an incubator to his own design, which he hoped would be ready in time for us to take to Switzerland in the Range Rover. This all seemed highly appropriate, and when I contacted the firm they were only too willing to co-operate.

Eventually, after a strenuous effort, the ambulance was completed in time and we set off to Switzerland, with the prototype incubator inside. The manufacturers had equipped this with a celluloid dummy of a very life-like new-born baby, with tubes and things running from it to various junctions within the incubator. This hardly being our usual metier, we were all looking forward to getting through the Show as quickly as possible and then heading for home. It ended on a Saturday afternoon, and we left Lausanne at about

4 pm. When we came to the customs post outside Geneva we had a bit of a shock: as we were in charge of a commercial vehicle rather than a private car, we had had to use the carnet system to get through customs, but the commercial section had closed down for the week-end and would not reopen till Monday. We weren't going to stand for that but didn't know quite what to do, until eventually I said, 'Come on, chaps: let's motor round the edge of Switzerland till we come to a nice quiet little crossing point where they might let us through, not being so caught up with headquarters administration ...' We motored for about half an hour and, sure enough, we came to just such a crossing point. There were four of us altogether: one driving, one in the passenger seat, one in the attendant's seat in the back and the fourth on the stretcher, opposite the incubator. We got through the Swiss side alright, but when we got to the French side, two dear old French customs men, togged up

The first ambulance on the 10-inch extended wheelbase Range Rover which we took to Switzerland.

in nice blue uniforms, came to have a closer look. As soon as they saw an ambulance with a man lying on the stretcher, they wanted to know whether he was 'très malade' and if there was anything they could do to help him, which was very nice of them. However, the chap on the stretcher, being the party's wit, said – in the most execrable Solihull-French – thank you very much, but he was alright; it was the baby in the incubator that we were worried about ... These two customs chaps looked at the incubator, looked at the chap on the stretcher, looked at us four men in charge of a premature baby, and then, with a lovely Gallic shrug and an 'eh bien', they got out of the ambulance, closed the doors and waved us on! I never knew whether the penny dropped or not, but we got home in time for tea on Sunday after all. However, it was rather a near squeak, not knowing whether they were going to lock us up for taking the mickey out of them, or what!

*A 28-foot operating height
and considerable reach.*

The hydraulically elevating work platforms, as made and marketed by Simon and others, were also becoming popular at this time. One of our fleet-users, the Southern Electricity Board, was very keen to have one of these mounted on a long wheelbase Land Rover, for off-road use on overhead power-lines and transformers. The manufacturers of the platforms were strangely reluctant to work on this, not seeing any future in it, and it was not until our fleet-user had specifically ordered the manufacturers to have a go at it that any action was taken. Progress was made eventually, and proved highly successful: in fact the firm concerned was kind enough to admit at a later date that for many years it was the most successful line of platforms it manufactured.

We experienced a rather tense period with these people because, parallel with their marketing of their Land Rover-based platform, we had also been doing tests with a chap who appeared from deepest Cornwall, with a device which he had fitted to his Land Rover for lifting hay bales, picking them up and placing them on lorries for transport from the fields to the barns. We thought this was rather an expensive way of picking up bales – as far as I remember it only picked up one at a time, and was a little bit slow and cumbersome. However, when the chap concerned saw our experiments with the elevating platform, he reckoned he could make a platform out of his bale-loader which would not lift quite as high but would be much lighter, easier to

The converted straw bale loader.

122

A Ministry of Transport snow blower in operation.

slip on and off the Land Rover, and sell for a lot less money. So he disappeared off to Cornwall again and about six months later, hey presto! – he turned up with his loading platform. Although this particular project was not successful, our investigations were sufficiently long-running for our original platform people to get to hear of it, and they became rather annoyed with us for actually talking to another manufacturer about a competitive unit. This was a somewhat parochial approach by today's standards but nevertheless very pertinent at the time. I never was able to convince them that we had no intention of doing any such thing, and that we could not help it if a man who produced a bale-loader for us to look at suddenly transformed it into a competitive working platform!

A very interesting project that arose during this period was one for operating snow-blowers. These are used in places such as Scandinavia, Switzerland and North America where they have large, predictable quantities of snow. They take the form of, you might almost say, an enormous cylinder lawn mower, which is pushed along in front of and driven from the operating vehicle. The snow is milled down by the cutting cylinder, and then blown forcibly through a

123

chute and sideways over the hedge to get it well out of the way. We were approached by the Swiss firm of snow-blowing manufacturers, Rolba, who were interested in doing a small unit based on the Land Rover, and we went to work. The concept was that these units would be kept at certain depots throughout the country, so that when a big snow-fall was reported in an area, the allotted depot's unit could quickly be trailed to the scene of operation, coupled up and put to work.

The system that Rolba suggested we develop was to have a separate engine mounted in the back of the Land Rover with a propeller shaft driving forward through the cab and over the bonnet, to propel the cutting cylinders of the snow-blower that was being pushed in front of the vehicle. There were two snags to this: the engine in the back of the Land Rover was not something that could be quickly removed and replaced, and making holes through the cab and the windscreen was not acceptable: in any case the Land Rover would not really go slowly enough. Coupled to this was the inevitable delay in operation on arrival at the point of work, where there would be snow and slush about and miserable working conditions, amidst which the Land Rover would have to be uncoupled, the unit turned round, and everything coupled up again, before the clearing could start. There was also the question of the low, or 'creeper' speed required for this operation.

Our final solution was to trail the blower behind the Land Rover in the normal way to the point of operation. There the trailing wheels were removed – quite simply because the blower itself was height adjusted by hydraulic skids which could be used as jacks when removing the wheels. The trailer coupling was made rigid so that it was part and parcel of the Land Rover. The driver then moved across into the passenger seat which was a swivel seat, enabling him to swivel round 180° and look out through the back window and over the rear floor and snow-blower. He coupled up a steering wheel mounted on the rear cab so he could steer the unit, while the blower itself was driven at a constant speed from the rear power take-off, which also drove a variable control hydraulic pump. By connecting it to a hydraulic motor coupled to a secondary lower power take-off it was possible to transmit drive through the vehicle's transfer box to the road wheels. Thus we achieved an infinitely variable 'creeper' gear to adjust the speed of the unit, forwards and backwards, through control of the flow from the pump.

Initial tests in the UK came at a time when there was just no snow about anywhere. The snow-blower people told us to try to find a water splash instead, as this would work almost as well as snow, and show us how effective our combination was. We found one at the Motor Industry Research & Proving Ground, and when we pushed the blower into it, it was so effective that it very nearly emptied the water splash completely. Our next move was to take the vehicle out to Switzerland and try it out in real snow. It worked well, but one could not help feeling that the Land-Rover was just a little bit too small and under-powered and that the whole unit was not quite up to scale. This was

Once the blower has been trailed to the point of operation, its wheels are removed ...

... the operator's seat is made ready and the steering wheel connected to the vehicle's steering column ...

... tie bars are put into position to lock the blower rigidly to the vehicle and the skids are set at the operating height and it is driven into work.

highlighted the next year, 1962-3, when we had terrific snowfalls in the UK. One of the northern county councils had some of these Land Rover blowers in operation, but they were simply not hefty enough for the mountainous snow drifts that they had to move. In fact, the vehicle was almost in danger of milling its way underneath the snow drift and burying itself. All in all, it was just too much of a good thing, and of course it was a pretty pricey little outfit. Since then, the demand has never been as strong and we have never had a winter quite like that of 1962-3 again.

Land Rover-on-the-Railway lines had been a dream for many people, and eventually we were approached by a firm of railway equipment manufacturers who had formerly made steam engines for the Indian railway system. They felt that a light unit for small sidings, generally private ones owned by manufacturing organizations, could be of interest as the normal small shunting engine was hideously expensive. In addition, it was thought that specially equipped road/rail vehicles that could easily get on and off the railway lines and take people to a point where maintenance was required, could be of interest to British Rail. In a way, the shunting unit proved the most difficult, because to get any traction at all with such a light tractive unit, it was necessary to make flanged railway wheels to replace the standard Land Rover wheels. These had to have a special composition of rubber tyre shrunk on to give the necessary co-efficient of friction. The wheels also had to be dished out by 3 inches on either side in order to match the standard railway gauge, and it was feared that this would throw extra stress on the wheel hub bearings. Furthermore, when braking it was only too easy to lock the wheels with the standard automotive brakes, and any harsh application leading to wheel lock immediately caused a flat to appear on the rubber composition tyre, and set up unacceptable

Shunting and marshalling.

Inspection.

The road/rail vehicle lowering its front guide wheels prior to moving off.

vibrations. The standard rolling stock was also much too big for the Land Rover which would have to be equipped with buffer gears to match up with the rolling stock buffers. Some form of braking system was required to operate the rolling stock which was equipped with a vacuum-braking system, as it was not considered to be wise to operate it with the old rolling stock which didn't have vacuum-brakes. Then again, when you go up a railway line you can't just turn round and come back; you have got to return in reverse. The vehicles were just not made for sustaining long periods in reverse: the speedometers got a bit upset for a start, and the speed wasn't very high, so something would have to be done about that. The real thought behind this whole project had been to see if something could be offered to fit on the smaller gauge railways throughout the world, at a much reduced cost, but the major 'carve-up' required in order to reduce the track of the Land Rover made it quite uneconomical and eventually it had to be abandoned.

With what we called the Road/Rail Vehicle, things were much more interesting. These vehicles were made so that when they were on the rails they actually rested on their tyres, and the tyres in turn rested on the rails. The wheels had to be packed out to match the railway gauge, and small guide wheels were lowered front and rear and the steering locked simultaneously to keep the vehicle on the rails. We then had rubber/steel friction which made for good, standard braking – it didn't matter if the wheels locked. The speed was high, and any convenient place would do for turning the vehicle around. All the driver had to do was drive off the rails, turn round, drive on again, lock himself on the rails, and back he went! The vehicle could carry personnel, equipment for maintenance, elevating platforms, welders, compressors and electronic gear for signalling. The one big snag was the signalling system, as operated by British Rail and most other railways. This is based on a track circuiting system, whereby a low voltage current is passed down the railway line. When conventional engines or rolling stock are on the line, they form a connection between one rail and the other, and this operates the signal in the box controlling the relevant section, alerting the signalman. The system operates on a very low voltage, and depends for really good contact on the sheer weight of the engines pulling the trains, which may take up to 7 or 8 tons on each axle. Even then, they don't always make contact if the rail is very greasy or has not been used for some time, and has become rather rusty. Thus, with the Land Rover and its rubber tyres, there was no hope of operating this system. The only other hope was that when the engineers were actually engaged on a major job of work on the railway, they would take possession of that section of track and control the traffic through it. If they were in control they could then bring their Land Rovers up the point of work and get them off the line before letting any more traffic through. This seemed to offer a solution, but unfortunately, at the same time that all this work was going on, Dr Beeching was also going on, at British Rail – closing branch lines and small stations which would have been the very meat and drink for this Land Rover operation. The prospects generally looked rather poor, and so our friends who were interested in marketing this equipment decided to withdraw.

Good as the cross-country ability of the Land Rover is, there are always demands that it should be made to go further in even worse conditions. In this context, two special projects, quite different in scope, might be of interest: one was a tracked vehicle devised for conversion by the firm of Cuthbertson & Sons, at Biggar in Scotland, and the other a special big-wheel Land Rover devised by the Forestry Commission Experimental Establishment at Alice Holt. The Cuthbertson conversion was really a sub-frame which carried track bogey wheels at each corner. The dimensions were so arranged that you could drop your Land Rover on top of this sub-frame, remove all four wheels and then put a track round the bogeys and round a sprocket which replaced the road wheels on the Land Rover. The front tracks were steerable in the conventional way, but with the aid of power-steering fitted to the sub-frame. With 4-wheel drive each track was powered at each corner but with differential motion, and there was no side to side scrubbing of tracks when turning as on a conventional tracked vehicle. The very nature of the conversion also meant high ground clearance, which (although not adding perhaps to the

The Cuthbertson conversion.

A Cuthbertson conversion used in Holland. The hollow drums are lowered hydraulically and support much of the vehicle's weight across the mud flats being surveyed. When the tide comes in, the vehicle floats on these drums and an outboard motor propels it back to hard ground.

The Roadless Traction conversion.

stability of the whole) at least made it more appropriate for operating in marshy and muddy ground, which was the intention. The Forest Rover, as it was called, had to have special axles made of considerably wider track so that they could carry the big wheels and tyres, 10 x 28, that were required, and also to give the vehicle a reasonable steering lock. The idea behind this was not so much the low ground pressures of the track vehicle, but rather what is known as step-climbing ability. The large diameter of the wheels really meant that with any luck the vehicle could climb a step the same height as the wheel radius. Thus, it could be driven over fallen logs up to a reasonable diameter, while its increased ground clearance meant that it could also straddle them and then carry on its way. The Forest Rover was made by a firm called Roadless Traction Ltd and proved to be an impressive performer on cross-country work, as did the Cuthbertson vehicle. However, they both had their drawbacks. With its 16 inch diameter track bogey, the tracked vehicle had poor step-climbing ability, so that if it was confronted with a bank to climb in marshy ground or in a river-bed, it was quite likely to mill its way straight ahead if it couldn't lift itself up. The Forest Rover, on the other hand, had such big wheels that it tended to become unbalanced and was not very controllable on the road, unless the speed was strictly limited. Accommodating the wheel arches also took up rather a lot of valuable load space.

During this period we were greatly preoccupied with extra-special cross-country equipment. One item we were asked to evaluate was the big, low-

A Land Rover converted to accommodate Goodyear Terratyres.

The Vickers cushion craft conversion, fitted with crop-spraying equipment.

pressure tyre marketed by Goodyear, known as the Terratyre. Here again, its major function was to have the biggest possible ground area of tyre in contact with the ground, thereby improving flotation. One year we took it down to Romney Marshes where we thought we would find the sort of conditions that the operators required. Most of the operators were oil-field exploration companies who were gradually reaching out to find oil wells in more and more difficult terrain. The tests on Romney Marshes were very impressive, but again, because the tyre equipment was still at the pioneering stage, it was extremely expensive. Inevitably, it also made the Land Rover a little less versatile and a little more cumbersome to handle, and so didn't find immediate favour. Today, of course, tyres of this nature are becoming increasingly commonplace on all-wheel-drive vehicles.

Perhaps the most bizarre application of all was the Hover Rover. This was developed in parallel with the hover-craft, an adaptation of a Land Rover being carried out by Vickers, near Swindon, at the time they were building the first big hover-craft. Strictly speaking, the Land Rover was more correctly termed a 'cushion craft'. The idea was to apply the hover-craft principles in such a manner that absolutely minimum ground pressures would be exerted by the vehicle's tyres on the surface, just sufficient for traction, steering and braking. The problem was that by the time the fans creating the air cushion had been fitted and another engine put in the back of the vehicle to supply the increased horse-power required, very little pay-load space was left, and really

A trailer or a boat on wheels? When traversing very marshy ground, the vehicle could proceed first and then winch the water-tight trailer across.

no pay-load capacity. The manufacturers claimed that as a lot of weight was taken by the air-cushions this was less important, and that in any case these things should be reassessed. However, the vehicle still had to be driven from depot to point of operation in the conventional way, and on many of the applications for which it was intended (for instance, one firm were interested in it for spraying purposes), it scattered so much stuff around the countryside due to the downward force of the air-cushion that it was rather impracticable. Vickers themselves said they wanted to use it simply as a means of publicizing their real hover-craft, and so it was left to private enterprise, in the form of Soil Fertility Ltd, to try it out on spraying jobs. Eventually, I believe the idea was abandoned.

Special Projects never became very involved with the military aspects of the Land Rover business, chiefly because the military customer would usually complete the vehicle under his own auspices if the Rover Company was not building the vehicle to the full specification required by the military contract. However, two or three years ago Lairds of Anglesey approached us with the

The beacon and floodlight unit are supported on a mast which is coiled up into the roof box and does not intrude into the driving compartment. This is done using spring steel strips just exceeding semi-circular form so that, when pressed together, they interlock to form the column: a fall-out from the American space programme, in which the astronauts' probes were made in similar fashion.

A complete mobile cinema with public address and recording facilities – a popular unit with government eduation departments in African countries.

idea of manufacturing and marketing a half-track vehicle for military use. The stimulus was the imminent production of a Land Rover with the V8 engine installed: the combination of this engine and the Land Rover's other well-known features would give them a reasonably cheap half-track with a very good power/weight ratio, which would in fact be the first all-new half-track vehicle made since the Second World War. They encountered a spot of trouble with their initial approach to Leyland Cars (as we were then), as some of the newer young executives were unsure of how to handle such a request and whether it had any future. I at least had the advantage of having dabbled in the possibilities of selling the sawn-off front half of Land Rovers in years gone by, and so when they came to see me I was very interested to see this idea cropping up again. Lairds set about the project in a very thorough-going way and did a superb job. Apart from day-to-day help on some aspects of specification, and details of design with transmission, I think all we did to steer them out of trouble was to help them obtain a Stage I prototype Land Rover chassis frame and all the special components that went with it, to enable them to build up their prototype. They had originally intended to modify a Series III diesel engined vehicle that they had bought for the purpose before we suggested using the Stage I, and this would have involved an awful lot of time-consuming detail work before they could put everything together. We had to agree on a mutually acceptable test programme which would be appropriate for this unusual vehicle. A cross-country course in a worked-out ore mine in Anglesey, and high speed work on the nearby RAF airfield and on the ordinary roads were included to give a very searching test cycle.

In the mid-1960s I had a letter from a woman who said she had 'invented a device that would go very well with the Land Rover', and could she come and talk about it? I was rather reluctant to spend time with a woman inventor (male chauvinist pig?!) but for the sake of our public image I asked her to let me know the next time she was in the Midlands, when I would be pleased to see her. Eventually the day came, and the good lady arrived. Far from being a battle-axe in a tweed skirt and flat-heeled shoes, with straw sticking out of her hair, she was a most charming and elegantly dressed young woman who breezed confidently into my office, sat down in the visitor's chair and proceeded to tell me about her invention. She lived on the East Coast and apparently had been much concerned with the problem of the disposal of manure from the many battery hen houses in farms round about. She had then conceived the idea of compressing this mixture into a form of fuel which could be used for heating the hen houses. To cut a long story short, she had talked to various authorities who agreed that there was some reasonable heat potential from this form of fuel, and she had subsequently processed some of this material through a rubber-extruding machine. At this stage in our discussion she dived down below the level of my desk top and reappeared with a sample from her briefcase. This took the form of a sausage-like affair of indeterminate length, some 2 inches in diameter . . . Her idea was that we should develop a compressing machine to sell as an attractive adjunct to the Land Rover, which could then trail the machine from chicken farm to chicken farm, compressing their surplus manure for a reasonable profit. Though this idea was not up our street – no way could we spend time developing such a suggestion – our young lady was very determined. (It emerged later that she was the niece of Douglas Bader, the legless pilot; she was certainly imbued with the same degree of determination!) I spent a pleasant day chatting about the project, showing her round our new P6 assembly hall, and taking her out to lunch. I couldn't convince her that her plan just was not practical for us. She seemed determined that we should put it into development and even supply the machine as an optional extra in the back of Rover P6s – but we could not, alas, accede to this. Later that year, at the Royal Show at Stoneleigh, I happened to be walking past one of the Ministry of Agriculture stands, which was advertising 'Fuel Conservation on the Farm'. Out of curiosity, I looked in, and who should be lecturing to a group of young farmers, but my elegant friend of a few months ago! The young farmers seemed quite enthralled by what she was saying, or was it by how she looked? She came back to our house

To prepare the Land Rover for wading in water up to seat level, a waterproof dynamo and ignition were fitted together with engine and transmission breathers, connected by plastic tubes to the carburettor 'snorkel' arrangement on the windscreen pillar. The fan belt was carefully adjusted so that the fan would slip if it became in any degree submerged.

Internally, the wipers and all instruments were raised except for the speedometer. This was left in its normal position for easy reading, and water-proofed.

for a meal that evening, and that was the end of that episode.

Special Projects was rather a sitting duck for way-out inventors, and we had our quota of them. One or two of them stand out as being exceptional, like the one just referred to. Another, also introduced by letter, was equally vague at the start. The letter just said, 'Dear Sir, I have invented an adaptation for the Land Rover, are you interested?' This landed up on my desk, and I simply had to do something about it. It didn't give me much to go on, perhaps intentionally, so I was obliged to ask the chap to come to see us and tell us what he had got in mind. An afternoon was appointed, and I got back from lunch in time to be followed into my office by a young man who said he was The Inventor. It transpired that he had been developing a one-man forage harvester. This was an aspect of farming about which I knew very little, but events were to ensure that I learned quite a lot in the future months. Our inventor, by the name of Mike Fisher, had observed on his father's farm that cutting silage and taking it to the clamp was a very complicated operation. They used one tractor with a silage cutter in the field, cutting the grass for ensiling. Behind the silage cutter was towed a trailer specially adapted to catch the grass. When the trailer was filled, another tractor would come up, couple up an empty trailer to the cutting combination, and take the full trailer back to the place to be discharged. This process often employed two, if not three, tractors because they were running a shuttle service, plus two or three trailers, at least one silage cutter, and the labour force, plus a man on the clamp controlling the discharge and build-up of silage.

Our inventor's idea was to couple up a silage cutting machine to the front of a 4-wheel-drive vehicle and push it along in front, driving the cutter from the front. The discharged silage would be blown by duct over the top and into the body at the back of the driving cab (this body would replace the trailers). When it was full of ensiled grass, the driver would stop the cutting machine, lift it well clear of the ground, and then drive at high speed to the silage clamp – bearing in mind that he had all the advantages of a 4-wheel-drive suspended vehicle. Once at the clamp, he would reverse up, start up the moving floor of the body at the back – similar to that of a manure spreader, and discharge his load straight into the clamp. Mike Fisher was interested in developing something with the Land Rover and, as far as I could judge, his system seemed to work quite well. However, it demanded a machine far bigger than any Land Rovers we were making, and I could not see any future for it at that time, so we parted company.

A few weeks later, when I was considering a vacancy in our department, I thought of our young man again, and wondered whether he might like a job with us anyhow. Special Projects had just been made responsible for the maintenance of the adjoining 100 acres of Foredrove Farm, put in our charge when the farmers pulled out. Cutting the grass was a major problem, and I had in mind the development of some sort of super lawn mower from one of our old prototype Land Rovers. He was well-trained in hydraulics and 4-wheel

138

drive practices, and such a project would certainly benefit us while teaching him a bit more about his ideas. I dropped him a line, and he replied that he would like to take up the appointment. He hadn't been with us long when I realized that a particular prototype Land Rover was about to be scrapped – this had been built originally for the Ministry of Defence, who did not require it in the end. It was a big machine of some 120 inch wheelbase, with forward control, rated by the Army as a 2-tonner but obviously capable of carrying a lot more, and fitted with a 5-litre Perkins diesel engine. I was able to stop it being scrapped, and we set to work to convert it into our Super Lawn Mower. (At this stage I should mention that Mike Fisher had conceived a name for his invention, which was SMOMOT, standing for Single Machine – One Man – One Team).

The super lawn mower which became SMOMOT.

With the wire cage removed, and spreaders fitted at the rear, the unit became an efficient manure spreader.

We obtained on loan nearly all the equipment we required: hydraulic drives, a forage harvester to go at the front, and a discharging body to go at the back. We put the machine together, fairly rapidly, and tried it out. It seemed to work well, but having got this far, we weren't quite sure what to do with our SMOMOT, apart from just mowing the Rover Company's 100 acres of farmland. One of the firms who had loaned us equipment pointed out that there was a Grassland Demonstration taking place at the Royal Show grounds in a few months' time, and that the organizers were asking for entries in the machinery section from anybody who had made a machine that contributed towards more efficient farming. He suggested we would be entitled to enter SMOMOT: even if we didn't get anywhere, at least we would get an expert panel of judges to tell us what they thought of it at no expense. This seemed a splendid idea and so we dispatched an entry form forthwith. In due course the area judging committee came along and we gave them a demonstration. They seemed to be pretty impressed, and later we heard that they had passed on a strong recommendation to the national judging committee, which meant that we were faced with a second demonstration before some very learned gentlemen. After this, we were asked to demonstrate the machine at the exhibition before the public, whereupon we won the machinery prize! Considering that all we had set out do was to make a lawn mower for the Rover Company's park, to end up winning a highly specialized agricultural machinery competition was quite a feather in our caps.

Auntie Rover's management was getting a bit nervous by this time, wondering if Special Projects was pushing them in a direction in which they were very reluctant to move. However, they need not have feared, because it was quite obvious to me that this SMOMOT machine was really the start of a whole new farming process. Even if there was money in it, it was going to be a very long-term plan, and other uses would have to be found for our 4-wheel drive lorry (which was virtually what it was) during those times of the year when it was not collecting silage. There were interesting possibilities here, such as swop bodies for liquid fertilizer, manure spreading, granulated fertilizers, cattle trucks, and so forth. But again, this was hardly up our street – it was all a bit too way out to graft onto the engineering base that we had available at that time. In due course Mike Fisher left us and went off to start his own company, which is very successfully manufacturing tankers for waste disposal, gully-emptying, and so on. The SMOMOT concept, although copied by two or three firms at later dates, never got off the ground. Maybe it is still lying around, waiting for someone with plenty of money behind him to develop it seriously.

Another inventor who came to see us with a likely idea was a chap by the name of Peter Moy, whose family had been much involved with the coal

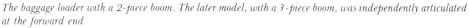

The baggage loader with a 2-piece boom. The later model, with a 3-piece boom, was independently articulated at the forward end.

industry. His particular interest was to develop a continuous-belt loading machine which would have cross-country ability and be able to traverse open-cast coal sites and assist in loading coal lorries on site. He had got so far with his invention, and came to see us about adapting the Land Rover power supply, hyraulics, axle-loads, brakes, and all the usual things that inventors want to know about when they are trying to make a Land Rover do something that wasn't in the minds of the original inventors! During the course of our discussions, I mentioned that we had had approaches at various times for aircraft baggage loaders for use at aerodromes and that I thought his device could be equally well adapted for this purpose. In fact, as I recollect, Moy found this a more attractive proposition than his open-cast coal site loading, and henceforth concentrated his energies on developing a baggage loader.

We went through several stages with him, starting with a single boom which could be raised or lowered hydraulically, and finishing up with an articulated boom in three sections. The uppermost and forward section could actually be poked into the baggage hold and adjusted according the baggage loader's desires, then came the main belt with boom, while at the bottom a further small adjustable boom could be adjusted according to the discharging baggage from the trailer or truck on the ground. This was an interesting project, and Moy eventually sold several units to British Airways which were to be seen operating at Heathrow Airport. But I think it was a question of timing, here, because although certain aircraft were very suitable for Moy's loaders, the trend was towards containerization, and most new aircraft were being designed so that baggage could be loaded into a container, taken out to the aircraft and elevated to the cargo door level, thus giving the loader in the aircraft an opportunity to size up the whole load before deciding how to stow it. So, while this was a very interesting project, it eventually had to give way to changing demand.

There have been various attempts to develop the Land Rover for deep wading and swimming, but the majority of these have been for military requirements, and are referred to in the Military chapter. However, we did receive a series of massive communications from an American who wanted to have his design for a swimming vehicle for leisure purposes built in the UK. We became involved because the basic components were to be Land Rover as much as possible. The scheme was very ambitious and I could see that if we continued with it we would almost certainly find ourselves contributing to an expensive development exercise. I was unconvinced that there would be a worthwhile leisure market for what would surely be a very expensive form of transport. If there was a military requirement, then it was up to the designer to get the authorities to say so, and if they then approached us, it would be a job for the vehicle development sections. Also, my conservation conscience rather pricked me when I thought of such vehicles rolling out of the sand-dunes into the sea at otherwise peaceful seaside resorts. My impression is that such places

A mass radiography unit of the late 1950s ...

... and the power supply from the Land Rover.

By the mid-1970s, miniaturization of much of the equipment made it possible to fit self-contained units on the Land Rover.

already have enough problems controlling noisy in-shore speedboats without adding to their troubles!

Mass Radiography was another activity with which we became quite closely involved. It seemed that after the Second World War, the equipment available for mass radiography was rather unsuitable. The generators and some equipment and personnel were carried round in large, immediately post-war, if not ex-WD lorries towing a big caravan containing the X-ray equipment and records. All this equipment was gradually wearing out. Development had taken place resulting in a reduction in the size of the X-ray equipment, and there was a move to replace the old transport with something like a Land Rover, which would be a mobile generator as well as being capable of towing a light caravan with all the X-ray equipment and accessories. One advantage of the Land Rover was that, once on site, it could be moved away from the caravan, and parked where the noise of its engine operating the generator would not intrude. We co-operated with several firms on this activity, notably Siemens in Germany, Phillips in Holland, and one or two firms in the UK. The problem was that a local authority wishing to buy one of these units had to shop around a variety of different suppliers for the X-ray equipment, the caravan, the Land Rover, the generator, and so on. What was really required was somebody to take over the rôle of main contractor, so that complete units could be specified and quoted for. This was an operation that Tooley Electro-Mechanical Ltd of Earl Shilton, Leicester, was prepared to undertake. However, although technically they did a very competent job, there were many branches of specialists involved: those concerned with caravans were jolly well going to continue to buy the caravans, those concerned with X-ray equipment were going to continue to buy the X-ray equipment, and so the problem of getting a main contractor to do the job remained. However, over the years, quite a few Land Rovers were sold in this capacity. In some cases, particularly overseas and in out-of-the-way places, the units would consist of one caravan and two Land Rovers, one carrying and driving the generator, and the other being a ferry vehicle, ferrying people in from the surrounding villages to be X-rayed.

As a mobile generator the Land Rover has many uses, but one particular intended application gave us yet another slant on this aspect. A TV company, concerned with outside colour broadcasts, raised the problem of silent operation for their generators. They were anticipating a situation where an outside broadcast could be taking place at night or after working hours, possibly in a quiet suburban area, where they might not have access to mains supply electricity. In such a situation they visualized something highly mobile like a Land Rover transporting a generator to its operating position and then driving it virtually silently. The unit would have to be capable of producing some 10-15 kva, which would in turn demand high output from the Land Rover engine, requiring it to turn at nearly 3,000 rpm to meet peak demand – and at this rate, the noise output would also be at peak.

The boxy utilitarian shape of the vehicle does nothing much in the way of sound deadening, particularly in the engine area, and this had to be attended to as the first obvious source of improvement. Adding sound deadening material all round the engine bay produced some improvement but not nearly enough, as the TV company were asking for a unit that could not be heard at all at about 30 yards' distance. To cut down noise from beneath the vehicle's engine which bounced off the ground, we experimented with mattresses. This showed some improvement, but as so often in operations like this, as fast as you reduce one noise source another one, previously submerged, becomes prominent, and we now had clutch and gear noise at one end and cooling fan and air intake noise at the other. One means of reducing the latter, much more prominent noise, was to reverse the cooling air flow and use electric fans, situated low down at the rear of the compartment, to blow cool air over the engine and out through the radiator, with a baffled exit in place of the standard grille. This showed further improvement, but this time at the expense of engine temperatures which rose unacceptably because the air exiting through the radiator had been heated more than we expected after passing over the exhaust manifold and engine block.

The silent generator vehicle. Note the high level carburettor air intake made necessary by the partial sealing of the engine bay.

By this stage of development it was becoming fairly clear to us just how far we could reasonably go with adaptation, and the likely results in noise suppression. This led to our final specifiction which included –

1. Fibreglass undershield from No 2 cross member to No 5 completely sealing off the underside of the vehicle.
2. Special exhaust line routed through above.
3. Air intake baffle at front of vehicle to quieten air intake through radiator.
4. Sound deadening trim around engine bay, front wings, driving compartment.
5. Roll down 'skirts' of sound deadening material fitted all round vehicle's outer extremities, as further baffling of noise emanating from underneath the vehicle.

Although this wasn't quite sufficient to meet the TV company's standards, they realized that it was about as far as it was practical to go with the Land Rover on a cost effective basis, and made arrangements to have several vehicles converted. Details were handed over to a small company experienced in this kind of work who would be capable of fulfilling any further orders likely to arise.

Although not much of a Land Rover activity, a fascinating enterprise we became involved with was what was known as balloon photography. This was a system thought up by a photographer by the name of Conrad Nockolds, well-known for his *Motor Sport* photographs and others, and the brother of Harold Nockolds, the motoring correspondent for the *Times,* among other publications. Conrad Nockolds was obsessed with the problem of getting elevation for his cameras – not hundreds of feet up in the air, but just 50 to 100 feet or so. He devised a system of fitting up a small balloon, a miniature of the war-time ARP balloon, so that he could suspend a camera from it. The height of the whole assembly could be controlled from the ground while the camera could be controlled individually for traversing and elevation. I think he used a light-weight bicycle wheel rim with a little carriage on it, so that the camera could be rotated around for traversing and elevated or lowered accordingly. The system worked well, but he found the balloon was rather bulky. As he couldn't afford to spend time blowing it up when he got to a site, he had to take it already inflated on a trailer. I believe it measured something like 12 to 15 feet long by 6 feet in diameter, so it was quite cumbersome even on a trailer. Once he had arrived at a parking place, he found that by the time he had dismantled the balloon from the trailer, let it out a bit, fitted the camera gear, let it go up in the air, and then walked it along to the site he was photographing, he ended up rather like the Pied Piper, with all the small boys in the neighbourhood following him and making appropriate comments!

He wanted a less conspicuous method for carrying out his balloon photo-graphy, and his solution was to have a telescopic mast on the back of a Land Rover which could be elevated and put into action quickly, and which would not excite the same attention during the course of its operation. He came to see us about masts and loading. He evantually found a chap who developed and built a mast that would go up to 100 feet and take his camera with it. When it was fully extended, this really was a most impressive sight. Conrad told me how, when he was first trying out his balloon photography, he once walked round the Bank of England on a Sunday afternoon, taking aerial photographs as he went. He couldn't help wondering what the Bank's security was and what they would say if they knew he had got photographs from the air of all their premises! He also showed me a most impressive aerial photograph of the Albert Hall, which I believe was taken with the mast and featured on the front cover of an early *Sunday Times* colour supplement. Masts for this and various other purposes are now made by Clark Masts Ltd in the Isle of Wight, and Land Rovers are frequently equipped with them, though nowadays not so much for photography as for airfield work, radio communications, emergency landing strips and items of that nature.

It may be appropriate at this stage to make reference to various matters of policy which have affected the course of Special Projects over the years, to correct any impression that it has been one continuing saga of happy-go-lucky engineering playtime! The first important matter of policy was probably our transfer from the Sales Division to Engineering in the early days. When the department was first formed it was known as Technical Sales, and took into its orbit a few people, principally Robert Hudson and David Good, who had been operating Technical Sales as such, prior to our appearance on the scene. We linked up and formed a complete Technical Sales Department within the Sales Division. Our Sales Manager, and subsequent Director, Geoffrey Lloyd-Dixon, was never very happy about having us under his wing as he found himself having to deal with problems which seemed to be of an engineering nature, although they were in fact just problems peculiar to the Land Rover which Sales should have been capable of dealing with. But Lloyd-Dixon, being a car-man, felt that it was engineering decisions that were required in many cases. He got fed-up with me badgering him, and – frankly – I was getting a little frustrated myself, being unable to get decisions when I wanted them. Then there was the other side of the coin: the Engineering Department was rather resentful that an engineering activity – or what was regarded as such – should be carried out under a Sales umbrella. So, inevitably, the crunch eventually came, and consideration had to be given as to whether or not we should be transferred to the Engineering Department. William Martin-Hurst took up the problems of this transfer, and we had a long talk together. He finally persuaded me that a move to the Engineering Division would be in everyone's best interests. I had a feeling that we might lose some of our freedom, but otherwise had no particular axe to grind, and the change-over, when it took place, presented no great problems. In due course we had as much freedom as we had enjoyed before, and in large measure this was thanks to Tom Barton (successor to Jack Pogmore as Chief Engineer, Land Rovers). He recognized our role and allowed us to get on with it, and it has been like that ever since. In more recent years the problems have centred around top management never being quite sure whether a project that was put forward should be handled by the factory itself, or whether it could be left to Special Projects to sort out. From time to time I would be called to high-level meetings to discuss such projects, but I always felt that to involve me was a mistake: any job should either be carried out by Special Projects out of plant, or be done in plant. In certain cases, problems did overlap, and one instance of this concerned air-conditioning. Approved manufacturers had undertaken to supply and fit air-conditioning after production, but since it was almost mandatory for certain export markets, it had to be fitted and exported under the seal of factory approval, rather than that of the manufacturer/installer. I recall having to attend a meeting on behalf of Special Projects on this subject which was really convened to consider in-plant possibilities. As the 10 or 11 people sitting round the table discussed production problems – of which I had limited experience and with which I was not very concerned – I had very little to say for the duration of the meeting. It was chaired by Spen King, and I remember telling him afterwards, 'You know, Spen, that meeting reminded me of my school days: I joined the school orchestra and at our first concert had to play the triangle. In the first piece we played they had me counting through about 50 bars, then giving one beat on the triangle, and that was it – my total contribution!'

Another trend has been the move from the earlier, sometimes rather ad hoc planning committee decisions, to the creation of a full-time product planning department. I consider this to be an important move in the right direction, so long as the tendency to cramp Special Projects activities is resisted. A product planning executive once admitted in my hearing that had his department been in existence in 1948, there would probably have been no Land Rover! So, by the same token, it is vital that Special Projects continues to retain some freedom for limited exploration in directions which at present produce no statistics to help and guide planning or market research.

The problem of special installations for the Land Rover is one which has been steadily mounting since the early days. I have already mentioned the fact that Land Rover is in itself almost a 'special project', and that once all the factory facilities are exhausted for supplying the different shapes, sizes and equipment for Land Rovers, outside help is still needed to meet the demand. The vehicle is built to four very basic specifications, i.e. 88-inch wheelbase and 109-inch wheelbase pick-ups, 88-inch and 109-inch station wagons. From these basic specifications, a number of workable specifications are built up: petrol or diesel, 4-cylinder, 6-cylinder, or, latterly, V8, with varying wheel sizes, tyre sizes, etc, etc. When you have a basic working specification you can still go on and add extras, or E-numbers, which provide extra facilities over and above those required to make the vehicle work, such as heating and de-misting equipment, folding steps, fly screens, oil pressure gauges, heavy duty suspension, rear door instead of tail-board and flap on hard top vehicles, etc. Then further on there is a system of Specification numbers, or S-numbers, of which there are about a hundred. These are specifications built up principally for fleet-users (GPO, MoD, overseas armies, civil engineering firms, etc). Going on still further there is a Non-Standard Request Form, whereby we endeavour to supply customers with what they want according to our abilities. This very often takes the form of special paintwork, external holders for jerry cans in various forms, modified tool kits to suit customers' requirements, and additional fuel tanks. When all these resources are fully utilized, we still do not meet all our customer's demands, and some work has to be farmed out.

It struck me early on in the course of our operations that we could well do with a Special Installations Division, which could be set aside on a paying basis, and given the responsibility for looking after all this work. They would have facilities of their own for the majority of the work, but they would also be the main contractor in those instances where they might sub-contract to advantage for certain work to be done. Such things as winches, of which there is a great variety for diverse purposes, could come under this umbrella, and possibly complete front-end units, ie from the seat box forward, to be offered for front-wheel-drive, low-loading trucks or as a power-pack for other purposes, and powered-axle trailers and ordinary trailers. Customers using trailers with their Land Rovers generally require auxiliary brakes to be fitted to the Land Rover for operating the trailer brakes, and this was something else that a Special Installations Division could encompass. And then there was the awkward question of composite vehicles, eg a Simon elevating platform with a compressor fitted to operate compressed air tools. If Rover agreed to become the main agent for such vehicles, they would supply the Land Rover but go to Simon Engineering, or Spencers, to fit the platform, and then go elsewhere to fit the compressor. By the time the vehicle had travelled between all the sub-contracting firms, it would have clocked up quite a mileage before the customer ever laid hands on it: nobody was fully responsible for the final entity, for its working efficiency, or for the quality of workmanship. This was a situation that a Special Installations Division could very well control, thus making sure that the customer got what he wanted. Such a division could also take over some of the production extras which did not fit in very well with the nature of the work at Solihull, such as supplying and fitting auxiliary fuel tanks (of which there are many variations), heaters and de-misters, air-conditioning and independent fuel-burning auxiliary heaters. Later on one could contemplate undertaking wheelbase extensions for special-purpose vehicles. The 1967 summary of the situation shows that in the preceding year, in the Non-Standard Extra business at Rover, 1,823 vehicles were painted with special colours, and this was spread over 69 different colours! There were 6,206 other vehicles all fitted with some form of the Non-Standard Extra or Extras, all adding up to quite a big problem which seemed to warrant a more orderly system of administration.

My first effort in this direction was made in the early 1960s, and again a fairly long period of lobbying was necessary for everyone concerned to see the problem and then agree to it. At long last I was able to convene a final meeting, to enable us to ratify the various agreements. We all sat round the table but five minutes later the whole thing was over. The Sales Director said that he didn't want to have anything to do with the scheme – he had completely changed his mind since I had last spoken to him – and so that was the end of that. Some years later I tried again, reinforcing my case by pointing out that a similar scheme had been highly successful with Bedford Trucks at Dunstable. The Manager there had very kindly showed me round all his facilities, and was quite happy to entertain a further party of visitors from Rover. After this visit, a massive and most interesting report was written by our then Production Director, WJ Robinson, which subsequently disappeared upstairs. Like so many reports, it then got itself pigeon-holed somewhere and I was never able to flush it out to get it discussed again. I think the reluctance was to some extent caused by a fear of industrial relations problems, particularly on the question of labour mobility/flexibility from a small unit operating within a union-dominated mass assembly plant. But, surely, with some firm management this was something which could have been overcome? A certain amount of disruption would also have been caused, as there were various little workshops situated around the site at Solihull undertaking bits and pieces of special work, some of which would have had to be eliminated, the others merging into an 'all-can-do' Special Installations Division. The other telling point – which could always be brought to bear when a decision had to be deferred – was that the plant was bursting at the seams with existing work, particularly with car assembly, and there wasn't the space to accommodate such an activity. This was very short-sighted, however, and I am sure that, today, had we pioneered such an activity in the late 1960s, we would have had a very useful adjunct to Land Rovers at Solihull, operating smoothly and efficiently to Land Rover's great advantage.

In the end, what Rover was reluctant to do turned into benefit for Spencer Abbott & Co Ltd, a company fairly well-known to Land Rover users and sub-contractors. I had started to use them intermittently for such jobs as winch installation, and we eventually got this going quite well. This was in the late 1960s and early 1970s, when the Range Rover was about to come on the market, and, as I have related elsewhere, the prospect of using this chassis for a high-class ambulance became an attractive one. Since it was too short for a 4-wheel-drive ambulance, it was essential that we engineered a wheelbase extension. Tests of a prototype proved satisfactory, indicating that it would be of value to the ambulance field. Through the Product Planning Committee we made sure that the management was fully aware of the rather bigger than usual step taken by Special Projects, but the project was passed without any comment. We then decided that since it couldn't be done at Solihull, we must select one contractor to manufacture all the chassis extensions for us and for all our approved ambulance body builders. We got Spencer Abbott interested and trained up to carry out this work, but this was a job that could have slotted in very nicely had we had a Special Installations Divison functioning; as we hadn't, the work and profit had to go outside.

As already mentioned, when the Land Rover came on the market one of the first customers for it was the War Office, who took away a quantity of vehicles to modify by installing 4-cylinder Rolls-Royce B-series engines. These were another wheeze of the War Office: Rolls-Royce built 4-cylinder, 6-cylinder and 8-cylinder engines for them, with many common features and maximum interchangeability of parts, so that they could then be used to power anything from Land Rovers to heavy tanks and big transporters. I remember SB Wilks himself telling me, when we were discussing some Marauder problems, of his first reaction on seeing a little 80-inch Land Rover fitted with a B-series engine. 'You went to drive the vehicle away, but found that the engine had got there first! There was scarcely room for anyone in the front driving compartment!' As a result of this policy, and the suggestion from the War Office that we should give them independent front suspension as well, we turned down military business at that time, deciding to stick to the commercial field. It was partly due to this that the Austin Champ came into being, as described elsewhere. I was always a little worried about the military business, as I felt that it would eventually become powerful enough to have a disproportionate influence on our production specifications, possibly to the detriment of the commercial world, apart from slowing it down. We can safely say that our military business has been both successful and profitable, but I would still maintain that it complicates life when we want to make specification changes to keep up to date with the demands of the commercial market. The 1-tonne, 101-inch vehicle was a good case in point: although extremely good for military purposes, it was so orientated in respect of size and overall weight, that we found no worthwhile civilian market application for it. Today, however, the complexity of international legislation in respect of safety, emission, noise, construction and use imposes a far greater burden on engineering resources.

One of the things I had always been interested in was the possibility of Land Rover producing what might be called a 'Poor Man's Unimog'. The 4-wheel-drive Unimog produced by a subsidiary of Mercedes-Benz in Germany was an excellent vehicle which I had always admired, but it was very expensive. I believed that with the knowledge and expertise we had garnered over the years with Land Rovers, and with the units available to us, we could have built a similar sort of vehicle but sold it for rather less money. In the early days, when we were looking at the front-wheel-drive low-loader previously referred to, known as the TempoWerke, and with the intermittent demand for a Land Rover much bigger than anything we had contemplated, I felt that as a matter of policy we ought to develop an all-wheel-drive speciality, thereby ensuring that anybody wanting an all-wheel-drive vehicle would automatically think of coming to us first. Such vehicles, particularly those of the more expensive and exotic types, would use a high proportion of sub-contractors but would still be profitable. I touted this policy around without much hope of success and, indeed, it got scant consideration. Again, the perfect answer was that Solihull was bursting at the seams with present production and there was no room for it. There didn't seem to be much room for people who looked very far ahead either. Later on, at the time when SMOMOT came along, had we developed some kind of all-wheel-drive speciality, we could have looked at the proposals that SMOMOT seemed to offer rather more intelligently. If we had taken this route, it is hard to say whether we could have made it profitable, but the signs have been pretty positive. After all, there are several firms making a living from manufacturing all-wheel-drive vehicles to different and bigger specifications than the Land Rover, and they seem to be making a go of it. A Special Installations Divison would have been just the right place in which to assemble the lower production volume of these machines.

Another very absorbing activity involving Special Projects is the transplanting of mature, or semi-mature trees. This idea is not, of course, a new one – it was employed by Capability Brown two hundred years ago, when he was altering the landscape on large estates throughout the country – but in those days it was horses and men that supplied the necessary power, while today it is all done mechanically, with a minimum of man-power. Without going into too many details, when we first became involved, the technique entailed the use of a trailer, specially developed for the purpose, which acted both as a lever to pull the tree out of the ground, and then as a transporter to take it to its new place of residence. To haul the tree out of the ground, the trailer was used as a pivot by means of winching on the extended drawbar, which stuck up in the air alongside the tree trunk, and then hauling on it by winch cable. Thus, when the trailer drawbar was eventually pulled down parallel to the ground, it pulled the tree and its trunk down and out of its hole. Then there is the question of hauling this heavy load out of the forest or away from the site. This usually involves a fair amount of all-wheel drive traction, and often the additional help of the winch to get away from the site, which is frequently in rough or boggy terrain. The process is more or less reversed for planting the tree at the planting site, and again involves some nifty work for the Land Rover, or other form of traction. The trailer has to be backed up to the planting hole, with its tree clamped to it, and tree and trailer then have to be manoeuvred into a vertical position, again by judicious winching, so that the tree can be released and dropped into the hole. Amongst other things, this process was a good occupation for the Land Rover as a demonstration for training people on the versatility of 4-wheel drive. When we started our Foredrove Farm Demonstration Site, we often had requests from the sales people to give a demonstration of Land Rovers working off-the-road for visiting parties of salesmen, overseas

The special trailer is up-ended, attached to the tree through the collar around the trunk, and the telescopic draw bar is extended for greater leverage. A winch is used to haul in the draw bar which is then pulled down parallel to the ground. This action will lift the tree out of its previously excavated position ...

delegates and so forth. We had a tree at Foredrove Farm which we used for this demonstration, and in fact transplanted it at least half a dozen times. By all the laws of nature, this shouldn't have been very good for the tree, but it seemed to thrive on it! It was strong and growing well until they came along and plonked the Rover SD1 Car Plant on top of it; now that didn't do it any good at all!

When the Range Rover was first introduced, we made rather an administrative bungle of its air-conditioning system. During the development stage, our Managing Director, William Martin-Hurst, who was very keen on air-condi-

... and deposit the tightly wrapped soil ball over the trailer axle ready for transport.

The normal position for the roof-top air-conditioner.

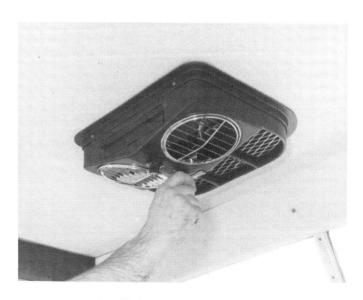

The cold air ejection louvres are immediately beneath, inside.

1950 Land Rover 80-inch basic model. (Neill Bruce)

1949 Land Rover 80-inch Chassis. (Neill Bruce)

An early 80-inch station wagon. (David Bowyer)

The new models at the launch of the Ninety, and improved One-Ten at Eastnor Castle in Spring 1984.

One of the first Ninety models.

Glenfrome's 'Ashton' power-operated convertible.

Glenfrome's 'Facet' built on the Range Rover chassis, a bold step into futuristic design. (Andrew Morland)

The 127-inch crew carrier: the perfect vehicle for a round-the-world trip.

Our expedition crew taking advantage of the driving facilities at Solihull. The members of the driver training team are Land Rover's best ambassadors.

US spec. Range Rovers doing what comes naturally.

130 being inspected by Indonesian Army Officers before leaving for Bosnia.

Ken and Julie Slavin on a Sahara expedition in the '60s, with vastly overloaded vehicles.

Range Rover North America and the Great Divide Expedition.

Line up of 1995 model year Discoverys in Belize.

One of our testing expeditions in the Sahara Desert.

An encounter between "Ships of the Desert"!

A silhouette now familiar in the Third World.

A Range Rover is roped through tropical conditions during the 1972 Darian Gap expedition

A 110 during The Camel Rally in Brazil sponsored by the 'Camel' cigarette company. (Land Rover Ltd)

101 Forward Control with WWF/London Zoo proved to be the king of load carriers for expedition use.

Prototype V8 towing 101 in soft sand.

Slavin family with aid convoy bound for Niger and Nigeria, 1987.

A stone-age setting for two Land Rovers.

Director of London Zoo, David Jones, using Range Rover tailgate to pack grasses collected in the Sahara for Kew Gardens, 1979.

Range Rover fitted with a roof-top air-conditioner.

High temperatures can build up in a closed security vehicle making air cooling essential. The unit on the roof of this vehicle is the self-contained Hubbard CT 140.

157

An air-conditioned security vehicle supplied by Glovers of Hamble. The additional petrol tank on the roof at the rear is a temporary fitting to make sure the long delivery mileage could be safely accomplished.

A radar surveillance vehicle also generates high internal temperatures. The vehicle is fitted with a roof-mounted refrigerant condenser and the cooling evaporator pack is fitted internally.

tioning, started a project to develop a system for the Range Rover which would cover the most extreme requirements the vehicle would ever be likely to meet. It was pretty massive, and as the units had to be specially made it was very expensive. Development progress did not keep pace with the launching of the vehicle, which had been speeded up by Leyland Cars as a matter of policy – I think we were told to announce it a whole year ahead of the original schedule. As soon as it was announced, several firms came along offering air-conditioning alternatives which they were prepared to supply and/or fit, and we had to have an audit to examine all these different systems. By this time William Martin-Hurst had retired and AB Smith was in command. We looked at systems which were fitted on the Range Rover roof, including our own, and those which were fitted inside the vehicle in various places, and AB Smith decreed that if we were going to have an air-conditioning system at all, it must be inside and not an external protrusion – which was fair enough. Anyhow, the Range Rover met with such an enthusiastic response that we were churning them out, in rather a halting fashion because of our premature start, which meant that we didn't have much time to devote to air-conditioning.

The Swedish ambulance conversion had a 1-meter wheelbase extension but did not increase the Range Rover rear overhang.

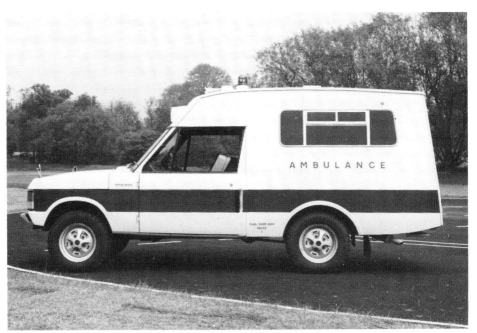

The specialist body builders welcomed the 10-inch wheelbase extension and added an additional 10 inches to the rear overhang.

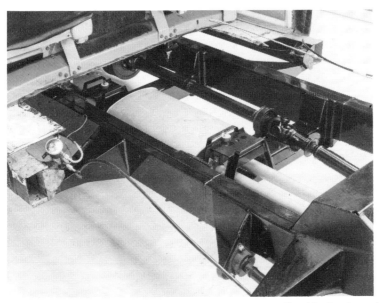

Our 35-inch wheelbase extension was made up with two cross members joined to the 35-inch-long side members and positioned within the Range Rover frame, so that the central silencer and split propeller shaft mounting could be correctly located.

When we made a 35-inch wheelbase extension available, the specialist body builders welcomed this too but retained their 10-inch overhang! The Swedish vehicle (below), however, remained the same.

Besides fire appliances, Carmichaels produced a 6 x 4 personnel carrier.

The problem caught up with us all of a sudden, when the sales people said that we *must* have air-conditioning for certain developing export markets, principally those in the Middle East. As there was no factory-developed system, they turned to Special Projects and said, 'Can you find us a proprietary system for the vehicle to tide us over until we can get a fully fledged factory installation going?' The only quick solution was to take a system already in use on commercial vehicles in America, the main part of which consisted of a big box of components which sat on top of the cab roof – unsightly but efficient. This solved one problem worrying us at the time – that of having to place the condenser for cooling the refrigerant in front of the radiator. As the condenser in this unit was incorporated in the box, there could be no question of the engine over-heating due to obstructions in front of the radiator. So, rather ironically, and in spite of what AB Smith had decreed, we had no immediate alternative but to offer an externally fitted device. It kept us going for a few years and helped us along, but now of course fully engineered, internally fitted equipment can be obtained ex-works.

We introduced a 10-inch wheelbase extension principally for ambulance purposes and 10 inches was chosen as it appeared to be enough to get a standard stretcher into the compartment, while not requiring extra expenditure in the form of a lengthened and split propeller shaft: it only had to be lengthened. We noticed later on that a firm in Sweden, untroubled by our inhibitions, was producing a very fine ambulance on the Range Rover, to which they had given a wheelbase extension of 1 metre (about 39½ inches). We inspected one of these vehicles when it was over on a visit to the UK and a very fine-looking machine it was too. This gave us further thoughts about introducing a longer wheelbase extension than our modest 10 inches. Another reason was that while the original conception had been that an extra 10 inches was sufficient to convey a standard stretcher, it wasn't quite enough to satisfy the ambulance body-builders who wanted more space still, and they were therefore simply building the bodies with an extra 10 - 12 inch overhang at the back. This wasn't altogether satisfactory and we thought that to build an even longer wheelbase would get us back to a better balanced vehicle again. Our deliberations showed that a 35-inch wheelbase extension would be about right. Alas, plans didn't work out very well because some of the ambulance body-builders, once they got hold of the 35-inch extension, *still* went on and built a

Scottorn Trailers' 6 x 6 conversion.

10 - 12 inch extra overhang at the back, resulting in a rather monstrous vehicle. We also had to take into account the question of legislation over brake performance and such like with this larger, more heavily laden vehicle, and for this reason it had to be abandoned. However, this 35-inch extension was used by some body-building firms for luxury personnel carrying vehicles and, provided the rearmost extension did not exceed the standard Range Rover one, and the gross axle weight wasn't exceeded, it made quite a satisfactory vehicle for this purpose.

At the time of the vehicle's introduction, we were approached by Harry Carmichael of Carmichael's, a firm which builds fire appliances. He had conceived a scheme for converting the Range Rover into a 6-wheel vehicle, which he wanted to use as a first-rescue fire appliance. This struck us as a bit unusual, but once we had talked about it, and seen what practices of this nature were carried out in the commercial vehicle world, we felt quite happy about going along with him. Eventually we drew up a jointly agreed specification which was, basically, a Range Rover chassis with an additional trailing axle and frame extension added on at the back. This configuration then became known as a 6 x 4 chassis. We carried out comprehensive tests on this vehicle as it was a

All body conversions undergo a tilt test.

fairly fundamental chassis change, and ever since Carmichael's have had much success with this particular conversion. The next step was to make it into a 6 x 6 or all-wheel-drive chassis. Carmichael's studied the problem but I think we all came to the same conclusion, that such a conversion would really be very expensive and probably not cost-effective either to develop or for customers to purchase, so we let it lapse. To get the ball rolling again, it took the initiative of a young Frenchman who linked up with the Scottorn Trailer Company to develop such a configuration. This is now taking shape, and it will be interesting to see what sort of market it achieves.

Having become such a 'prestige' vehicle, the Range Rover has attracted a great many motor-car body-builders to the possibilities of restyling and making variations on the theme to suit certain customers. The first step was to have available a 4-door conversion, and the pioneers of this particular work were FLM (Panelcraft) in London. This company has been in the luxury end of the body conversion business for many years and has built up good contacts, not only in the UK but overseas – particularly in the Middle East. They found a ready market for the 4-door conversion, and other varieties, including special hunting vehicles for Middle East potentates. Their hunting entails the use of hawks for tracking down the prey, and as the hawk is a very valuable bird and takes a lot of training, they obviously don't want to lose it during the course of a hunting expedition. So everything on these special vehicles is designed to prevent this happening: perches are built in the back of the vehicle for the hawks to rest on, and in some cases, when they have been dispatched in pursuit of their quarry, the owner, sitting alongside the driver in the front, can elevate his seat up through the open roof and keep an eye on his valuable bird, making sure that in due course it can be safely recovered. There have even been vehicles made on the extended wheelbase with two elevating seats at the rear as well, so that the owner and observers can emerge through the Range Rover roof as it cruises along the desert, looking rather like a triple-headed Loch Ness Monster!

Automatic transmissions was another area we investigated, as we had been informed by the ambulance people that this would almost certainly be a requirement on the more de-luxe ambulances that they were contemplating making. We did the first installation ourselves, identified most of the problems and mastered many of them. But when the motoring journal *Autocar* published a road test of a Range Rover which had been converted by Automatic Transmission Services Ltd and wrote of it in glowing terms, it became clear to me that we should test and approve their installation rather than become involved ourselves. Automatic Transmission Services went ahead doing conversions mostly on basic vehicles. The call from the ambulance world never really materialized and only in a few special cases could the combined cost of lengthening the wheelbase and installing automatic transmission be justified.

With a span of over 30 years watching Land Rover markets develop, it is interesting for me to see how the organization has changed. In 1948 we had

Our ill-fated post-hole borer.

hardly any Sales staff even for motor-cars, let alone Land Rovers, and no clear identity within the Engineering Division, but such a lot has happened over the years that we have now passed through an over-kill situation, where we have had far too many jobs and people overlapping. These circumstances seem so often to beget complications in an organization. Organization charts for old *and new* departments proliferate and eventually lead to overmanning, then overlapping and confusion, and inevitably to loss of flexibility. Now that Land Rover Limited has been formed as a separate entity with a bit more control of its own destiny, the situation should stabilize itself but – my goodness – we have had some peaks and troughs in the intervening years, with personnel and management changes.

S B Wilks was the first to see weaknesses in his staff and decided that we must have a Sales Director on the Board, and strengthen up the Sales Department. Then there was the merger with Leyland in the mid-1960s. At first all was quiet for us, as we were in what was called the Specialist Car Division which was profitable at that time; attention was given rather to building the Austin/Morris part of the organization into a more profitable concern. But, as history records, there were problems with Austin/Morris, and eventually along came Ryder, appointed by the Government, to put everything right. As far as I was concerned, for Special Projects and probably for Land Rover Limited, this was not a good thing, because, amongst other things, a centralized accounting system was put into effect. Those of us who had had budgets to operate in the past and had taken pride in operating them, making sure that we ended the year well within budget, lost all control. My belief is that centralized budget control is generally a sign of weak or uncertain management. They may think that by doing this they are getting everything under their own control, but in reality they aren't, because in a large organization it is impossible to be all things to all men when it comes to authorizing expenditure: it has got to be devolved to some extent. Fortunately, people who have been around the organization for some time knew how to side-step some of the incompatible restrictions which appeared from time to time.

A good example of how centralized budget control can be self-defeating occurred over the development of a post-hole borer for the Land Rover. Due to interest expressed in one or two overseas zones, we had developed and tested a post-hole borer specially for the Land Rover. The unit was seen by a buyer of a well-known civil engineering firm who thought it would be suitable for a surveying contract they were about to embark on in Africa. On its arrival in Africa, the company had difficulty in getting the machine to function properly. They offered to accommodate our engineer free of charge, if we would release and fly him out there, to get the machine operational as it had been demonstrated to them at Solihull. The unexpected sale of the prototype unit for £1,000 was in my view a 'windfall' profit, as it would otherwise have been eventually written off. The cost of the engineer's return air fare was £300, so it seemed to me that we would merely be reducing our windfall by this amount, to £700. But since the engineering budget would have to finance the air fare while receiving no benefit from the sale, the customer's offer was refused. The net result was that:

1) We lost our machine. It could not be shipped back due to export restrictions in the African country.
2) We had to agree to cancel the sale and therefore lost £700.
3) We lost some goodwill with an important customer.
4) We lost the opportunity of further field experience in the development of a piece of equipment which could well have been very suitable for Land-Rovers and would have enhanced its work-horse image.

I am convinced that a strong management, which has real product knowledge and knows what it is doing, is much more likely to be effective if it devolves budget control as far as it possibly can, and then sets up an inspection team to go round monitoring the budget holders to find out what they are doing, what they are spending and why, and particularly whether they are within or over their budget. In this way, it will exercise much more control and find out much more about its business and what is going on at lower levels. I am sure that Land Rover Limited will continue to improve as its new young management gains experience in handling what must surely be, in the context of the motor industry, a very odd-ball product – one which, after all, is sold as private transport, fleet transport, military and para-military hardware, industrial units, public utility vehicles, to all classes of people from heads of state downwards, and is one of the few vehicles that can be tolerated when seen operating in the dirtiest of workhorse conditions, or acting as a review vehicle to transport royalty past guards of honour or public displays.

My previous reference to the post-hole borer we devised for the Land Rover reminds me of the circumstances connected with its first display. This was to be at an Earls Court Smithfield Show. Our exhibition section had submitted details of all the exhibits proposed for the Land Rover stand to the Society of Motor Manufacturers and Traders, the organizers, as required by the regulations. I was surprised and not a little irritated when I was told that the exhibition secretary had objected to the post-hole borer on a technicality – when attached to a vehicle, the overall length of the combined unit was too long, or something like that. This prompted me to write a sharp reply, stressing the raison d'être of an exhibition to sell products, the aid to Land Rover sales by the addition of a new implement to increase its versatility, and so forth. I also mentioned that post-hole borers were coming into use in some countries for grave digging, as they saved labour and with vertical burial saved ground. I concluded with the dire stricture that this might be the case when the exhibition secretary's turn came, and that he would surely like to think he had not in any way impeded development of such important conservation! In his reply the exhibition secretary conceded my arguments and gave his assent to the exhibit. He also requested that, should I be officiating when the time came to lower him into his hole, would I make sure that he was facing in the direction of Earls Court!

During my career with Special Projects, I have often been asked if I thought that ideas for special equipment and conversions would ever dry up. I have never been able to foresee this happening and it is still the case today – so much so, that in writing these notes, I have had to leave out a great deal. Although, as I have said earlier, we sometimes seemed to be in danger of becoming a unit getting to know less and less about more and more, one could write again almost as many words as have been written on each of several of the conversions or equipment mentioned. In selecting items for discussion, I found the same problem intruding as when assessing the worth of some of the schemes put forward for approval. That was to resist the temptation to spend more time than sales potential seemed to justify on speculative projects with a high degree of engineering interest, and devote it instead to the sometimes more mundane sellers.

Changes for the eighties

The wind of change – and beneficial change – continues to blow, and for the Special Projects this brings about a rising status and better recognition of its function. Final cleavage from motor car activities has much to do with this new situation. What is this new situation? For conversions, the co-operation and approval of the converter/manufacturer is assuming more importance as it is realised to what extent he can become a strong arm of the overall sales promotion effort. Because, however, consumer legislation is gaining in complexity in so many markets, the obligation has increased of Special Projects to judge carefully the extent of approval tests required. This, of course, must be considered in the context of the number of extra Land Rovers the conversion is going to sell.

A reorganisation within the Engineering Division has resulted in Special Projects, Military Contracts and Engineering liason with Spanish Land-Rover Manufacture being grouped together as 'Special Operations' under a Chief Engineer.

A procedure has been developed enabling the converter to carry out a large measure of self-certification towards his approval – a procedure that rightly throws a fair proportion of the testing cost onto the conversion firm. The proposed conversion is studied by a small vetting committee of members of the Marketing, Product Planning, and Special Operations departments before being accepted for self-certification. It can be seen that such a representative vetting committee has a very wide scan to bring to bear in assessing conversions. If the committee likes what it sees there follows, among other things, a very close appraisal of the converter's resources, financial standing and integrity. Finally, a programme is drawn up to cover all aspects for gaining Engineering Approval. Thus the handling of conversions by the Engineering

Back row: *basic vehicles – 88-in canvas hood, 88-in hard top, 88-in cab and $\frac{3}{4}$ hood, 109-in hard top, 110-in FC rear view, 110-in FC front view, 109-in canvas hood, 109-in cab and $\frac{3}{4}$ hood, 109-in Station Wagon.*
4th row: *elevating platform on 109-in, articulated trailer conversion on 88-in with trailer, belt conveyor on 109-in.*
3rd row: *mobile cinema on 109-in Station Wagon, Shorland armoured car, compressor unit on 110-in FC.*
2nd row: *mechanically driven drum winch, hydraulically driven drum winch and mobile compressor conversion on 109-in, emergency stretcher gear in standard Station Wagon body, ambulance-bodied 109-in, motor caravan conversion on 109-in Station-Wagon, fire appliance conversion on 110-in FC.*
Front row: *pto-driven saw bench at rear, cable storage drum of Plumett winch between seats on 88-in, snow blade on 88-in, crop sprayer 109-in, car recovery crane on 109-on, fire appliance conversion on 109-in, air-conditioner on 88-in Station Wagon.*

Division and Special Projects is now on a firm and recognised footing and is processed by one of two sections within the department, the second section concerning itself with the activities connected with factory-produced specials, optional extras, designing, and liason with all other relevant departments. A good example of this function is how refrigerated air-conditioning has moved from a proprietary, approved extra for the after market, to a factory option available ex-works. I do not think it would be entirely inaccurate to say that the

The last word in communications? This is CAP's 'Mobility '84' system which is equipped with a satellite earth station and provides round-the-world communications via voice telephone, VHF radio, facsimile, video text and slow scan video. In addition computer facilities allow data and word processing integrated with the communications equipment. The whole assembly is here mounted on a 110-inch crew cab.

advent of and demand for air-conditioning on Land Rovers and Range Rovers precipitated, and *made* us solve this problem, as referred to on pages 159-168.

There seems a likelihood at the time of writing that a 6 x 6 chassis may be added to the Land Rover model sales list, based on the new 110-inch. However there are some fairly expensive engineering hurdles to cross here – and how cost-effective would such a chassis be? One result of the advent of the 110-inch and 90-inch is that all the active approved conversions must now be re-assessed for adaptation and/or respecified for these vehicles, which is in itself quite a workload.

This is a good opportunity to mention that Special Operations now include a recognised function for correctly specifying Land Rover units, engines, gearboxes, axles etc. for sale to other manufacturers. In the past this tended to be a sideline, supply being on an ad-hoc basis, which was understandable, in a way, as there was rarely any spare manufacturing capacity to cope with any

The Branbridge Mk. IV fire appliance from Pilcher-Greene Ltd.

significant demand that might arise. For a time the Gas Turbine Department became involved for no better reason than that, after the turbine car project had been shelved, they specialised in selling stationary engines.

It would be nice to think that a Special Installations Division (page 149) will be given further serious thought. When Special Projects was formed in 1957 our then Chairman told me that as long as I could convince him that Special Projects could cause the sale of an extra 200 vehicles per year he would feel the cost of the department justified. I went to great pains to do this, by circulating an annual report of our activities. In some years, when the company was desperately short of vehicles against the order book, it nearly had the opposite effect, with suggestions that our activities should be halted as we were diverting vehicles away from the main sales stream! This situation is unlikely to occur today, with more enlightened and integrated sales and marketing organisations, which haven't had to form their opinions only after dealing with apparently similar, but really diverging, problems affecting motor cars. Mind you, today we have computers and here is a temptation to let them produce lots of statistics in quite minute and idiotic detail. A close eye is required to be kept on the pendulum here, but the capability for assessing the value of a Special Installations Division is now much better.

Not long ago, I read Sir Michael Edwardes' book 'Back From the Brink' and what a much-needed and refreshing blast of common sense he caused to blow through BL. Even down at the level of Land Rover Special Projects the benefits will be felt. I think of a conversation I had many years ago with one of our directors, the subject of which was the staff Christmas bonus, usually two weeks' extra salary. The year in question had been a poor one and profits were down. I suggested that it would be sensible and logical to reduce the bonus. All I got was a chilly nil response! From what Michael Edwardes said, I am confident No More Shall Confusion Reign when a MOD/Carmichael situation arises again (page 84). No more confusion for Sales Management having to grapple with car and Land Rover problems, which are frequently far from compatible; this odd-ball product requires total commitment. No More of the situation that once occurred concerning the Engineering Department who were working against the clock to prepare two or three prototype vehicles, urgently required for submission to a foreign government who might award us a big contract. For the vehicles to be shipped on time some weekend overtime was required, but the union shop steward wouldn't budge. The situation was so desperate that Peter Wilks, then Technical Director and a persuasive speaker, offered to address the men. He was firmly discouraged by the management negotiator, such a move being considered 'improper' and creating an 'undesirable precedent'. The vehicles were delivered late. No More of the situation that I experienced more than once trying to put together a 'special', similar to the example quoted on page 72, with Rover as the main contractor. The sub-contractors had to give us their prices so that we could quote the customer for the whole package, as requested. A newly-arrived accountant of the Ryder régime flatly refused to do this: it was no business of his or mine, he said! Orders and requests such as this were sometimes quite incomprehensible to some of our transient masters from the car world. And No More post-hole borer situations please!

On a personal note, my feelings are that in work of this nature it is important to maintain the thread of product knowledge of the conversion, or special equipment, all the way through, for obvious reasons. What is not perhaps obvious is that this thread must also include practical experience, because theory and practice so often diverge. Product knowledge must include as much as possible of both. I felt strongly about this when I was actively engaged and I only hope that re-organisation, which so often elevates the importance of a tidy organisation chart above that of the flexibility of people and things, will not submerge this aspect.

Land Rover can now recognise itself for what it is and it would even be fitting if it considered itself; **The World's Most Versatile Bespoke 4 x 4 Manufacturer.**

A final cautionary word though. In the 1960s the British motorcycle industry thought of itself as the makers of the world's superbikes, content to leave the manufacture of small bikes and scooters to the Japanese. Who makes the superbikes today? In the 4 x 4 world there seem to be a great many small Japanese vehicles about.

In this case, history is unlikely to repeat itself. Having met and talked to several of the new management team and had the opportunity of trying out the latest models – the 110 and 90 as well as the latest versions of the Range Rover – I am convinced Land Rover are now making, and are determined to continue making, the world's **Super 4 Wheel Drive Vehicles.**

Land Rover Special Vehicles Operations
As George Mackie has amply illustrated above, the Company has always taken a keen interest in major conversions and, through its close involvement with customers and suppliers, has built up an unrivalled fund of practical knowledge in designing, building and equipping specialist vehicles. Since the last edition of this book, it has now all been vested in Special Vehicle Operations, (SVO), an independently managed division within Land Rover Limited, staffed by a highly motivated team, and flexibly structured to provide the dynamism, fast-response and personal skills traditionally associated with small businesses. It can perhaps best be described as the 'bespoke tailoring' unit of the plant and was established in July 1985. Handling all aspects of project management from feasibility studies to approval of completed vehicles, SVO must ensure that each converted Land Rover is built and equipped to the same demanding standards as production-line models.

For customers' convenience, specialist vehicles, be they luxury conversions, specialised military vehicles or custom-built 'workhorses', can be ordered through the normal sales channels. Thorough consultation with an SVO project engineer follows, after which a detailed vehicle design specification, to meet precisely the requirements, is submitted.

The specialised vehicles are manufactured either in SVO's unique unit, which has a highly skilled workforce based at Solihull, or with one of several carefully selected body-builders whose engineering quality and manufacturing standards are known to match those of Land Rover. Security and customer confidentiality are observed at every stage, and customers can, in conjunction with SVO, safely discuss detailed requirements direct with the body-builder/ specialist equipment manufacturer.

In its first year of operation, SVO signed a number of collaboration agreements with some of Britain's top specialist vehicle converters, and was

174

thereby able to supply customers with 'specials' including ambulances, armoured cars, skip loaders, breakdown recovery trucks, backhoe diggers, snowplough-gritters, armoured cash carriers, and even mobile cinemas. A typical SVO task was to prepare a very special Land Rover for Band Aid – a mobile workshop kitted out with enough equipment to be the envy of a small garage. Based on a Land Rover 127-inch with box body built by SVO, it was airlifted to North Africa to help keep Band Aid's food truck convoys moving. This box body proved an instant success: the first went to the Ministry of Defence, quickly followed by another to the BBC as a mobile workshop. As word got round, demand for the 4 x 4 'box on wheels' grew, for applications such as mobile police communications centres, mobile radio and TV recording units, mobile cinemas, mobile banks, and even a mobile lubrications unit for servicing aircraft.

SVO have developed a range of vehicles based on the Land Rover 127-inch chassis, in either crew cab or chassis cab configuration which can incorporate either a high or low box body. The vehicles are built to the customer's individual requirements which can include a variety of internal features; the versatility of the box body is virtually unlimited and lends itself to manifold applications.

The crew cab version provides seating for up to six people, ideally suited to multi-purpose use, where mobility is an important requirement, allowing a full work crew to be delivered on site with equipment. The design of the box body allows easy access to all equipment which can, if required, be through side flaps, which greatly increase work station capacity (and provide shelter from the elements), the main body can be kitted out to suit almost any situation or purpose to suit customers' specific requirements.

Apart from 'the box', in SVO's first year it supplied 6-wheel drive Land Rovers to customers ranging from the Dorset Fire Service to the Southern Electricity Board, worked with the Beaver company to launch the Land Rover Backhoe loader ('the 80 mph flying digger'), launched the Land Rover Towlift with BRIMEC Hydraulic Recovery Systems and introduced the Land Rover Multi-Loader in conjunction with Skip-Tip Engineering.

Throughout the building and fitting out processes, SVO maintains close collaboration with the body-builder and relevant suppliers, before the finished product gets formal Technical Approval. This acknowledges that the completed vehicle bears full Land Rover warranty covering both the chassis and the specialist contract content together with an assurance of Land Rover worldwide service and parts support. Wherever possible, standard parts and mechanical units are used assuring fleet users of the convenience and economic benefits of parts commonality.

SVO are pleased to discuss customers' individual requirements for conversions and special vehicles, based on the Range Rover and the Ninety and One Ten Land Rover, including the 127-inch chassis. For further

175

information contact can be made through Sales & Marketing at Land Rover Ltd (see appendices for details).

Typical Land Rover and Range Rover Specialised Vehicles

Urban Ambulance
Military Ambulance
Command Post
Mobile Audio/Visual Theatre
Discreetly Protected Vehicles
High Profile Armoured Vehicles
Agricultural Applications
Mobile Military Communications Centres
Educational Communications
Cinema or Video Theatre
Fire Appliances
Trenching and Land Drainage
Waste Disposal Vehicles
Luxury Vehicles
Leisure Motor Homes
Winter Maintenance
Mobile Workshop

Medical Dispensaries
Mobile Clinics
Veterinary Centres
Hydraulic Platforms
Mobile Banks and Cash Carriers
Surveillance Deployment Vehicles
Vehicle Recovery
Tanker Applications
Generator and Compressor Units
High Pressure Pump Units
Rapid Intervention Vehicles
Military Patrol Vehicles
Troop or Personnel Carriers
Police Communications Centres
Tipper Units
Lubrication Dispenser Units
Rotary Drilling Rig

THE ROYAL LAND ROVERS *by Roger McCahey*

The Royal Review Land Rovers are actually three Land Rovers and a Range Rover, each specifically built for the use of the Royal Family whenever the Royal Person would be better seen standing in the back of the vehicle by the assembled crowds.

The history behind this concept is that shortly after the Amsterdam Motor Show in March 1948 the Company received a request from the Royal Mews that King George VI would be interested in inspecting and driving a Land Rover.

The Company had to decide who would show the new vehicle to the King. The Technical Service Workshop and Training School were under the control of two young men just discharged from the Royal Air Force where they served in the same squadron: Peter Wilks (nephew of S B Wilks and M C Wilks), and Ron Phillips. Peter went on to become Chief Engineer and an inspiring member of the team responsible for Land Rover development, the Rover 2000 range and the Range Rover. His early death at the age of 53 in the 1970s was a tragic loss to the old Rover Company. Ron Phillips became a Director of Land Rover retiring in the early 1980s as Director of Quality.

Obviously a request from the Monarch could not be put to one side, but the

Land Rovers produced to date were all hard at work in various parts of the world doing sales demonstrations. As soon as a demonstrator became available it was checked over and sent to the London Service Depot, whence Peter Wilks proceeded to the Royal Mews, collected a Buckingham Palace representative and went on to Sandringham where the Royal Family was in residence.

On their arrival Her Majesty Queen Elizabeth (the present Queen Mother) accompanied by HRH The Princess Margaret duly appeared, as too did eventually the King, who climbed in and set off with Peter without escorts around the roads of Sandringham. After a few miles he decided to drive, and to Peter's astonishment asked how to select four-wheel drive, before turning off the road into a dark wood. The track got muddier and wetter and Peter got more nervous, but the King drove competently and finally emerged from the wood safely, said he liked the vehicle better than the wartime jeep, and thought he might obtain one.

Having taken his leave of the King, Peter was invited to see the gardens of Sandringham by a Palace escort. Exploring the many paths, a voice behind them suddenly boomed 'Just what are you doing here?', and Peter found himself facing the formidable figure of the then Queen Mother, Her Majesty Queen Mary. After explanations, she went to some trouble to explain the lay-out of the gardens and showed an expert knowledge of plants by advising them what to see!

In the summer a letter came from Buckingham Palace: the King would like to acquire a Land Rover for extended use.

Land Rover chassis number 861010 was delivered to the Palace that autumn, but the Company then discovered a serious design fault. Contrary to conventional practice, the swinging shackles of the front springs were mounted at the front of the springs. As a result any wear or even easing-off in the shackles would result in a drastic alteration in the castor action of the wheels, giving an alarming wheel wobble. In production the shackles were moved to the conventional rear mounting but for those in service it was decided to stiffen up the location with large washers. So far very few vehicles had been sold, so modifying them via the dealer network was relatively simple. By now the vehicle supplied to the King was at Balmoral and a Company representative had to journey to Scotland to carry out the modification. This time it was Ron Phillips who set off with his bag of tools by LMS Rail for Scotland. Arriving at Ballater he was security vetted at the station before being driven to the Castle, given a room in the chauffeur's quarters, and taken to the Castle Garage to start work.

There is no record available on the effect of the modification but it would appear that unknown to the Company the King had a personal interest in its performance, because his failing health restricted his shooting activities, and he wished to use the Land Rover at Balmoral for the more arduous cross-country work that traditionally was done on horseback.

The suggestion from Scotland that a Land Rover should become the King's official means of transport around Balmoral created a flurry amongst his London-based advisers, all of whom, probably, were even less familiar with such vehicles than was the King.

As a result the King's Private Secretary, Lieut-General Sir Frederick Browning, wrote to a certain General at the Cavalry Club in September 1948 asking advice on cross-country transport. The General's reply makes interesting reading today.

'The Land Rover is a good vehicle and we are considering buying a few of them as a stop-gap. It is, however, not suitable as a military jeep owing to its lack of clearance and to the fact that it is not too good cross-country.' The Land Rover had precisely the same ground clearance as the Jeep and, with permanent four-wheel drive, an improved cross-country performance, so perhaps the General was out of touch. Since then the Services have bought probably in excess of 70,000 Land Rovers so presumably such doubts were dispelled. The General's reply, however, led to the first ever competitive trial for Land Rovers. The Private Secretary's enquiries were passed over to the Crown Equerry, who as the Royal Household officer in charge of the Royal Mews was and is responsible for the Monarch's transport. He in turn approached the Ministry of Supply for advice. The Ministry arranged an extensive trial of suitable vehicles at the Military Testing Ground at Chobham, as a result of which Land Rover was pronounced the most suitable. Land Rovers have since been engaged in competitive trials all over the world but the very first was for King George VI.

It was reported that the King was very pleased with the results of the trial, and between 1949 and 1950 three more Land Rovers were sent to Buckingham Palace. However, the original had become a source of embarrassment to Rover as it was very much a prototype, and subsequent production models had incorporated many improvements. As a result it was quietly taken back from Balmoral and a new one sent off in its place.

Not only were they used on the Royal Estates but one vehicle supplied in 1951 was specifically painted and used for Review purposes.

The first recorded occasion was in 1951 at a Territorial Army Review in Hyde Park. Photographs show a very ordinary 80-inch Land Rover with one hood stick as the VIP grab rail. The rear passenger with the King was Field Marshal Montgomery, making his last official appearance before he left the UK to take up his post of Chairman of the Western Union Committee of Commanders in Chief. Given his own way he may not have chosen to be cooped up in the back of a Land Rover for his final military appearance!

Using a Land Rover for Review purposes by the King posed some difficulties for the Royal Mews as hood and rear tailgate had to be removed. For the front hood stick to do duty as handrail it had to be replaced and stiffened (to prevent bending) and with the best will in the world, as Monty's picture shows, seated rear passengers do not look dignified!

During the Autumn of 1951 the Royal Mews was considering adapting the

Territorial Army review in July 1951 in Hyde Park, London, by HM King George VI which was the first occasion on which a Land Rover was used on a ceremonial parade. It was also the last official appearance of Field Marshal Bernard Montgomery before he went to Europe as the chairman of the Western Union Committee of Commanders in Chief. It was possibly the Field Marshal's squashed posture that encouraged the authorities to consider developing a special interior for review purposes. The Land Rover is a standard 80-inch model with rear seats and with doors removed.

14

rear of the Land Rover to make it a true Review vehicle, but such considerations were cast aside by the death of King George VI in February 1952, and the accession of Her Majesty Queen Elizabeth II.

After the Coronation, however, Buckingham Palace and the Government had planned a rigorous tour of the Commonwealth by The Queen and Prince Philip, a large part of which would take place in front of crowds in the open air, and a Land Rover was the obvious choice for such a tour. However, it was The Queen herself who pointed out that one cannot stand up in the back of a moving vehicle and hold on tight while also holding onto one's skirt and one's hat. So therefore considerable thought went into the design with emphasis on ease of access at the rear, screening rear occupants from high winds, and placing grab rails and body supports conveniently in the interior for standing passengers.

Also fancy ideas of perspex hoods and electric sliding roofs were submitted, but the Queen's retort was that should it rain umbrellas would be used! (A remark the company bore in mind, building in an umbrella locker 20 years later on the Review Range Rover.)

It was clearly impossible for a Land Rover to go on the tour as part of the baggage so it was decided that in those countries where the Royal Party were attending a large function and could use a Review Land Rover, such a vehicle would be made and despatched there to await the Royal Party. The Palace would notify the host Government that a Land Rover would be required and the local dealer would be responsible for importing the vehicle and handing it to the local Government in 'show condition'.

The logistics of the Australian tour proved that about ten Land Rovers would be required. The Mews had already approached several body makers to mock-up vehicles to be studied for their suitability for the purpose. The Company knew, however, that by the time of the Royal Tour, production Land Rovers would have undergone drastic design changes to body and chassis, and the last thing the Company wanted was for the Monarch to proceed to all parts of the Commonwealth with Land Rovers that were out of date! After due deliberation the Company approached the Royal Mews and asked for permission to take on the responsibility for the designing and building (and subsequent disposal) of all the Commonwealth Tour Land Rovers.

The Technical Sales Manager, the late R V (Bob) Hudson was to co-ordinate the project and his first task was to inform the body builders who had been approached by The Mews that their efforts were in vain – an extremely unpopular activity. The design and engineering team got down to building a vehicle similar to that envisaged for the late King which was to have been built as an 80-inch Series I Land Rover. *State I*, however, as it came to be known, was to be built on an 86-inch wheel base with vastly improved body features, incorporating an aluminium superstructure with wind protector and grab rails and two unobtrusive seats at the side over the rear wheel arches. Consideration was given to the possibility of Her Majesty becoming tired of standing up, so two fold-away supports were built into the side. These fitments did not leave a great deal of room in the rear, and during a visit to a town in New Zealand the local Mayor attempted to board the Land Rover carrying the Queen and Prince Philip, and His Royal Highness had to tell him to 'get on the one behind!'

Mounted on the rear cross-member was a step leading via a side hinged door to the rear of the vehicle. The whole interior was trimmed in blue leather with matching carpet, while the exterior was painted in a grey/blue drab awaiting final paint instructions. The Royal Mews informed the Queen that the first Royal Review Land Rover was ready for inspection, and shortly after, in the late spring of 1953, the Company was told by Commander Michael Parker, secretary to the Duke of Edinburgh, that the vehicle should be brought to Holyrood Palace for inspection by Prince Philip in Edinburgh.

Bob Hudson, Arthur Goddard, Chief Engineer, and Ralph Nash,

Experimental Workshop Manager, took the Land Rover up to Edinburgh and The Duke examined it carefully, making one or two suggestions for improvement that were easily carried out, but, to the dismay of the Company representatives, he suggested the vehicle should be painted in a special maroon (the colour of all Royal cars used an official occasions by the Queen) and be ready for The Queen's use at a review of ex-servicemen in Hyde Park in three weeks. This was agreed to, but Bob Hudson knew it was practically impossible to obtain the special paint and carry out that work at Solihull in the time, so he asked Hoopers Ltd to do it. Hoopers were and are coachbuilders holding the Royal Warrant. Even such an urgent request was within their capabilities and the vehicle was duly ready on time. Pictures show the vehicle being used for the first time at the ex-service review in Hyde Park in 1953 and clearly show The Queen holding on to her hat with both hands!

The Commonwealth Tour took place from November 1953 to May 1954 and visits were made to Bermuda, Jamaica*, Fiji, Tonga, New Zealand*, Australia*, Tasmania*, Cocas Islands, Ceylon, Aden*, Uganda*, Malta*, and Gibraltar.

Factory-built Land Rovers were used in all the countries marked*, local Land Rovers in most of the rest.

The success of the subsequent Royal Tour of the Commonwealth, coming so shortly after the Coronation, is sometimes overlooked. Not only can Land Rover be proud of helping towards that success, they are also very grateful. In the early fifties Land Rovers were still relatively unknown and The Rover Company Limited even less known. The use of Review Land Rovers in countries around the Commonwealth by The Queen and The Duke of Edinburgh, and particularly on occasions of the greatest crowd scenes, was a major factor in laying the foundation of the vehicle's own success.

After the tour, which was fully covered by newsreels and television all over the world, the Company found itself involved in an area in which they had little or no experience: Royal protocol. Whilst the attendant publicity to Her Majesty using Land Rover was welcomed as a marvellous boost to sales, the use of the vehicle by an unsuitable person or firm after the tour could be undignified and detrimental to the Monarch and the Company. It was decided that the ten Land Rovers despatched overseas should be repainted in normal colours and the bodywork converted back to standard. Factory representatives in various parts of the world were instructed to supervise personally this operation, which was efficiently carried out, all Land Rovers reverting back to anonymity. One problem did occur, in the West Indies/Central America region, when President Somoza of Nicaragua, having seen the newsreels in his private cinema in the Presidential Palace in Managua, decided he would like an identical vehicle, for reviewing his troops. A message to this effect was sent to the Land Rover dealer in Nicaragua who in turn called the Rover Company, but the request seriously embarrassed the Company. Their business was making Military and Commercial Land Rovers

The Land Rover 'gun carriage'. During the shooting season at Sandringham and Balmoral, large amounts of ammunition and guns need to be moved to various sites, The Land Rover Ninety is the current successor to the original 86-inch model, designed by Prince Philip, that was in service for nearly thirty years. The carrier on the bonnet is for ammunition and the side screens are for guns, both easily removed when the Land Rover is needed for normal duties.

The Queen and Prince Philip in a State I Land Rover during the 1953/54 Commonwealth tour.

HM Queen Elizabeth the Queen Mother on an overseas tour. The Land Rover is an 86-inch made in 1954, without the usual bench-type seating of other review Land Rovers.

and not hand-tooling for a few Review vehicles. Furthermore, advice was received from Buckingham Palace that to make and sell copies of the Review Land Rover all over the world would cheapen the image of the product and the Monarch. The decision was thereby reached not to supply any further Review Land Rovers outside the United Kingdom. The factory representative in Central America was instructed to go to Nicaragua and inform the Presidential authorities that the company could not supply his requirement. His awkward task was made easier by an unsuccessful revolutionary attempt on the life of the President, as a result of which the authorities asked for an armoured Land Rover. The Company was able to reply truthfully that it did not make armoured Land Rovers. That all came much later.

In 1954 the Queen and Prince Philip visited the Ugandan game reserves. This vehicle was specially built at Solihull for touring the reserves and taking photographs. It is an 107-inch Land Rover with two VIP seats in the centre and two at the rear. There is a platform in the centre for standing on and a sliding roof gives excellent vision. After the tour it was purchased by the Ugandan government and used for many years as a touring vehicle for VIPs in the game reserves.

Range Rover, State I
Chassis No 35506365B. In 1971, when it was thought that the oldest State
Land Rover should be replaced, A B Smith, Managing Director, suggested a
Range Rover would be more suitable. At that time, with sales at home slow to
pick up, a little publicity via the Royal Household would be most welcome, so
Colonel Pender-Cudlip, Military Sales Manager of the Company, with
responsibility for Royal Household Liaison, approached Buckingham Palace
to see if this would be acceptable. His memo of January 1972 to David Bache,
Company Stylist, asks for sketches to submit to The Queen, and sixteen
months later a letter from the Crown Equerry says that the Queen and the
Duke of Edinburgh 'were very interested in the new Review Range Rover and
were extremely pleased with it'.

*Range Rover State I, Chassis No 35506365B. Built 1974, despatched to sales May 1975. This vehicle is
used only by the Queen or Prince Philip and is still in frequent use. In order to give a high paint finish the
superstructure is built in steel and all the gaps have been lead filled.*

Between these two dates and perfunctory memos lies an immense amount of
detailed design and high quality workmanship.

With sketches approved in outline, an internal order was raised for a
standard Range Rover which in theory would be built anonymously under the
heading 'War Office'. However the body unit and wing panels were painted in
non-standard Royal Maroon, (the colour for Royal Household vehicles used
for public as opposed to private purposes, the latter being a deep green). On
the production line tongues began to wag and by the time it had moved a few
feet down the track the chassis sported a broomstick with a Union Jack

attached. Under the leather seats and special carpets are the signatures of the dozens of men who worked on the vehicle.

Once it was built, minus roof, tailgate and glass, it was delivered to the Jig Shop at Solihull, where the final engineering team and Styling took over. Headed by the co-ordinator, Tony Poole, the work was carried out by Ken Vaughan, Bill Badger and Terry Rowlands. Several items of interest are not visible. Like State II, the body was made in steel, but the fuel tank was moved from beneath the rear floor where the Monarch would stand. The bulkhead behind the driver was moved forward and, in the space this created, a small petrol tank was slotted. Over the tank in the new thickened bulkhead was placed a lectern in the hope that Her Majesty would place her notes there regarding the route and layout of the day's events. In fact the Land Rover Chauffeur says she used it to prop her handbag on. 'I'm grateful for this because previously when she propped her handbag on the grab rail she invariably knocked my hat off!'

The bulkhead also contains a gentleman's and a lady's umbrella (from Harrods naturally!) which, to everyone's recollection, have only been used

The original State I Land Rover, now on display at Hampton Court.

186

once. Cunningly concealed at the rear are two supports normally hidden by the seats which can be pulled out and used as supports or half-seats when the Queen and Prince Philip are standing up, the idea being that if the driver's foot slipped off the clutch the Royal Persons would not be thrown flat on their backs.

The removal of the petrol tank forward helped the engineers to fit an extra silencer, and also to move the silencer outlet away from the opening rear door, to come out on the opposite side. This is necessary because when in use, the engine is running when the Queen gets in, and to have to climb over a smoking exhaust would not be the best way to start a journey!

The rear cross-member was removed to make room for a step, and the roof over the driver was removed to give ease of access and improve styling, which meant the only connection between rear and front sections of the body was via the lower half. The strong, rigid chassis gave total security but does not prevent the body from flexing. Stylist Tony Poole says, 'We did not worry too much. We had a similar experience with the first Gas Turbine Open Tourer twenty years before, so we knew how to overcome it'.

Hours of work went into the vehicle, not only from Land Rover but from other suppliers, such as when Tony Poole required an item from a German to fit exactly their requirements. The Germans wanted to know why it was wanted, but all they could be told was that when they saw it the Queen would be using it. The response was: 'Have it free with our compliments'. It was carefully explained there would be *no* publicity and they declared they were not interested in publicity, it was a pleasure to supply.

This applies literally to practically every supplier. Of all the Royal vehicles made by Land Rover with special leather trim, an invoice has yet to be submitted for the leatherwork. And the same applies to the steel body panels, which to make as a one-off would be horrendously expensive. The suppliers who make Range Rover bodies said they would 'knock out a steel set at the end of a production run, with pleasure – no charge!'

Land Rover, State II. Chassis No 14190020. Built September 1958, and despatched April 1959 on an 88-inch wheelbase (Series III) with body styling and passenger comfort drastically improved.

With a steel superstructure, the heavier body gives a smooth ride at low speeds, and also the advantage of accepting lead filling which hides all gaps and gives a much better paint finish. The exterior is painted in Royal Maroon, and the vehicle has never carried as a passenger anyone other than a member of the Royal Family.

The interior is very much the same as the previous Land Rover albeit on a different chassis.

The photograph, probably taken in 1959, is on the farm site which subsequently became a Land Rover production block in 1983 (original farm in the background).

187

Land Rover State II, Chassis No 14190020. Built September 1958, despatched to sales April 1959. The previous State Land-Rovers were 80-inch and 86-inch, this being the first 88-inch. The principle difference is in the steel bodywork which was incorporated to allow lead loading over various rivet holes to give a high paint finish. It first went into use at the Three Counties Show, Malvern in 1959, and is still in service, stored at Solihull.

State II and III (the 86-inch and 88-inch wheelbase Land Rovers), taken at Solihull circa 1960. The farm in the background, owned by the company, and the fields have all been built over for factory expansion.

Land Rover, State IV. Chassis No 47100009. Built 1953, despatched June 1953. This is the first State Land Rover. As stated it was first used in 1953 at an ex-Servicemen's Rally in Hyde Park. It was also used for many review occasions for the next 23 years. However, when it was decided to build a Range Rover as a State Review vehicle in 1972, the original Land Rover State IV became surplus to requirements. It was clearly a special vehicle and as such should be preserved somewhere. The advice of the Crown Equerry was sought, and it was donated to the Royal Mews for permanent display at the Mews Museum at Hampton Court Palace in 1975.

Land Rover, State III. Chassis No 57102615. Despatched January 1955. Though never, strictly speaking, a 'Royal' vehicle, as it is painted an ordinary blue colour, this Land Rover is interesting in so far as it was the last of the Land Rovers built for the Royal Commonwealth tour of 1953/54. It was retained by the Company and was only issued in January 1955 well after the Commonwealth tour was over. Apart from the colour it is identical to the Land Rover built for the Tour and as such identical to the State IV Land Rover.

It first came into service in 1955 at the opening of the Hyde Park Under-ground Car Park and was used by the Prime Minister, Harold Macmillan, which occasion was typical of its use during its life. Because it is in 'non-Royal' colours it can be used by non-Royal persons. It still does loyal service as an extra vehicle during Shows such as the Royal Show at Stoneleigh. Its recent distinguished non-Royal users were Torvill and Dean when they made a tour of Nottingham after winning the World Ice Dancing Championship.

The vehicle is stored at Solihull, in the company of State I and State II. It would appear likely it will be retired during 1989, when it will be replaced by a later model.

Chapter 3
Land Rover Conscripted
by David McDine

The end of the Cold War and the demise of the Warsaw Pact brought some of the greatest changes to the international security scene in modern politico-military history – but the world is still a dangerous place. The threat is now unpredictable. Since the Iron Curtain came down, an extraordinary coalition has fought the Gulf War to eject the Iraqis from Kuwait, the hard-pressed United Nations have struggled to end the tragic ethnic strife in former Yugoslavia, and – in 1994 – more than 50 other conflicts smoulder or blaze around the globe.

Instant satellite television pictures beamed from the world's trouble spots make Land Rover's ubiquitous military vehicles a more familiar sight than ever. In the mid-1990s they are in service with more than 100 military and para-military forces world-wide, operating in all extremes of climate and terrain in a great variety of roles ranging from ambulances to weapons platforms, from troop carriers to armoured vehicles.

The changing nature of the threat coupled with diminishing defence budgets is leading to further evolution of the Land Rover go-anywhere, do-anything vehicle family and company ethos as new solutions are sought by military fleet procurers. The company is meeting the challenge, anticipating new operational requirements with products such as the Special Operations Vehicle (SOV) and the Multi Role Combat Vehicle (MRCV), backing up their combination of versatility, rapid deployability, mobility, sustainability, lethality and dependability, with the highest standards of reliability, maintainability and in-service support. Increasingly, the military buyer is looking for all this in a value for money, low whole-life cost package – and healthy sales figures indicate he is finding what he needs at Solihull.

In this post-Cold War decade, the vehicles are frequently seen in white UN livery on international humanitarian aid and peacekeeping duties, and increasingly the military are adding Discoverys and Range Rovers to their fleets

Impressive line-up of some of the Land Rover variants in service with military and paramilitary forces around the world.

of 90, 110 and 130 workhorses. For ambassadors, visiting princes and commanders, Range Rover and Discovery are often the chosen military flagships on the new battlefields of peacekeeping diplomacy, but it is the multi-role Land Rover workhorse – now aptly called the Defender – which underpins their success. From the Pink Panthers that went Scud-hunting behind Iraqi lines with the SAS during the Gulf War, to the Defenders leading aid convoys through mountainous tracks in Bosnia, they are usually to be found near the centre of the action as well as performing myriad vital, but often unsung, tasks down the line.

All this high profile operational service use could lead the uninitiated to assume that the original Land Rover was conceived as a military vehicle, and that the civilian variants were derived from it, but of course it was the other way round.

Although the Wilks brothers based their prototype Land Rover on the lines of the Second World War Willys Overland Jeep, their aim, as we have already seen in the opening chapter, was not to produce a British military version but a utility vehicle for farmers – 'a proper farm machine . . . to be used instead of a tractor . . .' – in an austere post-war period when horses were beginning to be ousted by machines and agriculture needed to become more efficient. Swords had already been turned into ploughshares and ex-military Jeeps were put to work down on the farm, but, in the words of the military, they were mostly 'clapped out'.

During the war the British Army had been impressed with the usefulness of the Jeeps and Chevrolet trucks which had been supplied in large numbers by the United States under the lend-lease arrangements. For Britain, the ending of lend-lease and a bankrupt economy dried up the supply of Jeeps and trucks, but the operational requirement for a home-produced rugged go-anywhere replacement that could out-perform the American vehicles had already been recognized.

This requirement was underlined in North Africa, where a handful of specially equipped desert vehicles commanded by Colonel David Stirling, founder of the SAS, caused havoc against Rommel's Afrika Corps. With simple modifications – fitting filters, sand-tyres, larger fans and radiators, mounts for machine guns, navigation equipment, jerrycan holders and sand-shovels – the Jeeps and Chevrolets were able to conduct long-range reconnaissance missions and hit enemy rear echelons with devastating effect. It was a type of warfare used again to brilliant effect nearly 50 years on by Coalition Special Forces during the Gulf War and it has given birth to some of the latest Land Rover variants, including the SOV, versions of which are already in service with the United States Rangers.

Realization by the War Office and Ministry of Supply that Britain needed to develop a 4 x 4 vehicle of her own came far too late for it to come into service in wartime, but there were plenty of other roles awaiting a British version of the Jeep. During the war British soldiers had served everywhere from the rugged, wind-swept Faroe Islands in the north to the humid jungles of South-East Asia. Although the British Empire was soon to be dismantled, the sun had not yet set on it. With the coming of peace, British troops were still scattered across the world policing the empire in every imaginable environment as well as maintaining a large post-war presence in Germany.

The British 4 x 4 project, known in ministry/military jargon as FV (Fighting Vehicle) 1800, required selected motor manufacturers to submit tenders to the Fighting Vehicles Research and Development Establishment (FVRDE) for the supply of components for the new vehicle, which was not intended to be the product of any one company. Rover was considered too small scale and specialist to be invited to tender for any part of it and, in any case, Spencer Wilks was said not to be impressed by the order potential of a vehicle intended for service exclusively with the British Army. In fact Rover were invited to tender for the *manufacture* of the FV1800 in 1950. They responded by offering a large quantity of Land Rovers at a huge saving – about £3 million.

The project was slow in getting started because of the unrealistic proposal that competitors should co-operate over its construction, and it was 1945 before the first prototype appeared. It was built by Nuffield which was given the contract to assemble the new vehicle, subject to many modifications being incorporated – a cause of further delays.

So it was 1952 before production of FV1800 – to be known as 'Champ' – went ahead, only after Nuffield and Austin had amalgamated to form the British Motor Corporation. New vehicles were sorely needed by an Army that was equipped largely with left-overs from the war, a state of affairs which, according to the Grigg Committee, meant 'units sent two cars on a journey in order to ensure that at least one of them arrived'.

Meanwhile the Wilks brothers had pressed on with their 'proper farm machine' and two of the 1948 pre-production Land Rovers – numbers L29 (L for left-hand drive) and R30 – went to FVRDE for evaluation by the military. Research by the Land Rover Register 1947-51 reveals that, incredibly, these first two vehicles evaluated by the military still exist – now in private hands.

The Army liked what it saw and ordered 20 more from the first few hundred of the 1948 production run, delivered in December for further field evaluation, seeing Rover's vehicle as a potential stopgap until the availability of the Champ. The vehicles performed well and this tiny initial order turned out to be the tip of what was to prove an enormous iceberg upon which the Champ would founder. In May, 1949 the Ministry placed what was intended as a Champ stopgap order for 1,878 Land Rovers, for delivery from June onwards at the rate of 50 a week. Among them were 33 which were to have the 2.8 litre four-cylinder engine of the Rolls-Royce B family on which the British Army intended to standardise. Fitting the B 40 engine involved raising the bonnet on rubber buffers and moving the rear axle back an inch, increasing the wheelbase to 81 inches. A colour change to 'deep bronze green' was selected as being more appropriate for military use than the original 'light green'. The Army versions were allocated numbers from 00 BC 01 upwards.

It was not until August 1950 that the Army was able to tell the expectant end-users – its soldiers – about the long-awaited Champ in any detail. It did so through a fascinating, watershed article in *Soldier*, magazine of the British Army, which predicted: 'There'll always be a Jeep – even if it is called by some other name.' The Army's official, authoritative and much-respected mouthpiece took the line that the Jeep had set the fashion for military motoring. It argued: 'A modern Army is incomplete without a midget car tough enough to tackle tank country and powerful enough to do the work of a small lorry.'

Soldier recalled the extraordinary so-called Jungle Jeep, built by the Standard Motor Company for jungle warfare. This diminutive vehicle had four motor-cycle-type seats, a canvas bonnet and was light enough to be lifted by two men into its own trailer which acted as a boat for river-crossing. Perhaps fortunately for its potential users it never saw active service because the defeat of the Japanese ended the requirement for it.

The Land Rover was given an altogether more positive reception. *Soldier* summed it up like this:

> 'The first product of peace-time reflection on the subject was the Land Rover, a squat-looking but more comfortable car than the original Jeep. The Army welcomed it: the King rode in it to inspect parades. Farmers enthused over it too; it carried them effortlessly over the roughest fields and towed the cattle-trailers to market as well.'

This was a remarkable welcome from the official Army magazine, recorded as it was within two years of the first Land Rover production.

Of the Champ, *Soldier* declared:

'Now comes the latest – "light car, 5 cwt 4 x 4" which has been developed by the Ministry of Supply and the Nuffield Organization. It has a powerful four-cylinder engine which gives it 60 miles an hour on the road, and independent springing for all wheels, to take it over rough ground at speed.

'The new engine, the B 40, is one of a standardized range of engines and many of its components are interchangeable with those of six and eight-cylinder engines. Many other parts can be exchanged with those on other vehicles in the post-war range: many of the components can also be used in more than one part of the vehicle. All this makes for easier and cheaper manufacture, less complicated store-keeping, and easier cannibalization.

'The new car is claimed to be easier to drive than the old jeep. It has a five-speed gearbox which, with its 80 brake horsepower engine, makes a "booster" gearbox unnecessary. All the gears are synchromesh, to give easier changing. There is a secondary gearbox, incorporated in the rear axle assembly which has two levers: one offers forward, reverse or winch; the other two or four-wheel drive.

'The car's electrical system is waterproofed, and for wading all that is necessary is to attach a breather pipe to the air cleaner and to close a ventilating plug to the batteries. The car can be loaded into a Horsa II glider when the windscreen and easily-removable steering-wheel have been taken off.

'The electrical system is completely screened, so as not to interfere with wireless, and the two 12-volt batteries give a good supply for wireless work. The vehicle is intended for use in extremes of heat and cold and there is a place for heating apparatus to keep the batteries warm in Arctic weather.'

That was the official Army line, but however eulogistic it was about the Champ's features, it was *Soldier*'s comment about the Land Rover – 'the Army welcomed it' – that was most significant. Ironically the vehicle intended primarily for farmers but welcomed by soldiers was to supersede the specially commissioned Champ within a relatively short time. At about the same time as the *Soldier* announcement, one of the Land Rovers fitted with the 2.8 litre Rolls-Royce B series engine was being tested against a prototype Champ with the B 40 engine and a standard 1.6 litre Land Rover. To the embarrassment of the procurement agency, the standard Land Rover out-performed the other two. It was a blow to engine standardization plans, a nail in the Champ's coffin – and no more 2.8 litre, B 40-engined Land Rovers were produced. The contract with the manufacturers meant it was too late to cancel the Champ project, but the writing was already on the wall.

Nor did Champ receive the same warm welcome that Land Rover won from the soldiers themselves. In particular its rounded lines did not meet the pragmatic end-users' approval. Then as now *Soldier* accurately reflected the squaddies' views in its letters pages and in a subsequent issue a Royal Artillery battery sergeant major wrote complaining:

> 'Streamlining may look pretty in a civilian sort of way but it is not so good when the vehicle has to take hard knocks on active service. And with no flat surfaces available, where are we going to carry all those spare tins of petrol, ammunition boxes, valises and so on ?'

He added that headlamps should be countersunk and/or covered with a grid, and a windscreen wiper should be fitted for the front-seat passenger who, besides being the senior rank in the vehicle, was usually the map reader. It was criticism that could not be levelled at the Land Rover which had plenty of flat surfaces – and Rover had also anticipated the end-user requirement for protected headlamps. Initially they were behind a grill and, although exposed from May 1950 onwards, were still countersunk and well protected by the wing fronts.

When the Champ finally appeared on the British military scene, it worked initially side by side with the Land Rover. There were clear differences: Champ had impressive mobility and power but the Land Rover was cheaper, more versatile as men and equipment-carrier, had lower fuel consumption and lower weight. An infantry officer who operated with Champ found it 'Fast, but too heavy, too complicated and insufficient payload. Bogged easily. A wonderful toy but quite impractical.'

The Army's criticisms of Champ were neatly summarized by co-authors Roy Fullick, who commanded a Parachute Regiment company at Suez, and Colonel Geoffrey Powell, in *Suez the Double War* (Hamish Hamilton, 1979).

They recalled the plan to replace Britain's post-war ragbag of vehicles with a standardized, all-purpose range capable of operating anywhere from the Arctic to the Tropics and snorkelling rivers, to be driven by Rolls-Royce engines in which nearly everything was interchangeable.

> 'It sounded too good to be true, but specialist vehicles which are not based upon commercial production runs have snags; the new models were not only bigger and heavier than anything which had gone before, but were so expensive that the Champ cost four times as much as the American Jeep which it was intended to replace. Moreover, the Champ was far from reliable, and seemed to have been designed by men isolated from military reality. The front and rear ends of the early model had the curved and flowing contours of the old Morris Minor, surfaces which were quite unsuitable for those essential military tasks of

spreading maps, carrying additional loads, or even for balancing a hot mug of tea.'

They added: 'It was discovered rather late that the new Champ when lashed upon its platform and prepared for parachuting was too bulky; slung beneath a Hastings, the load would prevent the landing wheels from touching the ground.'

Ironically, it turned out to be Land Rover that provided much of the all-purpose family with the high commonality of parts that British military procurers had been seeking. Fullick and Powell's comment about specialist vehicles that are not based on commercial production runs having snags is a truism that still applies today. Modern military procurers still pay lip service to the good sense of opting for commercially derived vehicles, but some seem unable to resist 'gold-plating' and insisting on performance criteria way beyond any real world requirement.

In the Suez year of 1956, 12 months after the last batch of Champs was delivered, the British Army announced its intention to standardize on the Land Rover. Four decades on, it continues to reign supreme.

Land Rover had first gone to war with the British Army as part of the Commonwealth Brigade – later the 1st Commonwealth Division – in Korea in the early 1950s. It was the first war to be fought in the name of the United Nations. Contemporary newsreel footage shows the Supreme Commander, US General Matthew Ridgway, visiting UN troops in a Land Rover with his British driver. James Taylor records:

> 'In Korea, the Land Rovers proved their worth in action over and over again. Not only were they able to duplicate the roles of the Jeeps the Army was still using, but they were also able to stand in as load carriers and carry out a number of tasks which the Jeeps could not. Moreover, it rapidly became obvious that they were also more versatile than the Champ would ever be, for that had been designed strictly as a Jeep replacement.'

Another of Land Rover's early campaigns was the Mau Mau Emergency in Kenya where the mountainous and forested areas were ideal proving grounds for its off-road capabilities. General Sir Frank Kitson – later to become well-known for the controversy sparked by his study *Low Intensity Operations* and as Commander-in-Chief UK Land Forces – served in Kenya as an intelligence officer in the early '50s. In his book *Bunch of Five* (Faber & Faber, 1977) he recalls sleeping in his Land Rover 'to avoid wasting time in bed' and singing to keep himself awake as he drove to give the driver a break as they negotiated tracks where the hazards included hairpin bends, thick mud, primitive log bridges, mounds of elephant droppings and passing leopards. The Land Rover took to Africa like a duck to water and it would not be long before the vehicles were a common sight – as they still are today – throughout much of the continent.

The British were not the only ones to see the military potential of the Land Rover from the outset. The Dutch Army was operating them as early as 1949, and 45 years on the Royal Netherlands Marine Corps is still equipped with Land Rovers.

In 1951 Land Rover competed successfully against the Willys Jeep to win a large Belgian Army order. However, the contract required the vehicles to be built in Belgium – the first of a number of such arrangements which today include the production of Defenders by OTOKAR in Turkey and the Perentie 4 x 4 and 6 x 6 variants in Australia.

The early off-set deal struck with the Belgian Minerva company called for the use of a high percentage of locally manufactured components. So Solihull provided Minerva with kits – basically 80-inch chassis, engine, gearbox and instrumentation – and they were built in Belgium to Belgian military specifications. They certainly looked like Land Rovers, but the Minerva versions had their own large badges, sloping front wings and differently shaped grilles, as well as steel instead of aluminium alloy bodies. Although production ended in the mid-'50s, many were moth-balled to emerge 30 years later and continued in use with the Belgian paras until recently.

The West German Border Guards also showed an early interest in the Land Rover. They were responsible for security along the Inner German Border and needed a large fleet of rugged go-anywhere six-seater patrol vehicles. The Land Rover matched the requirement, but import/export restrictions meant that a deal similar to that with the Belgians had to be struck. In this case, the agreement was that the Tempo company of Hamburg would build the Land Rovers under licence. The first were built on Solihull's 80-inch chassis, but a later version used the 86-inch. Again, the Tempo versions were instantly recognizable as Land Rovers, but had higher doors and sides, and the 80-inch had a locker on the bonnet.

Over the next decade there were a string of other orders, many from the armed forces of the emergent Commonwealth. Trade follows the flag and it was largely the halo effect of the British forces' professional reputation and widespread deployment throughout the former empire that led to these orders.

As the Land Rover took over what are today known as the light and medium utility truck roles with the British Forces, so the vehicles were deployed – like their users – world-wide. As the '50s gave way to '60s, Britain's Armed Forces were still far-flung with major deployments of substantial numbers with BAOR in West Germany, and in Gibraltar, Cyprus, the West Indies, Malta, Libya, Aden, East Africa, Singapore/Malaysia and Hong Kong. There were many 'penny packets' elsewhere, such as Sappers working on specialist projects, and frequent training deployments both major and minor in many other parts of the world. Additionally many students from the armed forces of Commonwealth and other countries came – and continue to come – to British

Military Defenders, equally at home in the snows of Northern Norway, the jungles of the Pacific Rim, or the deserts of the Middle East.

training establishments, where they are exposed to British doctrine and equipment. With the ending of conscription, the growing quality and professionalism of the British Armed Forces – already the envy of many other nations – became a byword. As the empire was dismantled and Commonwealth nations developed their own armed forces – often with the help of British training teams – the British Forces and their Land Rovers were seen performing well in all terrains and climates world-wide. It was natural that the feeling grew: 'If the British have a good piece of kit we want it too.' What's more, British equipment tended to be used for real – in Korea, Kenya, Malaya, Suez, Cyprus, Borneo and Aden to name but a few of the post-war campaigns.

To the smaller nations, Land Rovers, unlike major items such as main battle tanks, were readily affordable, highly versatile, adaptable, easy to maintain and support, ruggedly dependable – and virtually soldier-proof, an indispensable quality in armies whose drivers and maintainers were initially less professionally trained.

The halo effect grew over the next three decades. In 1963 the company could claim that the armed services of 26 countries and the police forces of 37 used the Land Rover. In the mid-'90s the spread is now global. The company, conscious of the confidentiality of some contracts, states simply that the Defender and its predecessors are in service with more than 100 military and para-military forces around the world. *Janes* lists many of them, a roll-call that reads like an atlas index, starting at Angola and ending with Zimbabwe.

For the next 40 Cold War years Land Rover vehicles in multifarious roles were to play an important part in the preservation of peace in Western Europe. In a growing number of armies they were also to participate in almost every conflict and brushfire campaign – large and small – through to the present.

The vehicles have been in particularly high profile in recent conflicts, notably the Gulf, Kurdistan, Bosnia, Somalia, and Cambodia. But this global spread was certainly not envisaged back in 1948 when those first two Land Rovers were acquired for evaluation by the British Army.

Continuous improvements were made to the original Land Rover in the early years. The military's cry – still familiar today – for more power and capacity was answered to an extent with the introduction of the 1997 cc engine in 1951 and the 86 and 107 inch wheelbases in 1953, but further wheelbase changes – to 88 inches for the standard and 109 inches for the long wheelbase version – did not significantly increase payloads. More engine and transmission improvements followed and in 1957 a Technical Sales Department was set up at Solihull to cater for the specialist adaptations required by armed forces and the growing number of other fleet customers, including police and other emergency services. This department, later called Special Projects, then SVO (Special Vehicle Operations) and now Land Rover Special Vehicles, could provide exactly the right solution to any requirement while maintaining the commonality of parts and inter-operability that is such a boon to military maintainers and logistics personnel.

A year later – and 10 years after the original vehicle was launched – the Series II Land Rover made its appearance. It was more comfortable, more attractively styled and offered increased payloads and even greater commonality of components. Its 2¼-litre OHV petrol engine had been developed from the same block as Land Rover's existing diesel engine, making life easier for military and other maintainers whose fleets included both types. The wider tracks increased stability, allowing an even wider range of conversions, adaptations and equipment fits to make the Land Rover even more versatile.

The British Army took several thousand ¼-ton (88-inch) and ¾-ton (109-inch), almost all petrol-engined, canvas-topped General Service versions. Among them were many with 24-volt electrics in the Fitted For Radio (FFR) role and some with ambulance bodies. But within three years the Series II was superseded by the Series IIA, which reigned throughout the remainder of the '60s. Although initially it looked almost identical to its predecessor, the old 2-litre diesel engine was replaced by a new 2.25 which had the same capacity and design characteristics as the petrol version.

An enormous variety of specialist vehicles could be created from the basic pick-up, hardtop and station wagon bodies on the standard and long wheelbase chassis of Series IIA. At the annual Royal Engineers' demonstration at the (now Royal) School of Military Engineering at Brompton, on the Medway, in 1962 – although not on 1 April! – two new versions of the Army's maid-of-all-work were on public show: a tracked version and another with a rubber skirt billed – somewhat inaccurately – as the 'Hover Land Rover'.

The tracked version was on loan from the Royal Air Force which had eight on bomb disposal work. Its attractions were impressive cross-country performance including the ability to negotiate swamps and heavily scarred terrain with a ground clearance of 27½ inches.

On the rubber-skirted 'Hover' prototype two large fans driven by a second engine on the back of the vehicle produced a downdraught of air to lift the weight off the springs so that the Land Rover could glide over boggy ground. On firm ground the idea was to raise the skirt for normal travel. The Vickers Air Cushion Conversion was said to be 'easy to drive once the driver gets the feel of the lift-engine throttle and maintains a balance between skidding and sinking'!

These were not the only odd versions to emerge during the 1960s, when there was much confusion in military vehicle procurement ranks and Land Rover's engineers were kept busy producing – sometimes excellent – 'one offs' to meet the latest perceived need, only to see the projects shelved as operational requirements changed or economies were enforced.

One such was a multi-fuel engine developed from the 2.25 litre four-cylinder diesel version. It interested the British Army – and the other NATO nations – but was 'binned' because of the cost implications.

At about the same time a number of 109-inch wheelbase amphibious Land Rovers were built. They had airbags inflated from the vehicle's exhaust and a propeller attached to the rear propshaft. These strange amphibians had a one-ton payload and could be stacked nose-to-tail and two high in the Argosy transport aircraft. But although the One Ton APGP (Air Portable General Purpose) vehicle actually entered service and underwent troop trials, it too was shelved because the advent of more powerful helicopters meant they could lift Land Rovers across deep water barriers and so there was no longer an operational requirement other than, as we shall see, for the amphibious landing role.

The ever increasing military demands for greater payloads led to the design of a Forward Control vehicle with a 112-inch wheelbase, powered by either a three-litre Rover petrol engine or a 5.8-litre Perkins diesel. However the military decided not to order any and the prototypes were put to good use – one was converted to cut the grass at Solihull, another was built from parts to become the transporter for the Rover-BRM racing car, and another is still in use as a recovery vehicle at Rover's Gaydon Test Centre.

Military interest then focused on a powered gun carriage to be driven by a towing vehicle through a universally jointed detachable propshaft incorporated in the tow hitch. Rover produced a gun tractor based on the 110-inch wheelbase with the 112-inch Forward Control's three-litre petrol engine and five-speed gearbox. It had wider tracks for greater stability and demountable body panels for airlifting.

But again the focus shifted. The 110-inch gun tractor joined the other 'one-offs' on the shelf, and it was a new Forward Control model that eventually went into service in the gun-towing role. Calls for increased capacity had resulted in the first Forward Control model, launched in 1962 with a 30 cwt payload. This was achieved by moving the cab over the engine to increase the length of the load-bed within the dimensions of the long wheelbase version. But the UK market version with the 2.25-litre petrol engine was not reckoned to be powerful enough and, with the 2.6 engine offered for overseas models only, the British Army gave it the thumbs down. Despite considerable re-engineering, the military ordered only a handful of the new Series IIB Forward Control for the Army Fire Service and, as sales levels were below the British Leyland minimum, it was taken out of production in 1972.

But the concept was sound and the new Forward-Control gun tractor known as the 101-inch one-tonne Land Rover went into production in the mid '70s. It was announced at the 1972 Commercial Motor Show and was specifically designed for military use, with a capability to tow a 1½-ton powered-axle trailer. A prime factor behind its development was the British Army's requirement for a vehicle capable of towing loads of up to 4,000 lb, and in particular the 105 mm Light Gun which was too heavy to be towed by any existing Land Rover.

The priority was power and durability, and the design team did not have far to look for the right engine. The V8 was already being used in Rover's newest product, the Range Rover. This engine/gearbox/transfer box assembly, combined with the most sturdy Salisbury axles, was married to a new design of chassis frame to provide the basis of the revolutionary new forward-control

201

military Land Rover – though with its snub-nosed, bonnetless front, 7-foot height and 6-foot width, it was not readily identifiable as part of the Land Rover stable! The V8 engine – a military version of the lightweight Rover 3.5 litre unit – was positioned more or less between the seats in the cab. With half-elliptic spring suspension and the 1-ton 109-inch brakes, this new military Land Rover was designed to have as many detachable parts as possible – like the 1/2-ton Land Rover. This simultaneously increased its versatility while reducing its weight for the purposes of air-portability by the later generation of helicopters, now capable of carrying loads of up to 3,500 lb – 1,000 lb up on the 1/2-ton Land Rover requirement some five years earlier.

In 1975, Squadron-Leader Tom Sheppard, one of Britain's most able explorers and more recently author of the superb official book *The Land Rover Experience – a user's guide to four-wheel driving*, led a Joint Services' Expedition across Africa from west to east – the Atlantic to the Red Sea, using four new 1-tonne 101 inch Land Rovers, all featuring constant 4-wheel drive with differential lock.

Three of the vehicles were fitted with the optional trailer drive and all were equipped with 9.00 x 16 Michelin XS tyres. The lead vehicle in the convoy was the very first production model off the line, and the subsequent report on the expedition amply illustrated the versatility and worth of these unique machines. This expedition covered a total of 12,054 km (7,494 miles) and took 100 days. It was the first ever major user-trial of a production 1-tonne Land Rover and was considered entirely successful.

Sadly, although the vehicle was excellent for military use, it was so orientated in size and overall weight that no civilian outlet was ever established for it. As a vehicle for the military the 1-tonne was sold overseas as well as to the British Armed Forces and at the annual military parade in Cairo, in 1980, the anti-

Defender 130 Ambulance on UN duty in war-ravaged former Yugoslavia.

tank missile Swingfire was seen fitted to the 101-inch.

Clearly there was a military need and it was a pity that the life-span of the 101-inch was so short in terms of production. After its announcement in 1972, even though the sole concept behind it had been its military function, it found an unaccountable lack of popularity in overseas forces and failed to attract large orders. At home it was steadily fed into the Army during the period between 1975 and 1978, when production was halted.

It is ironic that in 1992, as the British Army prepared its invitation to tender for its next generation of field ambulances, 1-tonne Forward Control models – 17 years in service and still going strong – were deployed in Croatia to provide medical support to the 14,000 men and women of the United Nations who were keeping the peace between the warring Serbs and Croats. How many civil ambulance authorities expect such longevity from their vehicles? However, in fairness it should be pointed out that the venerable 1-tonnes were supported, and eventually replaced, by some of the latest-generation Defender 130s which were already in service with the RAF.

Land Rover had provided military ambulances since the '50s when it was recognized that the rugged 4 x 4 could reach casualties in terrain that defeated conventional vehicles. The British Army's first were based on the long wheelbase chassis with bodies by the coachbuilders Bonallack and carried two stretchers. Eventually a four-stretcher version on the 109 Series II chassis appeared with bodies by Mickleover and Marshall, and the same design was used on the Series III 109-inch chassis until the arrival of the 1-tonne Forward Control. Land Rover-based military ambulances including the 130 were used during the Gulf War and are currently in service with a number of armed forces, many being used operationally on UN missions. The latest generation Defender 130 version can be easily adapted for four stretcher cases, two

Famous Pink Panther used by the SAS and other elite Special Forces.

stretcher cases and three seated casualties, six seated casualties – or for ambi-chairs. Stretchers have assisted lift systems to speed up casualty handling.

Special forces have used Land Rovers for many years and one of the most successful special variants produced in the late '60s to meet specific military requirements was a long-range desert patrol vehicle that Colonel Stirling and his embryonic SAS would have killed for in their Western Desert days. Based on the Series IIA 109-inch chassis with the four-cylinder petrol engine, they were converted by Marshall's of Cambridge, painted pink for desert use by the SAS, and were immediately dubbed 'Pink Panthers'. They were used to good effect in the 10-year Dhofar War against Communist guerrillas.

The Omanis also used Land Rover 'gunships' with .50 Browning machine guns mounted on them to patrol the Salalah air base perimeter and the Dhofar's gravel plain. Even today, the Sultan's armed forces use very similar 110 Desert Patrol Vehicles for long-range desert missions. Subsequent versions of the Pink Panther are still in service and, as we will see, played an important part in anti-Scud missions during the Gulf War. Special Force users of Land Rover vehicles include Arab nations, North American, Australian and European Nations – including, of course, the SAS who have used them for four decades.

In the same decade growing requirements for rapid deployment and mobility highlighted the need to deliver lightweight fighting vehicles direct to the dropping zone or close to the battlefield for instant use by parachute troops and infantry and the British were among the pioneers of airportability.

By the start of the '60s the technique of air dropping had made tremendous progress since the first experiments just after the First World War when Jeeps were carried under the wings of a Halifax. The Army's Airtransport and Development Centre at Old Sarum, Salisbury, worked out in close co-operation with the Royal Air Force – the delivery men – how equipment should be loaded in an aircraft and what protection was required so it could be dropped for immediate use. The medium stress platform in use at the time could carry a load of up to 14,000 lb, easily catering for Land Rovers which were no great problem to an organization that had successfully parachuted a fully equipped Saracen armoured personnel carrier on the 24,000 lb capacity heavy stress platform from a Beverley transport aircraft. Shock absorption achieved by using air bags, wooden struts and even honeycombed cardboard, was the key to successful platform dropping. But air-dropping was imprecise and there was no guarantee that the vehicle was going to land undamaged, or in a position where it could be driven off easily. Where the situation allowed, the easiest and safest way was to deliver Land Rovers and other vehicles direct to airheads within transport aircraft like the Beverley, Hastings and the new Hercules. Failing that helicopters were rapidly becoming the favoured method of delivery. The Airtransport and Development Centre had anticipated the rise of the helicopter, which could deliver men and equipment exactly where required, and set up its Helicopter Section in 1960. It was concerned with both internal loads – and with what could be underslung from the hook.

In an early experiment the Westland Wessex helicopter successfully carried a Land Rover and recoilless rifle, and the twin-rotored Belvedere was able to carry 25 troops in its cabin – or a Land Rover and trailer from its hook.

Despite the increasing dominance of the helicopter, air dropping is still practised and modern dispatchers can land a stripped-down Land Rover with trailer or 105-mm Light Gun with reasonable accuracy and in relative safety.

The 88-inch Land Rover was too heavy to be lifted by the early helicopters and it would have to lose a lot of weight to qualify. Land Rover engineers realized that a radical approach was required and removed not only obvious non-essentials, but some of the less obvious, such as the upper body, doors, windscreen assembly and tailgate panels, while keeping the same basic chassis, engine, gearbox and axles as on the 88-inch commercial vehicle. As these body parts were designed to be built onto the machine on the production line, they could not be simply taken away. Instead, the machine itself had to be taken off before that stage and then built up to its own unique body specification, designed for maximum flexibility in detachable parts. By the time this process was complete, the minimum weight was still above the target weight, by 150 lb or so, but this was shown to be adequate if the helicopter reduced its cargo accordingly. The vehicle became known as the 1/2-ton Land Rover, indicating the total payload. Its austere appearance came from the peculiar styling that was necessary for air-portability: flat panelled apart from a simple curve in the bonnet.

The 1/2-ton went on to perform an impressive range of functions, including load and personnel carriers for the military, the police and civil defence; command vehicles for artillery, infantry, and other armed services; recovery vehicles; emergency two-stretcher carriers; towing light support weapons; specialist trailer towing and operation; signals communications, radio transmission and receiving centres, and reconnaissance work. Its adaptability, and the fact that specific individual requirements could be accommodated, won orders for the 1/2-ton from NATO countries and others. The British Army continued to take delivery of the military lightweight until the mid '80s. It could be fitted with a full-length soft hood constructed of rot-proof, flame-retardant canvas, supported by galvanized hood sticks, and was manufactured with both diesel and petrol engine.

Although the medium and heavy-lift helicopters can carry Land Rovers over deep water barriers, there is still a need for marines to be able to cross substantial water gaps during seaborne landings. Research, development trials and training on all craft, vehicles and equipment used for these potentially hazardous operations are carried out at the Amphibious Trials and Training Unit, Royal Marines, at Instow in North Devon. One of ATTURM's aims is to reduce the risk faced by a landing force by ensuring that their vehicles can overcome the initial hazards of an unfriendly environment. 'Sand and salt water are a deadly duo perfectly blended to corrode and grind away electrical circuitry and mechanical components in a remarkably short time,' said ATTURM's Fred Noyce.

Military vehicles have been prepared for deep fording since the Second World War and most marks of Land Rover were covered by a wide range of installation kits and specifications. These early kits were of a temporary applique nature intended for one-off use only, but they still allowed the Land Rovers to negotiate water obstacles at depths of up to 6 feet.

More modern kits were of a more durable, semi-permanent design, capable of remaining fitted to vehicles including lightweights and the 1-tonne for a year. But the increased electrical complexity of Defender variants, including winterized, 24-volt dedicated radio supply and others, make the applique unsuitable. This has led ATTURM to design a permanent – although still removable – built-in system for the Defender. Vehicles are currently prepared for a fording depth of 1.5 metres and a duration of six minutes per single immersion, although this can be increased to two hours for specialist beach assault units. Fred Noyce explained: 'The intention is that the new Defender range of vehicles will be capable of undertaking deep fording missions at any time throughout its life with Commando Forces units, needing only minor scheduled refurbishment to final stage waterproofing tasks in between operations.'

The era of the military lightweights spanned Series IIA, from 1968–71, and Series III production, which began in 1971. They were especially suited to roles such as that of Britain's 3 Commando Brigade on NATO's Arctic northern flank.

The Royal Marines' vehicles did sterling service in what an official Army report accurately described as the 'bare-arsed and boggy' terrain of the Falklands War, some were used to support the Gulf War Commando helicopters and they were equally at home in exercise deployments from Turkey

A waterproofed Defender is put to the test at the Amphibious Trials and Training Unit Royal Marines at Instow in Devon.

on NATO's southern flank to the −40°C temperatures of Northern Norway and with the ACE Mobile Force in every type of European terrain.

Series III, immediately recognizable by its plastic grilles (except on the lightweight), continued in production until 1985 in both 88-inch and 109-inch, petrol and diesel versions.

They were bought in large numbers by the military for use in a great variety of roles. The multiplicity of uses could best be grasped by observing the two huge NATO Exercises, Crusader 80 and Lionheart (1984), the largest exercises ever held in Europe and emphatic demonstrations by the West of its determination to defend itself against the perceived awesome power of the Warsaw Pact.

The sheer numbers and range of Land Rover variants from Britain and its NATO allies was astonishing, and there is no doubt that had the Warsaw Pact ever hurled its huge quantitative superiority in armour against the West, the Land Rovers' superb mobility – especially in the harassing Special Forces and anti-tank roles – would have played a key part in the defence.

Their myriad other roles, as personnel and cargo carriers, command and communications vehicles, weapons carriers and tractors, ambulances, mobile workshops and even field kitchens, all would have contributed a great deal if the Cold War had become the Third World War, and indeed did contribute significantly to the overall deterrent effect of NATO's well-trained and well-equipped defence forces. And there can be no doubt that the effectiveness of NATO was a major factor in the eventual demise of the Warsaw Pact.

Series III included the 3/4-ton Land Rover, based on the standard commercial 109-inch chassis. This 3/4-ton development was available in two guises, tactical and non-tactical, and of the tactical vehicles there were a number of interesting variations, which gave a clue as to why Land Rovers are now so numerous in the military sphere.

There was the Ambulance 2/4 Stretcher, specifically designed to provide casualty evacuation in forward areas, with accommodation for up to four stretcher cases as well as a medical attendant (the body was fitted by Marshalls of Cambridge). An armoured patrol car and an armoured personnel carrier based on the 3/4-ton Land Rover heavy-duty chassis was developed by Short Bros of Belfast and was especially useful as a cost effective vehicle for internal security duties. Another conversion, by Shorland, offered protection for up to eight men against NATO 7.62-mm rifle or machine gun fire, and also has special features to protect them against nail, pipe or petrol bombs.

As a support vehicle, fitted with the 24-volt electrical system, the 3/4-ton Land Rover was capable of being used with the British Aerospace Rapier Blindfire low-level surface-to-air missile system, as a tow vehicle or as a mobile launcher for the Blindfire radar tracker. The vehicle could also be used for transporting and launching the British Aerospace Swingfire wire-guided anti-tank missile system and the pallet-mounted Beeswing launcher, fired using a remote controller. The 3/4-ton Land Rover was also used as a command post for the Marconi Field Artillery Computer Equipment system (FACE).

It was not until 1979 that the V8 engine eventually became available in the standard 109-inch wheelbase Land Rover. In military terms, it could be adapted to many variations but one notable conversion specially developed to utilize its greater power was the Centaur Multi-Role Military Half-Tracked range of vehicles. The underlying concept of the Centaur range was to combine the easy operation and road performance of a well-tried wheeled vehicle with the excellent traction, off-road capability and high load-carrying capacity of a tracked vehicle. The resultant high road speed combined with accurate steering allowed the half-tracked Centaur variants to be deployed with standard road vehicles, while their cross-country ability enabled them to be used with equal facility in company with fully tracked fighting vehicles. The V8 petrol engine drove both the front wheels and the track through a manually operated gearbox. The vehicle had eight forward and two reverse speeds, provided by a high and low ratio transfer facility in the four-speed gearbox.

Simultaneous track and front-wheel drive was arranged through a differential unit built into the gearbox which transmitted equal power to the track and the wheels. The half-tracked concept was battle-proved in many parts of the world and, owing to its extreme mobility on almost any terrain, its road speed and its ability to transport almost any combination of armour, weapon systems, bodies, equipment fits, cargo and personnel up to a total of 3 tonnes, was recognized as a most adaptable form of fighting and logistic vehicle. The driving controls, too, are identical to those on a standard Land Rover, so there is virtually no retraining requirement for drivers. Centaur saw service in the Oman and was an ideal vehicle for desert work.

Coil-sprung Land Rovers – the 90 and 110 – were introduced in 1983 and 127 in 1994. Early on the British Army placed a large order for 110s to replace its Series III 109s. Military 90s, many with the 2½-litre turbocharged diesel engine, were extremely popular and many military variants including desert patrol versions were produced in-house by Special Vehicle Operations. The powerful and highly adaptable 127 shelter range, providing 17 extra inches of wheelbase and a crew cab option, with a capacity of 6.7 cubic metres and payload of 1.3 tonnes, was used for everything from command centres to electronics repair units.

With the advent of Discovery, the company had Land Rover as a marque for all the products, but specifically as a name for the 90, 110 and 130. It was confusing. Mike Gould, of Product Planning, explained: 'This made the selection of a name and determining the optimum timing a matter of urgency.' The name chosen was Defender – checked in a variety of languages to ensure that it had no adverse connotations – and it was launched at the 1990 Motor Show. The Land Rover tape badge was replaced with the medallion used on Range Rover and Discovery to reinforce marque identity and engine designation badges were added to the front wing sides of Tdi-powered models.

Certainly in the military arena the new title more accurately reflected the

Defender 130 Crew Cab fulfils many useful military roles.

role. The name is particularly apt in the light of the recent UN humanitarian aid and peacekeeping operations on which the Defender family has been deployed in such numbers.

At the same time as the name change, all diesel Defenders were given the new 2.5-litre direct injection turbocharged diesel engine first introduced in Discovery in 1989. The new 200 Tdi engine boosted Defender's power by 26 per cent and its torque by 25 per cent while improving fuel consumption by 25 per cent.

It would take several volumes rather than just one chapter to tell the full story of the ubiquitous Land Rover family's part in the many campaigns and peacekeeping operations it has taken part in throughout the world over the past four decades. Sadly too, the successes of these great workhorses so often go virtually unnoticed as the vehicles merge into the background and get on with their multitude of tasks leaving the limelight to the strike aircraft, helicopters and tanks.

The Land Rover's involvement in the kind of Special Forces activity that would attract the media like flies if it could be filmed normally takes place far from public gaze – as in the Gulf War.

Land Rover was involved in each and every aspect of Operation Desert Storm, supporting British and other Coalition countries' air, land and naval operations to achieve the liberation of Kuwait in demanding desert terrain and extreme climatic conditions. Within hours of the Iraqi invasion of Kuwait, Land Rover was operating in the Eastern desert, giving vital all-terrain mobility to recce units, airfield support detachments and special forces. Its roles varied from liaison to ambulance, anti-tank, electronic warfare, command and control, military police, logistic, REME light aid, Royal Marine lightweights able to be lifted by Sea King helicopters, FFR, special weapon fits, Navy air co-ordination, and many, many others. Those deployed included the 90, 110, 127 – now known as the Defender 130 – or their recent predecessors, through to Discovery and Range Rover, much in demand as staff and command vehicles by Coalition commanders. At the height of the campaign some 2,000 Land Rover vehicles of all types were deployed with the British Forces alone and by the end they had covered many millions of kilometres.

Standing beside the main highway heading north towards Kuwait, or travelling along the Tapline Road, you could tick off dozens of Land Rover variants belonging to the British and their Arab and other Coalition allies: one tonne 101s and the newer 130 ambulances, lightweights, Series III vehicles and the later 90s and 110s in the FFR and a score of other roles, stripped-down weapons carriers, one tonne Rapier tractors and mobile repair workshops, and many, many more. Then there were the Range Rovers, much prized as staff cars, and Discoverys taking part in their first campaign. The Americans snapped up any commercially available Discoverys they could find, and other satisfied users included the Vickers Defence Systems teams who supported the Desert Rats Challenger 1 tanks throughout the war. Their three Discoverys were described as 'extremely reliable and ideal for this sort of support role in desert terrain'.

The Saudi Arabian National Guard had bought several thousand Land Rovers in the 1970s and some 400 were taken out of storage for deployment during Desert Shield and Desert Storm. The National Guard units were equipped with half-ton Land Rovers mounted with 106-mm anti tank rifles and

RAF Rapier anti-aircraft missile tractor.

they were used as a rapid deployment force with great success, notably at the Battle of Al Harrar. The SANG verdict was that 'it was the Land Rovers which won the battle'.

Not least, the Land Rover was highly successful in the Special Forces' role. Britain's Special Air Service (SAS) Group in the Gulf was equipped with two types, the well-proven Pink Panthers – 'Pinkies' – plus a new, smaller variant based on the Defender 90. These were soon known as 'Dinkies' to the men of 22 SAS Regiment. Unimog trucks acted as motherships, resupplying the patrols.

The SAS disrupted Iraqi communications and their behind-the-lines mobile Scud missile launcher hunting patrols were highly successful, as reflected in the winning of 41 gallantry awards. Britain's Gulf War Commander, General Sir Peter de la Billière, at the time the UK's most decorated serving officer and a self-confessed Land Rover fan, had been familiar with the vehicles throughout his own SAS career and had even made a four-day transit of the Nubian desert by Land Rover with his family in 1970. In the Gulf he instructed the SAS to plan and execute what he termed 'classic operations' deep in Iraq to cut roads and create diversions which would draw Iraqi forces away from the main front.

This role eventually crystallized into taking out the Scud missile launchers which disturbed the sleep of those of us back in Dhahran and Riyadh. In his book *Storm Command* (Harper Collins, 1992) he reveals that there was a debate about the best method of insertion: on foot by helicopter at night with less chance of being 'bounced' but lacking mobility, or by stripped-down Land Rovers and motor cycles. In the end two patrols went by helicopter and on foot – like the now-famous Bravo Two Zero – and the rest by Land Rover.

They successfully called down air strikes on the Scud launchers and in doing so helped keep Israel out of the war by ending provocative Iraqi missile attacks, and restored the sleep of everyone else in-theatre. Their behind-the-lines success was achieved with the help of Milan anti-tank missiles and at times it was so cold at night that the patrols had to light fires beneath their vehicles to stop the diesel from freezing. General de la Billière comments: 'Between them, Special Forces managed to give the Iraqis the impression that the Allied formations at large in the western desert were about 10 times the size of the units actually deployed there and so drew a useful number of troops away from the main theatre of operations.' Despite the dangers, the SAS patrols found time to pose with their Land Rovers for 'family snaps' in the desert, somewhere behind enemy lines. They also managed to hold a full meeting of the Warrant Officers' and Sergeants' Mess deep inside Iraq. Coalition Commander, US General 'Stormin' Norman' Schwarzkopf paid this tribute to their exploits: 'The performance of the 22nd Special Air Service Regiment during Operation Desert Storm was in the highest traditions of the professional military service, and in keeping with the proud history and tradition that has been established by that Regiment.'

When it was all over, senior British military spokesman, Nigel Gillies said:

'Land Rover is one of the unsung heroes of the Gulf war – it performed as required, giving the dependable service we've come to expect backed up by excellent in-theatre and home-base support from the company itself.'

Significantly some of the first B (soft-skinned) vehicles to re-enter Kuwait City on liberation were Kuwaiti, Saudi and other Coalition Arab forces' Land Rovers, and among the first British military vehicles were FFR Land Rovers, air-lifted in by C130 transports as Special Forces roped down from helicopters to re-occupy the embassies.

Having played its part in winning the war, Land Rover's Gulf Task Force – both in the UK and in theatre – continued to underpin the great effort to help get Kuwait back on its feet. Amid all the devastation a growing fleet of hundreds of Land Rover vehicles was used successfully in a multitude of roles, especially for the extremely hazardous oil well firefighting and bomb disposal work. Plans had been drawn up by meetings of Land Rover's Gulf Task Force, chaired by Ken James. 'We knew Kuwait well, having been there for 30 years, and realized that extraordinary action would be needed to rebuild the country with Land Rover vehicles leading the way,' explained Ken. Teams of specialists at the company's Solihull headquarters and in the Gulf co-ordinated the specific transportation, supply and servicing needs of companies involved in the reconstruction.

Within days of hostilities ending, Land Rover personnel had re-entered the war-torn city to assess the damage to their facilities. There was an immediate demand, mainly for Defenders and Discoverys, and within a short time more than 500 had been provided with orders continuing to grow following the appointment of a new distributor.

Another top priority was to restore a full parts and service back-up to Land Rover users. Military Support Manager Allan Oliver, who spent nine years in the Royal Electrical and Mechanical Engineers before joining Land Rover, recalls: 'All the parts had been stolen from our Kuwait dealership which was then burnt out by the Iraqis. So we sent out tailor-made, self-sufficient Defender 130 workshop and parts support vehicles, manned by a highly experienced team.'

The go-anywhere workshop, fitted with compressor, generator, welding gear and special tools, was highly successful in an environment where virtually no facilities had survived intact. Leading the team in Kuwait was Larry Kay, also ex-REME. Earlier, before and during the Gulf War, he and Allan Oliver were based in Saudi Arabia supporting British and other Land Rover-equipped Coalition forces. They even provided stickers for military drivers giving hints to those new to desert driving.

The entire Land Rover performance in the Gulf won praise from General de la Billière. He said: 'Land Rover played a significant part in Britain's contribution to the Coalition's Gulf War victory. They were great workhorses in every role from ambulances to fighting patrol vehicles and it was good to see Land Rover people out there, sharing the danger, to give direct support on the ground.' General de la Billière was given a warm welcome when he visited the Solihull factory after the war to thank everyone, and particularly the Gulf Support Team, for all they had done. He told them:

> 'In the Gulf the Land Rover played a vital role in the whole of our command and logistic infrastructure. Not only was what you achieved remarkable, but those members of Land Rover who served during the war and in the very difficult and dangerous time in Kuwait afterwards made a particularly important contribution to the image that British expatriates have in the Gulf. It's been noticed throughout the Arab world that the British stayed by their posts when the going got rough and didn't bug out. Land Rover's role in this was exemplary".

Vehicles are unable to choose sides and like most others, Land Rovers have turned up with the 'baddies' as well as with the 'goodies'. One long wheelbase version photographed in Belfast in the early '70s with a harp painted on the door and a seat mounted on the roof was allegedly used by the Provisional IRA for patrolling the so-called 'no-go' areas of the city. And, although the company always strictly observes Government export controls, Land Rover vehicles – either procured before sanctions or stolen from the Kuwaitis – were plainly to be seen among the jumble of vehicles in the shambolic Iraqi convoy that was caught fleeing Kuwait and shattered by Coalition aircraft on the Basra road in the dying hours of the Gulf War.

No sooner was the Gulf War over than Land Rovers were deployed with the Royal Marines and others on the humanitarian aid mission to the Kurds in Northern Iraq. In Cambodia, UN Forces, including the highly professional Dutch Marines – staunch Land Rover adherents despite the fact that their Army counterparts now operate Mercedes – and the Australian Army played a key role in bringing an end to factional fighting, overseeing the 1991 Paris Treaty and supervising the 1993 elections.

The Dutch commitment in Cambodia lasted for 18 months, but although their 60 Defender 110s remained in operation there throughout, the Marine Corps units were relieved after six-month stints in the tropical heat. Their 110s were used mainly for command and control and patrolling the laterite tracks through jungle-clad areas. Their deployment successfully completed, Marine Corps Colonel Leo Don, reported: 'The 110s were extremely reliable and could be kept in operation without any real problems due to the high quality of the vehicles and a flow of spare parts from the Netherlands to Cambodia.'

The Australians' Land Rovers, based closely on the Defender, were also part of the UN operation in Somalia, bringing relief to a starving people in a country ravaged by warring factions. The headlines went to the Americans because of media criticism of the way they conducted the operation and as a result much of the excellent humanitarian work done by them and Land Rover-equipped contingents such as the Australians, Turks and United Arab

Emirates went largely unrecognized.

Both four-wheel drive and Australian-designed six-wheel drive Land Rovers were used by the Australian peacekeeping troops in both Somalia and Cambodia. They are part of a 3,700 strong fleet of Land Rovers in service with both the Australian Army and Air Force. The vehicles operating in Cambodia and Somalia 'hardly missed a beat' according to Lieutenant Colonel Lee Osborne, Project Director for the Australian Army's Land Rovers. 'Our Maintenance Engineering Agency, which handles all vehicle problems, has had virtually nothing reported back from Somalia and only a handful of minor problems from Cambodia. We're very happy with their performance,' he added. 'We expected them to be rugged and reliable and they haven't let us down.' Land Rover had won the Australian Army's Project Perentie contract in 1984 after 18 months of tortuous trials in remote areas of Far North Queensland, South Australia and the Australian Alps. Named after the desert-dwelling Perentie lizard, the project aimed at finding a vehicle with the Perentie's legendary agility in trackless terrain, its endurance and adaptability. Project Perentie Land Rovers range from surveillance, command and communications vehicles to field ambulances, cargo and general maintenance vehicles. The 'jewel' of the Perentie fleet is the astonishing Long Range Patrol 6 x 6 Land Rover, which can cover 1,800 km on one 350-litre tank of fuel. The Project Perentie vehicles are based closely on Land Rover's Defender wagon and hardtop models, although the Army vehicles use 3.9-litre Isuzu engines rather than the Defender's more economical 2.5-litre turbocharged and intercooled direct injection diesel.

Also operating their home-produced Land Rovers with the UN in Somalia

Jewel of the Australians' Perentie fleet, the astonishing Long Range Patrol 6 x 6 Land Rover.

were the Turks. OTOKAR, the Turkish arm of Land Rover, produces Defender 90, 110 and 130 models for both the Turkish military and civilian markets. Like its Solihull counterpart, OTOKAR fields Military Support Teams of technicians equipped with 130 crew cab mobile workshops to operate alongside the military deployed on exercises and operations. Both the Australian and Turkish experiences are classic examples of Land Rover working with the customer to develop products to meet indigenous needs.

The Gulf War emphasized the requirement for easily deployable and sustainable rapid reaction vehicles capable of delivering a powerful punch. The rapid reaction, high mobility requirement is one that many military forces world-wide agree is likely to be of increasing importance in peacekeeping and security operations in the foreseeable future. The most recent figures from United States sources show that in 1992 there were more than 50 conflicts going on around the world and American Special Forces were deployed on 150 missions in over 100 countries. This represented a 35 per cent increase in US Special Forces deployments compared with the year before, and the increase was over 100 per cent in deployments connected with anti-drugs missions.

Land Rover had anticipated, understood and interpreted this changing operational requirement – not least because of emerging instability in the world following the break-up of the Warsaw Pact alliance – and were already well advanced with the development of the new generation of purpose-built rapid reaction vehicles: the Defender Special Operations Vehicle (SOV).

When the United Kingdom announced the major restructuring of its Armed Forces following the demise of the Warsaw Pact, British politicians and military planners acknowledged that there was a need to maintain 'well equipped,

Multi-Role Combat Vehicle (MRCV) emerging from a helicopter.

Defender Special Operations Vehicle (SOV) developed to meet air transportability and mobility requirements of Rapid Reaction and Special Forces.

mobile and flexible forces to be able to respond to developments in a rapidly changing world'. It was a statement echoed by many another nations around the world. Air transportability, mobility and flexibility were key design considerations for the SOV – as indeed they are for all Land Rover products. It – and the Multi Role Combat Vehicle (MRCV) that soon followed – had to have the mobility and range for extended reconnaissance and combat roles. It had to be reliable, airportable, capable of tackling the most demanding terrain and extreme climatic conditions, and able to carry a weapons mix enabling its crew to carry out missions against a wide variety of threats. It also had to be easily maintainable and supportable far from its home base. Not least, for smaller friendly nations with tight budgets but a real defence need for such a vehicle, it had to be affordable, and the Land Rover view is that this should not just apply to unit cost but in overall value for money, low whole-life cost terms.

These qualities make the SOV ideal for rapid intervention and screening deployments, giving its operators the capability of snuffing out a problem in a swift surgical strike, whether in peacekeeping, internal security, counter-insurgency, anti-Scud style operations and a wide variety of other roles in hostile areas. It is lighter and much narrower – and therefore more easily airportable – than its rivals such as the American Humvee, and has more of everything than the limited-role, space-frame dune buggies used by some armies for reconnaissance and the various light strike vehicles currently on the market.

The SOV has greater mobility, with its coil sprung suspension and 750 x 16 tyres, carries more payload than the light strike vehicles – up to 1,500 kg with heavy duty suspension – and has a range of up to 850 km on a standard 79.5-litre fuel tank. Increased range can be obtained by fitting an additional fuel tank and/or carrying jerrycans. It also has greater firepower, being capable of carrying a variety of weapons including grenade launchers, GPMG, Carl Gustav, Stinger and personal weapons – an easily adaptable platform for multi-roles depending on individual requirements. A typical powerful mix includes a 30-mm cannon, 81-mm and 51-mm mortars, LAW 80, 7.62-mm general purpose machine gun, 5.56-mm assault rifles, 40-mm grenade pistols, 9-mm sub machine guns and Blade – or equivalents. The main weapons mount ring is attached to roll bars and subsidiary weapons have easily-detachable clamps. There is also ample space for ammunition, with stowage for Claymore mines, smoke, stun and standard grenades, plus personal kit and pioneer tools. The SOV is powered by a choice of either Land Rover's own highly successful and economic 200 Tdi 2.5-litre direct injection turbo charged diesel or the 3.5-litre V8 petrol engine. The engine range is common to all Land Rover vehicles, simplifying logistics and support activities and providing high levels of interoperability. The standard version has seating for a six man crew, with full kit and safety features include the roll bars and harnesses for all crew.

A version of the SOV is already in service with the United States Rangers. Known as the Ranger Special Operations Vehicle (RSOV), it is vital to their role which includes 'infiltrating and exfiltrating by land, sea or air: conducting direct action operations; raids; recovering personnel and/or special equipment; and conducting light infantry operations in a conventional or special operations environment'.

Rangers are required to be ready to deploy anywhere in the world within four hours – fully trained and equipped for operations and the mobility, reliability and airportability of their RSOVs is a crucial factor. Acquisition of the RSOV followed a market survey for a dedicated Ranger vehicle in early 1990, which recommended the Land Rover Defender 90 and 110, the Austrian Pinzgauer and the standard US Army HMMWV as the candidate vehicles. Extensive testing and an Integrated Logistics Support analysis were completed to determine which vehicle would best meet the requirements for the RSOV, and a contract was awarded for the Land Rover 110 on 19 July 1991. Fielding for the RSOV began in February 1992 and was completed in July 1993.

The diesel-powered, light special operations vehicle, which replaces modified MI5I Jeeps, comes in three configurations: a weapons carrier, a communications vehicle (SHARK), and a logistics/medical vehicle. The standard vehicle is 70.5 inches wide, 79 inches high, 175 inches long and has a ground clearance of 10 ins. It will accommodate a generous payload. The weapons carrier is capable of firing a 50-calibre machine gun, M60 machine gun and MK19 grenade launcher.

The RSOV fits into CH-47 and CH-53 helicopters and C-130, C-141 and

C5A aircraft. It was also tested for sling load operations with an MH-47D and was flown successfully to 140 knots for dual hook-up and 100 knots for single point hook-up and for single point sling loading with the UH-60.

Latest in the military range and likely to attract many customers is the Defender Multi-Role Combat Vehicle (MRCV) unveiled at the 1993 Royal Navy and British Army Equipment Exhibition. Fully airportable, it has been specifically developed as a highly versatile and mobile weapons platform with powerful firepower capability, readily adapted to respond to the rapidly changing threats encountered by Rapid Reaction Forces, reconnaissance and patrol units.

The MRCV has ready mountings for the Milan, the Mk 129 grenade launcher, and three mounting locations for .5 Browning or 7.62 machine guns. There is seating for up to six crew, mountings for ammunition panniers, and space is available for communications equipment, personal weapons and kit. Defender 90, 110 and 130 variants are available with very high commonality of equipment and the 'kits and fits' possibilities are almost endless.

Other recent arrivals on the military scene from the Land Rover stable include a new Discovery variant developed to meet the need for greater mobility for Investigative Explosive teams. It combines outstanding on and off road performance with a spacious interior for tools and equipment, providing an ever-ready, go-anywhere, cost effective IEDD vehicle.

An increasing requirement in the '90s is for light armoured vehicles,

Below left *The Defender is airportable for rapid deployment and can be carried underslung, complete with trailer, from the Chinook and other helicopters.*

Below right *Defender 110 fitted with Courtaulds Aerospace high tech Vehicle Protection Kit, which has already proved itself in Bosnia.*

particularly for UN humanitarian operations or other flashpoints where there is factional violence. Land Rover has long worked with manufacturers of armouring materials for urban work, border patrols and riot control, as well as in the specialist field of discreet armour for VIP protection and escort duties. The lightly armoured Shorland, produced by Short Brothers on the Land Rover chassis, and used for patrolling in Northern Ireland, was just one example.

The latest development is Courtaulds Aerospace CAV 100, based on the Defender 110 chassis, which is being used extensively in former Yugoslavia. Courtaulds' specially designed lightweight composite armour panels are moulded and assembled on to the vehicle to form a monocoque construction. The monocoque body is both tough and strong and forms a security cell for protection against ballistic threats and a safety cell for protection in road accidents and roll-over.

The SNATCH armoured patrol vehicle, as the military version used in Northern Ireland is known, has already withstood small arms fire, mortar attack and mine blast, saving lives and reducing the number of casualties both there and in Bosnia, where it is also deployed with humanitarian aid organizations and the press corps. The unique all-round composite armour of the CAV 100 provides outstanding lightweight protection against threats such as fragmentation from grenades and mines, high velocity ball rounds and blast with no behind armour effects – spall or splash. Its exceptional performance against mine blast was amply demonstrated when one hit a land mine, thought to have contained more than 4 kg of high explosive. The force of the blast destroyed the front wheel, badly damaged the engine compartment and deafened people standing a hundred metres away but the composite armour monocoque remained firmly intact and the three occupants escaped unhurt, although no doubt their ears were ringing.

As this edition went to press, a great many Defenders and Discoverys were serving under the UN flag in war-ravaged former Yugoslavia in the now usual bewildering variety of roles. They included the Discovery and 38 Defenders of the Malaysian contingent, part of a package of vehicles and equipment on loan from the British Government.

Among the many satisfied users was the UN Commander in Bosnia and Hercegovina – Lieutenant General Sir Michael Rose himself. He was having to spend much of his time travelling by Range Rover or Discovery between city streets and snowy mountain tracks in his efforts to get aid through, protect threatened ethnic groups and broker peace. His verdict?

'I have been personally most impressed by both the armoured Range Rover and the Discovery. I travel great distances at speed over very rough terrain and even during the winter months I have never failed to reach my destination. On one occasion, I woke in the middle of the night to find the Range Rover swerving violently from side to side across the road.

Range Rover on active service, with Lieutenant General Sir Michael Rose (centre) discussing troop locations with local commanders at a Bosnian Serb checkpoint.

> Far from the problem being caused by mechanical breakdown or a puncture, it was the driver trying to avoid the anti-tank mines that had been placed all over the road!'

Currently Land Rover is competing for the UK Ministry of Defence Trucks Utility Light (TUL), Trucks Utility Medium (TUM) contract leading to an order for some 6,000 vehicles to take the British Army well into the 21st Century. The company is also competing elsewhere around the world to provide military customers with the increased breadth of operational capability and adaptability required in the rapidly changing international security situation. Initially some 25 international 4 x 4 manufacturers expressed interest in the UK TUL/TUM contract but Land Rover alone was selected to provide trials vehicles for evaluation.

The Defender 90 and 110 trials vehicles were powered by the 2.5-litre direct injection turbo diesel engine (200 Tdi) and are safe and simple to operate, robust and rugged for military use – including airmobile and amphibious roles – with high levels of reliability and ease of maintenance, delivering greater availability and lower whole life costs. They have more than 90 per cent UK content and involve more than 750 British suppliers. Additionally, Land Rover has developed its new-generation, battle-proven Defender 130 for international competition for Field Ambulance requirements.

Rover Group Chief Executive John Towers said the new military business was highly significant, explaining, 'Armies and other customers world-wide are well aware that Britain's highly professional armed forces accept only the best.'

Land Rover has for many years maintained a dedicated Government and Military Operations function which looks after the interests of military and public service fleet operators – and supports them in the field as it did throughout the Gulf War. Its Director, George Adams, is clear about what is required of the company today – and in the future:

> 'Our aim is to provide the performance, payloads, reliability, mobility, rapid deployment capability and in-service support to satisfy military customers' needs into the next century with the minimum cost of ownership.
>
> 'We are confident that Land Rover will continue to do well in the military arena because of the company's great depth of experience in this field. The adaptability of the product meets the changing needs and profiles of armed forces and formations – like the Allied Rapid Reaction Corps – in this very complex post-Cold War environment.
>
> 'It is our experience of military customers that enables us to exploit the multi-role aspects of the vehicle family – Defender 90, 110 and 130 – with new versions like the MRCV, which is a brilliant concept, and the SOV which has evolved way beyond the original Pink Panther SAS vehicle. Another growing requirement is for the use of the latest composite armour which is where Land Rover's strong links with the specialist suppliers and converters is of great benefit. There are close links with defence manufacturers and suppliers all over the world, and with us they are constantly looking at adapting and validating the vehicle to take the next generation of electronics for communications, command, control and surveillance – or the latest weapons configurations.
>
> 'But above all in the '90s there's a realization within the company of the need for a strong focus on the specialist needs of military and para-military customers and the need to be responsive and attuned to their changing needs. This applies not only to the product and its performance and reliability, but also to in-service support and whole life cost of ownership which must represent good value for money.
>
> 'We are also fully attuned to changing government budgetary needs and market testing leading to contractorization and privatization in which industry takes on more responsibilities – as is already happening with Land Rover dealers providing contract maintenance and genuine parts supply for military fleets.'

Whatever direction the international security situation takes as we prepare to enter a new century, all the indications are that Land Rover – with its focus on customer satisfaction and dedication to total quality and world class performance – intends to ensure it retains its place as the supplier of the unbeatable 4 x 4 for military fleets.

Chapter 4
The Range Rover Story

What is a Range Rover – primarily a load carrier or a people carrier? And does anyone care which? Emphatically, yes: Range Rover of North America cares a lot, because thanks to the US Customs Service, the difference between the two classifications now means a reduction of several thousand dollars on the price, with all that that implies in the market place.

So, it's a people carrying vehicle .... OK, prove it.

Late one evening, in the first days of 1989, we received a call from the Range Rover headquarters in Maryland: 'Can you track down the earliest data on the concept of the Range Rover? It's urgent. We need to know the kind of vehicle it was intended to be ....'

Who better to instigate this search than George Mackie, a contemporary of the key figures involved with formulating the Range Rover concept. He agreed at once, and within hours had spoken to Spen King and Gordon Bashford. The next day George went to see Gordon who had already produced a lot of old papers. Together they sifted through them until at last they located the crucial evidence. Lodging the originals in the Company Secretary's safe at Solihull, George then had the copies faxed through to America.

Late one evening, some six weeks later, we received a fax from Range Rover of North America which began: 'Eureka! We're out of the soup on the Customs issue .... The decision, favorable to Range Rover, was handed down on Thursday last.' Much credit for this was rightly given to George Mackie and Gordon Bashford who never imagined that, years into their retirement, they would still be saving the day for the old Rover Co!

*   *   *   *

The advent of the Range Rover stems more from the vehement and consistent resistance to 'tarting up' the Land Rover on the part of its management than from any other single factor. Time and time again, proposals have been submitted for modifying the Land Rover design, to make it more stylish, more comfortable, and more luxurious, to cushion the ride and widen its appeal. However, with the wisdom of long experience, the management have always dug their toes in and maintained that the function of the Land Rover is well-defined and clear cut: it is a utility vehicle, and no more than that. Too much styling and softening could only detract from what has made it so universally useful, and successful. It has often been aptly described as 'the workhorse of the world' – and no one vehicle can be all things to all men. If the Land Rover team were to bend their ideas towards a more prestigious vehicle it could never be called a Land Rover, and could certainly not resemble a Land Rover in appearance. The resemblance would be concentrated entirely on performance, toughness and versatility – the invisible assets, but the crucial ones.

Within the organization there were many who were single-mindedly loyal to Land Rover, and so committed to its utilitarian, functional features that they were unable to view a revolutionary new design of 4 x 4 vehicle – aimed at a different sector of the market altogether – with anything but pessimism and scepticism. One of the main arguments was that the combination of power and speed in a 4-wheel-drive cross-country vehicle was courting disaster: it could only be a danger off the road as it would be driven too fast, and would most likely fall to pieces anyway ... The other familiar argument, particularly from the sales and production areas was 'why mess about with new models when there's a waiting list for existing ones?' – the age-old trap!

Fortunately, there were those enthusiasts who predicted the emerging trend for multi-role 4 x 4s, and doggedly worked away at the design of a vehicle that would be quite unlike anything yet produced. Serious research into the design of a car-type Land Rover vehicle had already taken place in the 1950s when Maurice Wilks had encouraged Gordon Bashford and his team to explore the

The first Road Rover prototype.

223

potential of producing such a machine – but the concept was not sufficiently far-reaching. At the time, funds were limited and the only chassis available on which to base the new vehicle's design was that of the Rover saloon car, known as the P4 chassis, apart from that of the Land Rover itself. Economy required that this be used. The expense of an entirely new body would have to be met, and this was as far as funds would stretch: the rest had to be an inspired jigsaw puzzle of existing components. Although the first complete prototype was with 4-wheel drive, the demand at the time seemed to indicate that conventional 2-wheel drive would be preferred. Thus the vehicle that evolved, which was known as the Road Rover, did not have 4-wheel drive, which of course immediately curtailed any cross-country ability. Based on the P4 chassis, it was fitted with a 2-litre Land Rover engine, but its styling was far from satisfactory or aesthetic, quickly earning it the nickname of 'The Greenhouse', for its angularity and flat-sided clumsiness. This concept even entered a second phase (with the MK 2 Road Rover) with a more modern body shape bearing some resemblance to the 3 litre (P5) saloon car, but the difficult balance between an all-purpose off-road vehicle and one that handled well on the highway had not been struck and – to cut a long story short – it died a natural death in 1958 before it had been launched. Its relevance here is that it illustrated that the much later Range Rover idea was by no means totally innovative, even if the end product turned out to be just that.

The time lapse between the two projects was to provide a clearer definition of the requirement for such an entity, although while the Car sections were looking at the Road Rovers, the Land Rover sections were still engineering all sorts of 'improvements' for the Land Rover, like independent front suspension, levelled rear suspension, deluxe trim, large heaters for cold territories, 2.6-litre high compression engines in North American 10-seater Station Wagons, 3-litre engines in 88-inch Station Wagons, and so forth. Of course, throughout this period body styling and production techniques had progressed by leaps and bounds. Peter Wilks, who was the nephew of Spencer and Maurice Wilks, took charge of engineering during the early 1960s, and had long believed that the time for a 'luxury Land Rover' would, in due course, come.

Various 'concepts' had been under discussion including, most recently, a new Land Rover Series III, the 'One-Double-One' (111-inch wheelbase) having a 3-litre 6-cylinder engine, or a 3.5-litre V6!

Two factors now came together to create a more positive atmosphere for change: a cut-back in military orders for Land Rovers, and the results of a market research survey showing an upsurge in the 'leisure market' and a greater requirement for passenger carrying (as opposed to payload carrying) vehicles.

By late 1965 early 1966 discussions were beginning to gel around a new (not modified Land Rover) vehicle, of station wagon type, as another 'stop-gap' measure, and the title 'Interim Station Wagon' developed.

The V8 3.5-litre engine had also recently appeared on the scene as a result of

William Martin-Hurst's trip to General Motors in 1963, and was being shoe-horned into the P5 (3-litre) car and the P6 (2000). Of greater interest however is the fact that three 88-inch Land Rovers were already running with these engines, two with manual transmission, and one with Borg Warner auto transmission (and low range 4WD), and they were already showing what could be achieved off-road and on-road with the right combination of torque and power. No one was really surprised when this engine found its way into the Interim Station Wagon concept.

By July 1966, Gordon Bashford's design engineers had developed a five-seat station wagon layout with P6 standards of seating comfort, on a chassis allowing wheel travels never before seen on off-road vehicles, and within a wheelbase giving acceptable drive line angles and standards. The wheelbase was 100-inch – the 'Interim Station Wagon' overnight became the Land Rover 100-inch Station Wagon!

William Martin-Hurst that evening had the last word when he turned to Joe Brown (Gordon Bashford's deputy) and said, 'Is the chassis strong enough for a pick-up version?'! An extra $^1/_2$-inch depth was put into the centre section of the chassis frame, and the vehicle has been over-engineered ever since! It did, however, help people's confidence in 1972 when the four-door model was designed.

Police Range Rover Tdi in action.

An expedition-equipped Range Rover with roof-mounted air-conditioning.

Because no similar vehicle existed, the designers had to be sure of the basic aims of their product, having no yardstick to help them along their way. What the brief boiled down to was that the vehicle must be faster, larger, more 'civilized' than a regular Land Rover, but quite as practical, and recognizably a Rover product. In designing the new transmission system (the 88-inch V 8s had proven, if such proof were needed, that the Land Rover gearboxes were not strong enough), 4-wheel drive was the jumping-off point. The vehicle had to have the versatility that this would engender (and therefore the high ground clearance, wheel mobility and ruggedness it entailed), but it was only later on that permanent 4-wheel drive was decided upon, making it completely different to the Land Rover, rather than merely a smartened-up version of it. A transfer box was located behind the new main gearbox, giving high and low ratios on all main gearbox speeds. Front and rear drive was permanently engaged via a third differential, lockable by a vacuum control switch. The third differential was incorporated on to a system that was in other respects similar to that of the Land Rover, to obviate transmission 'wind-up' between front and rear. This increase in traction gave it an even greater cross-country ability – which in itself demanded vastly improved suspension design. Long-travel vertical coil spring suspension was devised, with axle location by radius arms front and rear, and initially with transverse location links similar to the Ford Bronco. The initial design did not include a leveller, but had conventional long stroke hydraulic telescopic dampers similar to the 109-inch Land Rover.

No. 1 prototype was built in June/July 1967 to this layout, with Land Rover drum brakes and transmission.

Experience with this first vehicle exposed problems of axle location and steering fight, so this system was abandoned in favour of the system we now know so well including the Boge Hydromat levelling device.

The changeover from the 6-cylinder 3-litre to the V8 3½-litre engine was warmly welcomed by Peter Wilks, Spen King and Gordon Bashford who were the mainstays of the enterprise. They considerably developed and modified it, and most of the engineering details and design of the vehicle had been adjusted to accommodate it by 1966. The last big hurdle was still to be overcome, however – that of styling. While the precise market for the machine was still rather vague, it was generally accepted that it had to look good. The engineers who had laboured so long over it had their own notions of body style. Spen King and Gordon Bashford worked out the lay-out and built a mock-up themselves rather than waiting until the Styling Department could undertake it. The decision to make it a 2-door vehicle was made early on in the design stage, because of doubts about the strength of the body structure on a 4-door model, especially for cross-country work. A 2-door vehicle was also a lot cheaper to produce, which would be reflected in the final cost price – even though the 2-door design finally necessitated the inclusion of expensively designed and manufactured seat belts. The usual seat belts, anchored to the BC posts, proved awkward and hazardous when the front seats were tilted forward for access to and from the rear seats, so it was decided that they be incorporated in the back of the front seats. Although successful, this was a costly development, and tended to reduce the 2-door cost saving. However, Spen King and Gordon Bashford achieved a body style in their own prototype which even then was recognizable as the Range Rover of today.

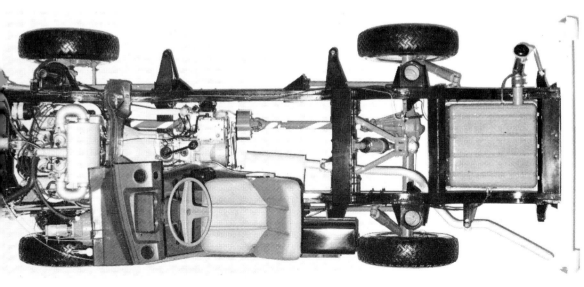

A Range Rover chassis.

In 1967 Rover was to merge with Leyland (the latter becoming the dominant partner) and it was anyone's guess how the new management would view the production of a vehicle like the one Rover was now offering, the actual outlet for which was still fairly indeterminate. Luckily, they seized upon it enthusiastically and couldn't wait to get it out. They may have thought it would represent the auspicious start they all hoped for. Whatever its shortcomings, it would be a product of the Land Rover stable which could only stand the company in good stead – even though it shared practically no common component with the Land Rover vehicle. Two prototypes now existed, No 1 (SYE 157F) with the old suspension and drive line, and No 2 prototype (ULH 696F) still with the King/Bashford body, but with the new levelled suspension and disc brakes.

No 1 prototype was passed to Styling (who still insisted on calling it a Road Rover) (see photo), for assessment and to be modified under the eye of David Bache. He must take the credit for the overall styling detail that has made the Range Rover, bulky as it is, into such an elegant machine. Photographs show the main areas where his influence created such marked improvements. Its graceful proportions and pleasing lines conceal its ruggedness and its power, as well as the fact that, unlike so many commodities these days, it is designed and built to last, and to withstand punishment. It was subsequently exhibited at the Louvre in Paris as an outstanding example of modern sculpture – an unusual accolade for a motor car!

No. 2 prototype completed a 'double' endurance test on the pavé and cross country circuits at MIRA, proving the durability of the complete chassis and running gear, and thus No. 3 prototype (AGN 316G) was soon to be built to 'production specification'. Approval was immediate and prototypes 4 (AMV 287H), 5 (WYK 315H) and 6 (AOY 289H) followed by late 1969. In fact Nos 5 and 6 were then prepared for the combined testing/filming safari in Algeria and Morocco, to run during November/December 1969. Production was aimed to begin before the close of the 1960s – but there was an enormous amount of detail to be finished off on the design and styling side, alternatives to be considered and tested, as well as the physical problem of where it was going to be built. Space had to be made available somehow, since although many parts of the vehicle had been contracted out to be manufactured by other firms (springs, dampers, self-levelling strut, some of the axle components, even the frame itself, and some of the alloy body shell panels), factory space was required for building the transmissions: of the major components, only the engine was already established. Right alongside the existing Land Rover tracks, Range Rover assembly commenced, the Pilot Build Shop having assessed and sorted out production build problems by assembling the final Engineering prototype 100-7, registered YVB 150H.

Facing page:
The styling department had built clay models for appraisal, still insisting on calling it a 'Road Rover'. Body details were finally agreed and No 3 prototype (LHD) was completed in February 1969.

No 3 prototype built early 1969. Production models would look relatively unchanged over a decade later.

Schemed as early as November 1971, the 4-door model first appeared 'in the flesh' as a 'K' registered prototype. Nearly two decades later, can you spot the differences?

The first vehicles off the production line were in fact the pre-production batch of 25 (intended to be 30 but no-one allowed for spare parts!) registered YVB 151H to 175H. These came off in the line in various states of finish, but fitted only with two front seats made up from Land Rover De Luxe units, no rear seats and very little internal trim.

The next batch of twenty vehicles (all right-hand drive), NXC 231H to 250H, were, after many visits and revisits to the rectification department, correct to specification and ready for the Press Launch at Meudon Hotel (near Falmouth) in Cornwall in early June. Range Rovers began to appear in public at last in June 1970, but even then it had been something of a rush job in the end, to the chagrin of the men behind the scenes who were indoctrinated with very high Rover standards, and would have liked another year in which to iron out the final wrinkles.

Not surprisingly, production was initially very low key. Teething troubles in assembly were inevitable at the beginning and it was months before a realistic number could be seen to emerge from the factory gates at Solihull. In the first 10 weeks or so, the average was less than 10 vehicles a week, building up gradually to more like a 100 a week by the beginning of 1972 compared with 250 a week by 1975. The first Range Rovers cost about £2,000, but not for long. The rate of price escalation has been sharp, as can be appreciated by the fact that a 1984 Range Rover (2-door) fetches in the region of £16,000 on the home market. But back in 1970, a £2,000 price tag was still placing the vehicle amongst the élite, which in itself probably contributed to its instant popularity: it was not only essentially practical, but it had snob value. Within weeks of its release, the public was clamouring for Range Rovers, and all previous speculation on the strongest potential outlets had been proved to be wildly below the mark. Far from appealing only to land-owners, horse-racers and gentleman farmers, it found favour with the many and diverse Land Rover fans who needed additional performance, comfort and space for certain purposes. The Police Force was a case in point: they could hardly clock a sports car exceeding the motorway speed limit with a Land Rover, but the Range Rover's maximum speed was only fractionally below 100 mph – quite remarkable in a 4-wheel drive vehicle. The sheer height of the vehicle when compared to any conventional saloon car also proved to be an attraction. Suddenly people could get above the rest of the traffic in towns, not to mention their improved vantage point when driving cross-country, allowing them to observe obstacles more easily and see beyond the usual obstructions of walls and hedges, while still feeling perfectly safe: for, despite its increased elevation, the vehicle remained stable because of the low centre of gravity ensured by the solid steel chassis and low mounting of axles, gearbox and engine. Ground clearance was, nevertheless, still exceptionally high (12.6ins – except below the axles where it was 7.5ins), allowing the vehicle to negotiate muddy, snowy, rocky, sandy, marshy or any kind of uneven ground with ease, and to ford rivers – for which reason all electrical components were specifically positioned at the top of the engine to avoid swamping of the ignition system.

Unlike the Land Rover, whose post-war development precluded the use of much steel in its construction, the Range Rover's inner skin was built up from pressed steel sub-assemblies bolted together, clad in a body of light aluminium alloy similar to that used on the Land Rover. The steel structure was much stronger than pure aluminium and in effect provided a safety cage for the occupants. One of the initial faults in the Range Rover was insufficient anti-corrosion treatment of the steel, which inevitably resulted in evidence of rusting before very long. This had to be rectified in all subsequent models by comprehensive protection against corrosion both of the steel body panels, and of the welded, deep box section chassis. Nowadays, the chassis undergoes two rust-proofing dips and an electrophoretic paint dip. The steel body components are also electroprimed and dipped twice in acrylic paint. All downward facing surfaces are undersealed, and steel and aluminium surfaces are separated by sealant. One other early amendment was the elimination of the limited-slip feature from the centre differential: with permanent 4-wheel drive, the vehicle's traction proved to be adequate for most off-road conditions without this additional feature, which was dropped only months after production got under way.

This 2-door Range Rover was specially converted by Spencer Abbot for Sir Alfred McAlpine.

An unusual crew-cab cum pick-up based on a standard Range Rover.

One of the Range Rover's most impressive built-in features has always been its towing ability. With a specially strengthened rear cross member on the chassis, it is ideally suited to pulling trailors, caravans, horse boxes or boats, which again broadened its appeal from the outset. The following gives an idea of its capability in this area:

	Trailer Weight	*(+ Vehicle)*
Off-road trailer:	1,000 kg	(3,504 kg)
On-road 2-wheel trailer:	2,000 kg	(4,504 kg)
On-road 4-wheel trailer with power brakes:	4,000 kg	(6,504 kg)
For emergency purposes:	6,000 kg	(8,504 kg)

In the early stages – apart from a hiccough at the disclosure that fuel consumption was as high as 15 mpg – the demand for the Range Rover grew steadily, far in excess of supply, and once it became available overseas orders began flooding in from all corners of the earth. The production volume couldn't hope to match the order books, and the frustrations of long delays in delivery eventually gave rise to a flourishing black market in Britain, where purchasers were known to pay well over £1,000 above the list price of a new vehicle. This was revealed in a television documentary exposé in the mid-1970s, which specifically investigated the Range Rover market. It is interesting to note that, whereas it was

233

one of the hardest vehicles to buy before the start of the recession, in the early 1980s the company was having to dangle carrots to tempt potential Range Rover customers, with a selection of up-market 'prizes' for purchasers ranging from salmon fishing and golfing, to tickets for Wimbledon, Badminton or the British Grand Prix!

No sooner had Range Rovers become an accepted part of the landscape – or the cityscape – than a tendency amongst certain Range Rover owners began to manifest itself: a desire to convert the vehicle into something even more special. The inspired blend of engine, transmission and suspension that provided its unique performance, coupled with its hardiness and style, had without doubt caught the imagination of the appreciative motorist – but some of them wanted more. The Special Projects chapter of this book describes some of the elaborate conversions – citing for instance the exotic Falconry Range Rover with elevating seats – but the most obvious inclination was towards building in two more side doors, to avoid all that clambering in and out of the rear seats. While 1981 at last heralded the introduction of Land Rover's own version of the 4-door Range Rover, it is worth looking back at some of the earlier, independent findings on the subject.

Although firms like FLM (Panelcraft) were converting 2-door Range Rovers to 4-door models on the existing wheelbase, there was a minority firmly in favour of extending the wheelbase at the same time, to increase passenger comfort and interior spaciousness: a constant criticism had been that leg room is restricted on standard models for the rear seat passengers. Without fitting a new, smaller front door, the existing dimensions demanded an undersized, narrow rear door which detracted from the advantages of the conversion, whereas by extending the chassis the rear seat passengers should be amply accommodated. During the late 1970s, our organization was approached to develop an extended, 4-door Range Rover for a Middle Eastern client, regardless of the fact that it would almost treble the cost. The concept was simple enough, but the execution was a lot more laborious: the idea was to insert 35 inches into the chassis between the wheel arches, and we have our design to the coach-builders, Smiths, of Kettering. The finished product looked well, was streamlined and capacious, but had it retained its versatility as a cross-country vehicle? Or could, perhaps, a 2-wheel-drive limousine do the same job? Too much tampering with the original only dilutes its basic attributes in the end – which is why so many of us welcomed Land Rover's own design of the 4-door with relief. Here was a trustworthy, practical, integrated version that had lost none of its flexibility or innate good looks in the process of development.

Although this new availability would have been welcome years earlier, as it happened it was timed perfectly to give the Range Rover a new sales boost when most needed, when the market was showing signs of flagging. The small but significant demand continues to exist for special Range Rover conversions by firms such as Wood & Pickett (who have produced their own exotic and stylish range, named Sheer Rovers, with a wide variety of well-thought out and

The FLM (Panelcraft) 110-inch Range Rover conversion.

The Vogue Range Rover for 1984.

Power-operated convertible Range Rover, converted by FLM (Panelcraft).

This Glenfrome Falcon is typical of the highly specialised sporting vehicles demanded by the Middle Eastern market.

unusual features), FLM (Panelcraft), and Monteverdi (of Switzerland). They were able to capitalize on BL's long overdue 4-door development by producing some interesting and exotic Range Rover versions of their own. FLM (Panelcraft), whose own version of the 4-door has been approved by BL since 1974, carry out approximately 50 special conversions a year, the majority of which go to Middle Eastern states and include variations on the existing 100-inch wheelbase, the 118-inch extended wheelbase, and 12-inch rear body extension. The most popular requirement is for the 118-inch 4-door conversion. Apart from the hunting Range Rover, which can be fitted with gun racks, falcon perches, refrigerators, supplementary fuel tanks, refreshment cabinets, drinking water containers, stone guards, dust deflectors, search lamps and winches, as well as the unique elevating seats (rising up to 23 inches) and folding roofs, other special conversions carried out by this firm are a power-operated convertible 2-door Range Rover, a 4-door open model with fold-flat windscreen, a 2-door open model with side-facing seats, detachable canvas top, roll-top side curtains and fold-flat windshield, while a further option is a power-operated metal roof, and automatic transmission.

Another interesting coach-builder/converter is the Bristol-based firm, Glenfrome Engineering Ltd, who started as a small family business a few years ago and now employ 65 people. While they concentrate on Range Rover conversions, producing in the region of 500 "specials" a year, they have also started playing with Land Rovers.

Of existing Range Rover conversions, the vast majority have always gone to the Middle East, but in-roads are now being made into the Far East and certain European countries. No two end-products are alike but the basis of their range is about 10 different models, including four extended wheelbase models, the Filton extended by 9 inches, the Clifton by 24 inches, and the Westbury, and Portway by 36 inches, each unit being cut and reassembled on their own manufactured jig. Another popular model is the very strange-looking Facet sports coupé, the basis for which is a wedge-shaped glass-reinforced polyester shell dropped onto the Range Rover chassis, which boasts the most comprehensive equipment of any all-terrain vehicle in the world, and is specifically designed for the more aggressive Middle East market so that it in no way resembles the Range Rover as we know it. It sells for about £55,000. There is an opulent-looking convertible model up there at the top of the range too, the Ashton, at £48,000, which is all Range Rover from the waist-down but fully modified above (except the windscreen) the end result being a spacious and elegant soft-top saloon car with top quality finish, which is the hallmark of Glenfrome's products, (as their prices reflect!). The Glenfrome Six is an ingenious 6-wheeler, either pick-up or saloon, with widened wheels for even better road-holding, the price of which starts at £24,000.

Glenfrome has not been slow to supply the demand in certain Arab countries for hunting vehicles, and have developed two basic options: the Falcon, an open-top adaption with two doors or four doors, and the Hawk

Range Rover's versatility makes it at home anywhere.

which has a closed cab.

The various optional extras available include a Hawk perch, with adjustable tail support, leash clips and dirt tray, and also dashboard-mounted or portable falconry radar equipment complete with aerial (hand held or vehicle-mounted). This latter seems to us grossly unsporting as it locates the direction of the falcon and indicates whether it is in the air or on the ground, leaving the poor prey with dismally low odds. One wonders why the 'huntsmen' don't stay at home and play video-games then they would have no grounds for complaining that the birds are being over-hunted and populations declining. However, that's another issue: the Falcon and the Hawk vehicles are very practical for their purpose, and can also be fitted with such refinements as long range fuel tanks and fresh-water tanks and elevated rear seats (the Falcon only). This company is certainly one worth watching, for the originality and perfectionism of its products.

The interior of the Range Rover has become increasingly luxurious. This is the 1984 model.

There is no reduction in the load space of a 4-door Range Rover when the rear seats are folded forward.

4-star fuel only in the 4-door Range Rover.

240

Range Rover with in-dash air-conditioning by ARA of Texas. Note new steering wheel design.

A 4-door Range Rover, built by Range Rover, had seemed a logical step for a long time when it was introduced in 1981, after the 2-door model had been on the market for 11 years. The Chairman of BL at the time, Sir Michael Edwardes, succeeded in securing the necessary government funds to implement the full-scale investment plan demanded by such a step. BL estimated that, with the vastly improved production facilities in the Midlands, the 4-door would account for four out of every five Range Rover sales, and rightly so: by 1984, on the home market, the 4-door had taken over 90% of Range Rover sales. Having been assembled for so long on a split track in cramped conditions alongside Land Rovers, the Range Rover's move into its own premises meant that, for the first time in its history, supply would have a chance to catch up with demand. All of this tied in with the massive £200 million investment programme which was instigated by Sir Michael Edwardes, and was the cornerstone of the BL recovery plan of the early eighties.

The site – North Works – is based on the old Rover 2000 factory which was totally gutted, renovated and extended to house the new complex, of 1 million square feet – or the equivalent of 10 football pitches. The high-technology plant cost £85 million to build and is effectively two factories under one roof, as it accommodates the Land Rover, in part, as well as the Range Rover.

Interior of the 4-door Range Rover, with left-hand side doors removed for the photograph.

The 4-door Range Rover was expected to account for 80 per cent of Range Rover sales.

The objectives were to up-date and improve their products, invest in new machinery for higher standards of quality and increased productivity, and also to improve the working environment. Originally the investment plan included development of facilities at Canley, not far from Solihull, but Mike Hodgkinson managed to convince the BL board of the advantages and good sense in keeping Range Rover and Land Rover together at Solihull – hence the blossoming of the North Works. Credit was also largely due to Mike Hodgkinson for the development that took place on both vehicles during his period as Managing Director of Land Rover Limited – before this, the emphasis was chiefly on increased output, rather than product refinement and development.

The move into North Works was effected early in 1981, giving 2-door and 4-door Range Rovers their own separate, self-contained assembly plant and paint shop, covering 565,000 square feet, divided up into six main areas: body and engine assembly; final assembly and trim; storage, panel preparation and paint; rectification and paint inspection; rolling road testing; and customer assurance line and final quality clearance. The manufacture of Range Rovers is by advanced mechanical handling systems, and stringently applied quality controls. The area of the plant assigned to Range Rover manufacture cost £15 million to complete and equip; it offers a capability of producing up to 600 vehicles a week, on two work shifts. The rate of production of each model is flexible according to market demand. This is a built-in feature of the plant, allowing variants to be accommodated readily.

This philosophy of meeting as many sectors of the market as possible, without detracting from the integral performance or quality of the product, led not only to the introduction of the 4-door Range Rover, but to the up-dating and refining of the 2-door model. This was first carried out in 1979, about six months after the introduction of the V8 engined Land Rover. By then improvements were long overdue, but the 1970s had not been a time for expansion of product development. Until Mike Hodgkinson took up the reins, and had access to the kind of funds that enabled progress in this direction, the Range Rover had quite simply failed to evolve and keep pace with the times. Having arrived on the scene with an impact and opened up an entirely new, dual-purpose, 4-wheel-drive market in 1970, by 1979 it was badly needing a face-lift. Many details of interior trim were up-graded, the air-conditioning unit was at last incorporated in the dashboard instead of on the cab roof, and the external lettering of RANGE ROVER was altered to adhesive plastic strip, easily applied and eliminating the rust-factor of the former individually mounted letters, as well as making cleaning more practical on the bonnet and tailgate. In 1981 further-reaching modifications were carried out so there were then two different basic versions of the vehicle assembled in Solihull: the standard improved model, and the 'Fleetline', which evolved in accordance with the requirements of a specific outlet, namely fleet-users (and the police in particular), and those wanting the Range Rover's combination of load-carrying capacity and speed, without the de-luxe fittings. In 1984, some three years after the introduction of the 4-door model, the original Fleetline model started to be phased out because by then over 90% of the UK market was using the 4-door unit. While a 2-door unit is still manufactured in limited quantity, the rather down-market vinyl seats, manual steering and uncarpeted floor of the Fleetline have gone forever: upholstered seats, power-assisted steering, and carpets are obviously a necessary part of the Range Rover, for fleet-users as well as the private owner.

As part of its efforts to widen the vehicle's appeal to the fleet market, Land Rover Limited has authorized a liquified petroleum gas conversion to be carried out by Landi-Hartog Limited, either on existing vehicles or to be ordered as a built-in feature. Liquified petroleum gas (LPG) is considerably cheaper than petrol for a VAT-registered company: currently, it costs about £1.41 a gallon as opposed to £1.85 or thereabouts for a gallon of petrol. Even though fuel consumption is higher, it is possible to make significant savings if mileages are sufficiently high. In the Landi-Hartog installation the normal fuel tank is reduced from 18 to 7½ gallons, and two LPG cylinders of a 6¾ gallon capacity give a total fuel capacity of 21 gallons. The LPG tanks are fixed below the floor of the vehicle, so that the load space is not affected. The fuel source can be changed while on the move by operating a simple rocker switch on the fascia, and the difference in performance between LPG and petrol is slight. LPG is a cleaner fuel than petrol and reduces pollution from exhaust emission, while it is also supposed to prolong engine life. In Holland – the base of the parent company of Landi-Hartog – 600,000 cars and vans are using it. With the introduction of the 110-inch V8 engine Land Rover, the same application can also of course be made to the Land Rover.

The conversion of the 2-door Range Rover to a 4-door model was executed by shortening the existing doors, converting the B-posts to BC-posts and inserting the D-posts to marry-up with the trailing edge of the rear doors. At the same time the rear seat was moved back 3 inches and the heelboard was realigned, retaining its original base-line and sloping backwards to meet the rear seat pan. This layout had, in fact, been schemed and built as a non-running prototype as early as 1972 (on a K registered vehicle) (see photo), but finances were not available and the scheme was shelved, to be dusted off and revitalised 10 years later. These modifications resulted in good access to the rear of the car while also giving increased leg room for rear seat passengers. To increase fuel economy and reduce noise, the compression ratio was raised and a low lift camshaft was introduced. This gave revised valve timing and lift, and meant that maximum power was achieved at 4,000 rpm instead of 5,000 rpm. The crankcase was stiffened, also with a view to reducing noise, by the use of lasers. The combination of higher compression ratio and revised valve timing increased torque – both maximum values and at lower speeds, which enabled the transfer ratio to be changed from 1.113 to 1 to 0.9962 to 1, increasing the overall vehicle gearing from 21.23 mph to 23.72 mph at 1,000 rpm in top gear, with consequent improved fuel economy but without affecting performance. The carburettors and ignition distributor were retuned to meet the changed engine characteristics, and sliding contact breakers were incorporated in the distributor, greatly improving contact breaker point life and maintaining more consistent ignition timing over higher mileages.

The most common criticisms of the old Range Rover tended to revolve around the inconvenience of access to the rear seats, the lack of legroom in the rear seats, the weight of the wide front doors when being opened or closed, the inconvenience of the wide front doors when opened in a restricted parking space, and the noise. The new 4-door conversion set out to rectify all of these points as neatly and efficiently as possible. By repositioning the rear seat 3 inches further back, the space behind the rear seats was reduced, but when the rear seats were folded down the interior load space was just the same as it always had been. In effect, therefore, better and more practical use was made of the interior space, without any alteration to the length of the wheelbase or any external dimensions. Now that there were two doors to do the job of one, the front door came down to a manageable scale in terms of weight and size, while the noise problem was tackled by revising the machining of the helix gears in the transfer box. This combined with the revised gate layout introduced in 1980, not only reduced the internal mechanical noise but made gear changes a great deal smoother. The compression ratio was increased from 8.13 to 9.35 to 1 (4-star petrol became a standard requirement, as opposed to the former 2-star requirement). Other refinements in 4-door models included a new windscreen wash/wipe system which was probably the most comprehensive ever developed. Mounted on a single stalk from the steering column, it combined a 2-speed wiper, single flick wipe, delayed interval wipe and an adjustable wipe cycle after windscreen washing. The interior light now remained on automatically while the ignition key was inserted, on a delay system – and if the key was already in place but a passenger was alighting, it stayed on for a shorter period. There were two lamps to light up the engine bay when the bonnet was lifted, and every model was fitted with twin door-mounted stereo speakers, wing-mounted aerial and full wiring (though not the radio/stereo equipment itself, obviously). The interior detail of the vehicle received considerable attention, and the result went a long way towards elevating the Range Rover to the luxury limousine category, with its vanity mirror on the passenger sun visor, lockable centre console with ashtray for rear seat passengers, elasticated map pockets on the back of both front seats, carpeted spare wheel cover, tool box cover and rear wheel arches, a ticket pocket on the driver's sun visor, and childproof locks on the rear doors (of the 4-door model). In addition to all these new standard fittings, there was a special option pack available for the 4-door vehicle – at a cost of £750 extra, or £1,575 including air-conditioning – to raise the image still further. This consisted of alloy wheels, wood veneer door cappings, metallic paint, and fully carpeted loadspace and interior of tailgate. One thousand 2-door Range

Rovers were built to incorporate these de-luxe extras as a limited edition, fulfilling a demand which was sparked off after one had been produced as a promotion for *Vogue* Magazine, for a photographic session in the South of France. It went by the name of 'In Vogue Range Rover', and was available in pale metallic Vogue Blue, or metallic Silver Birch. The price included air-conditioning and a matching picnic hamper, as well as the luxury optional extras.

A variety of amendments and alterations have been made to the Range Rover from time to time over the years. One of these was the inevitable inclusion of power-assisted steering, several years after its introduction, without which it was almost impossibly heavy to handle in traffic, or to park, although adequate for cross-country purposes. The main reason this feature wasn't incorporated in the original Range Rover package was the attitude of the old Land Rover die-hards, whose firm belief was that unless it was hefty and cumbersome to drive, it would be a danger to humanity. During this early period engineers were coming up with all sorts of potential improvements, most of which were shelved, but which would eventually appear in some form or another, once the stagnation period was over. Even the puritans eventually had to admit that its success was largely attributable to its curious mixture of characteristics – a tough performer, but smooth to handle and a pleasure to ride in – and began to recognize that ease of handling, speed and comfort need not necessarily be synonymous with fashionable, flimsily built, short-life cars. It is perhaps worth mentioning here that another argument in favour of four doors on the Range Rover came from certain sectors of the overseas market. In areas where security has to be a priority, potential customers would decline to buy a Range Rover for fear of being trapped in the back seats in the event of an ambush. It was rugged enough and fast enough, but the 2-door aspect was a definite deterrent. This also applies to the military market to a certain extent, where no real place for the Range Rover has been found. As a field car, the Land Rover still meets most of the cross-country demands, and less specialized 2-wheel-drive vehicles are considered adequate for the transport of officers and higher-ranking personnel on the road. So far, what the Range Rover has to offer has been beyond the requirements of the military user – though it is rumoured that they are used by the SAS on special operations.

When the Range Rover was announced in 1970 its market was, as has been said, somewhat vague, but it was a very short time before it attracted overseas attention. By 1975, two-thirds of the Range Rovers that were being produced were being exported, and this figure has never diminished. The up-grading of the Range Rover has become an integral part of its survival, and in 1983 it was the turn of the transmission to come under scrutiny. The end result was a two-fold development: the purpose-designed 5-speed manual gearbox, of great benefit to the long distance motorist, and the option of a fully automatic gearbox, with all the advantages of a high and low range transfer box. On its release, Land Rover gave us the loan of an automatic Range Rover for a couple of weeks to try it out. Dubious about the off-road handling, we determined to put it through its paces on hills, fields, rough tracks and beaches; a thousand miles later we had to admit to being impressed. The machine looked after itself very nicely, minimising the gap in the gear-change in dicey conditions, and generally saving on transmission wear-and-tear (not to mention driver wear-and-tear!). Up to now the Range Rover market has not extended to the United States, partly because in the past it failed to reach the necessary regulation standards, but the demand for 4 x 4 vehicles in America being what it is, this is surely a market worth attaining. Jaguar have already set a fine example by showing with what kind of success the British product can be received, but the potential for a top-quality all-terrain motor in America, with such vast tracts of rugged country and open desert to utilize, is without doubt a great deal more significant. The quality-conscious Managing Director of Land Rover Ltd, Tony Gilroy, ought now to be able to reap the benefits of his philosophy.

At the same time as the launch of the 90-inch Land Rover in 1984, Range Rover was ready to announce its latest series of refinements and design improvements, aimed to give greater value-for-money. In 1982 it had won the Design Council's award for "excellence in design and in recognition of an outstanding product from British industry", and in the same year the automatic transmission option was introduced. In 1983 the 5-speed manual gearbox option arrived and also in that year Range Rover production exceeded 12,000 vehicles; sales at home and in Europe were the best-ever. When the latest improvements were announced, Land Rover proudly boasted that over 400 changes had been made to the vehicle, all with the customer in mind. Be that as it may, the net result is unquestionably superior to all former models, and the list of modifications includes, internally, an entirely new instrument binnacle (with 15 warning lights), illuminated switches to operate all the lights and the rear window heater, an intermittent wipe-facility on the rear wash/wipe, a fascia-mounted clock, a 20-fuse fuse panel, side window demisting vents, new door trim (changing the position of handles and speakers), improved heater (with pipes to rear-seat passengers on the top-of-the-range models), and reclining front seats (not on 2-door models) which are also height-adjustable, as are the new seat belts. Externally, improvements include one-piece windows on the front doors to enhance visibility and reduce wind noise, aerodynamic mirrors, and easier-to-close upper tail gate (which also operates a new courtesy light).

The 'In-Vogue' limited edition of Range Rovers proved so popular that an equivalent super-deluxe model is now standard at the top of the range, known simply as the 'Vogue'. This model, launched concurrently with the improved standard 4-door and 2-door Range Rover, features such nice touches as electrically heated and remote controlled mirrors, electrically operated windows front and rear, headlight pressure washers, wooden door trims, front and rear headrests (as well as rear seat belts which were already standard on the

'In-Vogue' version), digital stereophonic audio system with four speakers, sumptuous grey upholstery and a clever cover for the rear load space which can be conveniently stowed when not required. Power-assisted steering is standard on all Range Rovers, as are servo-assisted disc brakes on all four wheels. We had the privilege of driving a Vogue model off-the-road just prior to its coming onto the market, and with automatic transmission as well as all the comfort and convenience elements, of superb seat-support, electric windows, mirrors, top quality sound system and so forth, it was genuinely impossible to make driving over fields and up rutted lanes, or through squelching muddy swamps and rocky streams, the least bit uncomfortable! All in all, the Range Rover has reached the stage of development where to drive it, no matter where, is to be instantly convinced of its supremacy in its class.

The following gives a resumé of the basic specification and the vital statistics of the 4-door and improved 2-door Range Rovers:

Engine: High compression 'economy' engine: eight cylinders in V formation, aluminium alloy construction with five bearing crankshaft and self-adjusting hydraulic tappets. Bore 88.9mm (3.5in). Stroke 71.1mm (2.8in). Cubic capacity 3,528cc (215 cu in). Compression ratio 9.35:1. Max power 93.2kW (125 DIN bhp) at 4,000 rpm. Max torque 258 Nm (190 lb/ft) at 2,500 rpm.

Transmission: Main gearbox incorporating four forward and one reverse speeds, manually operated with synchromesh on all forward gears. Transfer box on main gearbox output giving high and low ratios on all main gearbox speeds. Front and rear drive permanently engaged via a third differential which may be locked by a vacuum control switch. Overall ratios (final drive):

	High Transfer	Low Transfer
Top:	3.52:1	11.76:1
Third:	5.31:1	17.69:1
Second:	8.63:1	28.78:1
First:	14.34:1	47.84:1
Reverse:	12.92:1	43.07:1

Axles: Beam type axles front and rear incorporating hypoid spiral-bevel type differentials and fully floating axle shafts. Differential ratio 3.54:1. Front axle incorporates enclosed constant velocity joints.

Suspension: Long travel coil spring suspension. Axle location by radius arms (front and rear) with Panhard rod (front) and support rods and central wishbone assembly (rear). Control by long-stroke hydraulic telescopic dampers. Rear suspension incorporates self-energizing ride-levelling unit.

Brakes: Lockheed hydraulic disc brakes on all four wheels with servo-assistance and dual circuit piping. Drum-type handbrake operating on transfer box rear output shaft.

Steering: Adwest Varamatic power-assisted steering with damper and safety column, 3.5 turns lock to lock; or manual steering employing Burman recirculating ball, worm and nut system, 4.75 turns lock to lock.

Wheels and tyres: Styled pressed steel wheels, five stud fixing, size 6.00JK x 16, fitted with 205 x 16 tube type dual purpose radial tyres. Optional cast aluminium alloy wheels, size 7.00K x 16.

Fuel system: 82 litre (18 imp gallon) fuel tank, located between rear chassis frame members, feeding two Zenith-Stromberg carburettors via a Bendix electric pump.

Basic construction: Welded box section chassis protected by two galvanizing dips and an electrophoretic paint dip. Pressed steel body frame fitted with bolt-on body panels, most of which are of lightweight, corrosion-resistant aluminium alloy.

Heating and ventilation: Through-flow heating and ventilation system with two-speed fan providing fresh or recirculated air. Adjustable individual face level vents and rear quarter panel extracter grilles.

Windscreen wipers and washers: Single steering-column-mounted stalk operates two wiper speeds, flick wipe, intermittent wipe and programmed wash and wipe sequence. Single speed rear wash and wipe system operates from dashboard mounted rocker switch.

Seating: Individual orthopaedically designed front seats incorporating integral inertia-reel safety harnesses. 2-door vehicles are fitted with a mechanism allowing seat to tip and slide forward for ease of access to rear seat. Rear seat accommodates three passengers and may be folded to increase payload area.

Instrumentation: Main binnacle incorporates speedometer, fuel gauge, water temperature gauge, odometer, trip recorder and twelve warning lights. Supplementary instruments consist of battery voltmeter, oil pressure gauge, oil temperature gauge and electric lock. Soft green instrument illumination is switchable.

Electrical supply: 12-volt negative earth system incorporating 65 amp output alternator and 60 amp-hour battery.

Lighting: Quartz-halogen headlamps (60 watt main beam, 55 watt dipped beam), sidelamps, indicator lamps with hazard warning system, stop/tail lamps, reversing lamps, rear fog-guard lamps, number plate lamps, twin interior courtesy lamps with delay system, automatic underbonnet inspection lamps (except the Fleetline model).

Miscellaneous: Padded sun-visors with vanity mirror (passenger's side) and ticket pocket (driver's side), tinted glass with laminated windscreen, child safety locks on rear door (4-door model), integral parcel tray/passenger grab handle, spacious glovebox (except with air-conditioning option), provision for radio installation, opening quarter vents, two exterior rear view mirrors (door mounted), cigar lighter, heated rear window, lockable fuel filler cap, rear mud flaps.

*   *   *

1988: Range Rover has continued to evolve in line with consumer demand, its invasion of North America meant adaptations to its basic spec which, naturally, it has easily taken in its stride. On this side of the Atlantic the turbo-charged diesel is becoming a popular option, while the carburettor-equipped V 8 petrol has been dropped in favour of the EFI version.

The idea of 'dieselizing' Range Rover has been around nearly as long as the vehicle itself, but in practice it hasn't been easy to achieve because nothing came up to scratch, until the Italian specialists in tailor-made diesel units, Stabilimenti Meccanici VM SpA, were identified. The two firms worked hand-in-hand to develop and prove one of the most powerful, lightweight diesel engines of its class available anywhere. If development was laborious, proving was gruelling, but it paid off, and with only 2393 cc, the engine produces 112 bhp at 4200 rpm, maximum torque 183 lb ft at 2400 rpm. This translates into 0-60 mph time of less than 19 seconds, and a top speed of over 90 mph. This is certainly a very robust stablemate for its V 8 counterpart which, though it may be noisier, is a lot less thirsty.

In the middle of 1988 the Range Rover range has progressed to encompass many variants: four doors, turbo diesel, petrol fuel injection, 5-speed manual or 4-speed automatic transmissions. Optional extras include electric tilt-and-slide sunroof and air conditioning, but new standard incorporated features are horizontal-bar radiator grille, concealed bonnet hinges, fuel filler flap operated through the central door lock mechanism (one key for all locks), and the lower tailgate release has been relocated on the inside for convenience and added security – and it's a lot less dirty to handle!

Inside there's a revised steering column shroud, stronger central stalks, 16-inch diameter 2-spoke steering wheel, and warning lights for washer and brake fluid. The rear seat now divides asymmetrically for greater passenger/load carrying versatility.

Range Rover's latest and most aristocratic flagship is the Vogue SE which has the features like air conditioning, in-car sound system, automatic transmission, electric tilt-and-slide sunroof, and Pembroke grey leather upholstery on electrically operated seats all as standard specification, the whole image completed by polished walnut door pulls and cappings. It all makes one wonder how much further up market it is possible to go.

1989: For 1989 Range Rover has been developed further with increased interior refinement, including new colour schemes, trims, door inners and better heating and ventilation, and four new exterior colour schemes. More important, however, are the technical changes which include a new transfer gearbox which uses a Morse drain and sprocket drive system in place of the earlier two-speed helical arrangement. A viscous control unit is included in the transfer box which controls the centre differential in slippery driving conditions.

Range Rover Facts & Figures

Engine	*2.4 Turbo D*	*3.5 V8 pi*	*3.9pi*
Type	4 in line	V 8	V8
Bore/Stroke	92 x 90 mm	88.9 x 71.1 mm	–
Comp ratio	21.5:1	9.35:1	–
Cubic capacity	2393 cc	3528 cc	–
Output	112.6 bhp (84 kw) @ 4200 rpm	165 bhp (123 kw) @ 4750 rpm	178 bhp @ 4750 rpm
Torque	248 Nm (183 lb ft) @ 2400 rpm	280 Nm (207 lb ft) @ 3200 rpm	297 Nm (220 lb ft) @ 3250 rpm

Performance	*Turbo D*	*V 8 Manual*	*V 8 Automatic*
0-60 mph	18.5 sec	11.6 sec	11.9 sec
Max speed	91.4 mph	107.5 mph	104 mph

Fuel consumption			
Simulated Urban cycle	25.6 mpg	15.4 mpg	14.6 mpg
Constant 56 mph	34.1 mpg	27.2 mpg	26.2 mpg
Constant 75 mph	24.4 mpg	20.9 mpg	20.2 mpg

Transmission
No. of Gears:

Turbo D & V 8	5 speed
V 8 auto	4 speed

Transfer box
Ratios:

High	1.222
Low	3.321

Dimensions

Wheelbase	2540 mm (100 in)
Length	4449 mm (175 in)
Width	1818 mm (72 in)
Height	1792 mm (71 in)

Kerbweight:

Turbo D	2016 kg
V 8 manual	1927 kg
V 8 auto	1971 kg

General
Wheels:

Turbo D	6.00K x 16	or 7.00 K x 16
	Steel	alloy
Tyres	Michelin XM + S 200 205 R16	
Fuel tank	79.5 l (17.5 imp gal)	
Suspension	Coil springs	
	Panhard Rod	
Dampers	Hydraulic	
Towing Capacity:		
Unbraked	750 kg	
Braked	4000 kg	

RANGE ROVER UPDATE
by James Taylor

From the point of view of product development, the five-year period from 1989 to 1994 was one of the busiest in the Range Rover's entire history. It was a period characterized by the enlarged V8 petrol engines of 3.9 and 4.2 litres, and by no fewer than three new turbodiesel power units, each one an improvement on the last. It was a period in which the Range Rover was moved even further up-market, to smooth the way for the autumn 1994 introduction of the long-anticipated 'new' Range Rover. It was a period in which US sales became increasingly important, and in which US market demands to a great

Early 3-door Range Rover on St Kitts.

extent dictated the direction in which the Range Rover was developed, and above all it was a period in which the Range Rover fought off serious challenges from newer vehicles such as the 1989 Toyota LandCruiser VX and the 1991 Mitsubishi Shogun to remain the king of the luxury off-roaders. Sales certainly did drop – from over 28,000 in 1989 to less than 18,000 in 1993 – but a large proportion of those lost went to Land Rover's own Discovery.

Many people were surprised to find that the Range Rover is not a single vehicle but a whole model range. At the beginning of the 1990s there were already 2-door and 4-door bodies, plus van versions of the 2-door for certain markets. In addition, the Range Rover was available in chassis/cab form (that is, with front panels, windscreen and doors) for special bodywork. Those were just the basics: there were of course both petrol and diesel engines and both manual and automatic gearboxes.

By the middle of the 1990s, the basic variants had been increased by one – the long-wheelbase model with 108 inches between axle centres, which was introduced in autumn 1992. Two variants had also gone out of production when the last 2-door model was built in early 1994, and with it went the Range Rover van. However, the model range still remained complicated. In addition to the chassis/cab, buyers could order a base-model 4-door, and Vogue 4-door, a more luxurious Vogue SE 4-door, or the top-model, long-wheelbase Vogue LSE. In the USA the model range began with the Range Rover County, went up to the County SE and on to the County LWB.

Then there have been the special limited editions – the CSK 2-door of 1990, and the Brooklands Green 4-door of 1992 for the UK, the GDE (Great Divide Edition) in the USA, and a score of others with different names and

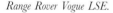
Range Rover Vogue LSE.

specifications all over the world. How about a Silver Fox or a Silver Spring in France, an Ascot in Germany, or a Countryman or a Balmoral in Spain? All have their own combinations of features from the Range Rover options list and sometimes a few unique items, in each case carefully chosen for maximum appeal in their intended markets.

The sheer complication of it all can be immensely confusing, and the simplest way of understanding what has happened to the Range Rover in these last five years is to look at the basic building blocks on which this wide variety of models has been created. These are most conveniently divided up into four sections: Powertrain, New features, Exterior changes and Interior changes.

Powertrain
Right through this five-year period the standard Range Rover engine has been the 3.9-litre petrol V8, always equipped with fuel injection and always available with an exhaust catalyst. The catalyst was not standard in all markets until autumn 1992, however. Before then, non-catalyst engines enjoyed a 10 bhp power advantage over the 178 bhp catalyst-equipped engines with their lower compression ratios. By 1992 Land Rover's powertrain engineers had developed the engine to a point where it pumped out 182 bhp in high-compression catalyst-equipped form and so this engine was standardized for all markets. There are those who argue that the 3.9-litre V8, especially in catalyst-equipped form, sometimes feels more strained than the older 3.5-litre engine, but performance figures give the larger engine a clear advantage on the road with or without an exhaust catalyst.

Even so, Land Rover needed more power for the long-wheelbase Range Rovers introduced in 1992. The 8 inches of length added weight – about 360 lb of it – and it would clearly never had done to allow this to make the flagship model *slower* than the cheaper models on the 100 inch wheelbase. A very much more powerful version of the venerable V8 was under development with a 'new' Range Rover in the early 1990s but Land Rover decided to keep their powder dry for the time being. So the 1992 long-wheelbase Range Rover had what was simply a long-stroke version of the 3.9-litre engine, displacing 4.2 litres. With 200 bhp and a useful torque increase, it made the Vogue LSE (or County LWB in the USA) marginally faster than the standard-wheelbase model, but there were many owners who found its performance disappointing.

In Britain and the USA, the popularity of the petrol V8 tended to obscure the fact that the Range Rover was also available with a diesel engine, and few people realized that 40 per cent of all new Range Rovers were by this stage being delivered with diesel power. The advantages were obvious: fuel consumption could be as much as 50 per cent better with the diesel engine, and in many countries diesel fuel was also cheaper to buy than petrol. The disadvantages were also obvious: diesel engines offered reduced road performance together with increased levels of noise and vibration, characteristics not generally welcome in the luxury car market. In 1989, therefore, the diesel engines could only be had in base-model Range Rovers; but attitudes changed quite quickly. The early 1990s saw a rash of diesel-engined special editions in Europe and for the 1991 model year it was possible to buy a diesel Vogue, while from early 1994 customers were offered the diesel engine coupled to automatic transmission as an option in the luxuriously equipped Vogue SE.

The 1990s opened with a Range Rover Turbo D powered by a 119 bhp 2.5-litre edition of the VM diesel engine which had been introduced in October 1989 to replace the original 112 bhp 2.4-litre type. However, it would only be a matter of time before this was abandoned in favour of Land Rover's own 200 Tdi engine, the direct-injection 2.5-litre first seen in Discovery in 1989 and widely acclaimed for its excellent driveability and fuel economy.

The problem with the Tdi engine was that it was noisy – too noisy for a vehicle of the Range Rover's class, but by 1992 the Land Rover engineers had reduced its diesel clatter to more acceptable levels, and so the Range Rover Turbo D became a Range Rover Tdi for 1993. With just 111 bhp the Tdi-engined model lost out to 119 bhp 2.5-litre Turbo D on top speed, but in all other respects it was a major improvement. Fuel economy was outstanding and a Range Rover Tdi achieved an astonishing 53 mpg during an economy run from Land's End to John O'Groats shortly after the model's launch. Even in everyday use, 30 mpg was within easy reach.

Refinement work on the Tdi engine continued and in March 1994 Land Rover announced that the 200 Tdi was being replaced by a revised version known as the 300 Tdi. They claimed considerable reductions in noise levels, although strangely had not increased maximum power or maximum torque. In

Range Rover Tdi.

countries like Switzerland and Germany, where the diesel engine was equipped with an exhaust catalyst to meet forthcoming regulations, performance and economy both suffered slightly; but the 300 Tdi looked like proving every bit as admirable as its 200 Tdi predecessor.

All the Range Rovers of the 1990s had the Borg Warner chain-driven transfer box with viscous-coupled centre differential which had been introduced in 1988; most petrol models came with a 4-speed ZF automatic transmission as their primary gearbox, while all diesels until early 1994 had the 5-speed manual transmission which was also available in petrol models. The original 5-speed LT77 gearbox was modified for the 1992 model year, to offer easier gear selection and was thereafter known as the LT77S. It went out of production in early 1994, however, and was replaced by the new R380 5-speed gearbox which had a very much more car-like change action, and revised shift pattern with reverse behind fifth instead of out to the left of first. When the R380 arrived on Range Rovers, the ZF automatic also became available behind the new 300 Tdi diesel engine.

New features

Now that the Range Rover was competing with sophisticated luxury cars such as the BMW 7-series, the Mercedes-Benz S-class and the Jaguar XJ saloons, equipment levels were of ever-increasing importance. These cars had very high levels of equipment both mechanical and electrical, and the Range Rover needed to be able to compete on equal terms. For this reason, a whole series of new features were added to the specification during the early 1990s.

The 1990 models had some important braking revisions. All models were given ventilated front disc brakes, partly, no doubt, because they were fitted to rival high-performance luxury cars, but also because the asbestos-free brake pads introduced with them generated more heat, which the ventilated discs dissipated of course. For the more expensive models, however, there was a much more important development in the shape of the sophisticated four-channel ABS system. This worked not only in normal road driving, but was also fully automatic in off-road conditions, unlike the systems favoured by Audi and Mercedes-Benz for their four-wheel drive models. A further extension of the BAS technology allowed Land Rover to introduce ETC – Electronic Traction Control – on 1993 models. This automatically pulsed the brake on a spinning rear wheel, so transferring torque to the opposite wheel through the action of the differential and thus improving traction.

The Range Rover's road manners also received attention during this period. Although actual road-holding had always been very good for a vehicle of its type, body roll on corners had long been a problem, and was certainly not in keeping with the requirement of a sophisticated luxury car. Aftermarket specialists had been offering anti-roll bars for the Range Rover since the mid-1980s and in 1990 Land Rover finally introduced their own.

These were first seen on the limited edition CSK 2-door in the autumn and were then fitted to the more expensive models as standard from that winter. They could be added optionally to lesser models – and before long, Land Rover sensibly introduced a retro-fit kit of parts which enabled older models to enjoy the same level of cornering refinement. There was one small penalty: the anti-roll bars limited axle travel by around half an inch. But very few customers ever took their Range Rovers into the sort of off-road conditions where this mattered, and most of them welcomed the softer ride which came from the new road springs supplied with the anti-roll bars.

Perhaps the most widely publicized refinement for the Range Rover in the early 1990s, however, was the Electronically Controlled Air Suspension (ECAS) introduced in 1992. This was standard on Vogue SE and Vogue LSE models (and on their equivalents in other markets), and was optional on other petrol variants. From early 1994, it was also available on the 300 Tdi diesel engine.

The air suspension looked good in the specification, and certainly added refinement, by substituting air-filled rubber bags for the steel road springs which transmitted noise from the road wheels to the interior of the car. Body roll was rather less well controlled than with conventional springs, even with the anti-roll bars which came as standard, but few buyers noticed. Most of them were more concerned with the system's other advantages.

The two most obvious of these were the most visible ones: when the vehicle exceeded 50 mph, the ECAS lowered the body on its air springs to reduce drag and improve stability, while when the vehicle was at rest the ECAS lowered the body still further to aid access and loading. Yet these were just two of the five height settings available. The third was normal running height – equivalent to the standard ride height with conventional springs – and above that came a manually selectable 'high' setting, which increased the ground clearance for off-roading. Right at the top was Extended Profile which was not really a running height at all but rather a feature which automatically extended the wheels

Tom Collins' Driving School, Colorado.

downwards to retain traction if the vehicle had bellied out while off-roading and the wheels had lost contact with the ground altogether.

Exterior changes
With the exception of the long-wheelbase shell, in which the rear doors had been lengthened, the 1995 Range Rover looked very much like a 1989 model from the outside. Yet there had been a whole collection of subtle changes. Thus the 1991 models were the first to have concealed front door hinges while the front spoiler had extra cooling slots in its lower edge after 1991 (after 1989 on Vogue SE models) and was fitted to diesel as well as petrol models after autumn 1990. Then there were other details, like the higher-mounted filler cap on 1991 and later models (which used the Discovery's plastic fuel tank with its longer filler neck), and like the increasing numbers of vehicles ordered with the single coach line, and body-colour wheels originally available only on the Vogue SE.

The wheels changed, too. Back in 1989, there had been either Rostyle pressed steel wheels of the original pattern for the basic models, or three-spoke alloys for the others, either in grey or in body colour on the Vogue SE and other top models. The Rostyles soon disappeared to be replaced by Discovery-style pressed steel wheels most commonly seen in the UK on Police Range Rovers. The three-spoke alloys were supplemented by five-spoke alloys for the 1991 model year, by star-pattern alloys designed by TWR for 1993, and by eight-hole alloys on the long-wheelbase models for 1994. These latter were actually made available in the USA in mid-1993, although they did not reach other markets until early 1994.

A TWR-designed body kit became available as an option for the 1994 model year, after making its debut on the limited edition Brooklands Green model and its continental European equivalents in spring 1992. This body kit consisted of body-coloured front and rear aprons, and of shaped sills which were available

Range Rover fire engine, St Lucia.

in two different lengths to suit both 100-inch and 108-inch wheelbase models. Lastly, the Range Rovers introduced in early 1994 had two small black protuberances on their front bumpers, resembling overriders. These were in fact impact-absorbing 'crunch cans' designed to reduce damage in certain types of frontal collision.

Interior changes

Only small changes were made to the Range Rover's interior between 1989 and 1994, although all of them added to its luxury appeal. The 1989 models had the first new door trims since 1986, with armrests and door-pulls integrated neatly into the trim itself. A new style of upholstery with larger plain panels arrived on 1990s Range Rovers, which also had new and clear instruments in the existing binnacle, plus higher levels of soundproofing. There was then a pause until the 1993 model year ushered in a more comfortable angle of rake for the rear seat backs, together with a raised loadspace cover which gave more height to the Range Rover's 'boot'. Special wood trim in Italian Poplar was used for the Vogue SE and the long-wheelbase models only, and the LSE also had a matching fillet on the transmission selector lever.

The most far-reaching changes came in early 1994, as part of the package which included the new 300 Tdi engine. The complete dashboard was changed for a more rounded and integrated one-piece moulding which was broadly similar to the one announced at the same time for the face-lifted Discovery, but differed in a number of details. At a stroke, it did away with the problem of poor fit and poor colour match on early dashboards. Most important, however, was that this new dashboard incorporated provision of twin airbags, one on the passenger side and one mounted on the boss of the new steering wheel. It also contained a new heater, with simpler rotary controls and separate adjustment for driver and passenger sides of the vehicle. To complement the new look up

Range Rover from the Madagascar Camel Trophy event, used for promotions by Range Rover North America.

Range Rover meets Discovery in the USA, 1994.

front, the upholstery panelling changed yet again, and the overall result was an interior which looked every bit as good as those of the best luxury models with which the Range Rover was competing for sales.

Who knows how long the Range Rover will remain in production? Land Rover themselves are not sure, but certainly do not plan to stop making it until demand dwindles to a level where continued assembly is no longer economically feasible. While the long-wheelbase models disappeared in autumn 1994 with the introduction of the 'new' Range Rover, the 100-inch, 4-door model remains available and will celebrate 25 years of continuous Range Rover production in 1995. That is an astonishing record – and one of which Land Rover can be justifiably proud.

Range Rover USA

Range Rover of North America, Inc has contributed the following account of how Range Rover appeared on the American scene. Would that more markets were able to respond with the same high standards of service!

On 27 October 1986, a crisp, sunny autumn morning in the capital of the United States, Princess Alexandra and her husband, the Honourable Angus Ogilvy, drove with the new British Ambassador, Sir Antony Acland, to a small town in the Maryland countryside just outside Washington to celebrate the

'Eagle' prototype in desert testing, Arizona, August 1986.

Range Rover of North America headquarters in Lanham, Maryland.

Interior of 1987 US Range Rover developed under code name 'Eagle'. Note cruise control operating buttons in steering wheel (only available in US). Power seat switch to right of seat cushion. Leather upholstery option.

Malcolm Smith and Alan Fieuw Leading for fourth place in the 1988 Paris-Dakar Rally in their much modified Range Rover.

beginning of a new British enterprise. In Lanham they stopped at a modern office building identified with two words above the main entrance: RANGE ROVER. The words were probably a mystery to passers-by, but not to British royalty.

This was the official opening of Range Rover's American headquarters, now incorporated as Range Rover of North America, Inc. The Princess and her party were greeted by an automobile company executive, chosen by Land Rover to lead this long-awaited Range Rover invasion. Charles R Hughes had spent nearly twenty years in the American automobile industry, marketing some very distinguished marques both from Detroit and from Europe, and knew what American customers wanted. But this was his first experience with a British company, and greeting royalty was just one intriguing new aspect of the job.

His task was to build a marketing and distribution organization from scratch for a car that most Americans had never heard of, at a price well above what they were used to paying, and to establish a maintenance and service network across the continent to equal the best available from manufacturers like Mercedes, and all of this in the world's largest, most competitive market place. There were many unknowns and his staff was tiny, but on that sunny morning he told his guests that, 'Launching the number one car in its category in the world's number one market is the kind of challenge every auto executive hopes for'. A certain excitement was in the air as Princess Alexandra presented framed charters to the first of the American Range Rover dealers, and chatted with the new company's first employees, one of whom was a longtime Land Rover marketing specialist, Roger Ball. (Before leaving for America he had been working hard to forge Land Rover's close links with the Royal Geographical Society, specifically with Land Rover support for its major Karakoram Expedition.) Sent to America in 1985 to study the selling potential for Range Rover there, his research was thorough and convincing. It showed that between 1982 and 1986 sales of sports and leisure related goods had increased 400 per cent. He explored the buying patterns of the post-war 'baby boom' generation, now in their peak earning years, keen to enjoy an active lifestyle, and able to spend on leisure pursuits on an unprecedented scale. They were buying cars and boats (and planes) to take them where they wanted to go.

Of all the four-wheel drive vehicles on the American market – dominated by the venerable Jeep – he found nothing to compare with the Range Rover in quality and performance. Specific changes would have to be made, however, before it could be introduced in America, some of which would be required by law to meet safety and pollution regulations, while others would be purely to meet customer expectations, including fuel-injection and numerous electrical accessories. Americans now expect electrically-adjusted seats, cruise control, window lifts, door locks and stereo AM/FM cassette sound system on expensive imported cars. Ball also advised that the tailgate operation would be unacceptable and would have to be simplified. Many of the suggested changes would eventually be adopted for the entire Range Rover fleet, but for this market they were essential now. The result was that on the first 'Americanized' Range Rovers, launched in March 1987, everything was standard except the colour (Caspian blue metallic, Astral silver metallic, Cypress green metallic, Cassis red metallic, Chamonix white and Cambrian grey) and the leather upholstery. It was the most completely equipped Range Rover ever.

Few markets had been so thoroughly researched, or dealer networks selected with greater care, for Hughes recognised that dealerships were the key to success. He wanted only those with outstanding reputations for service and for customer satisfaction, and the numbers to be kept small – no more than sixty to start with. This entailed turning down more than 800. One requirement for becoming a dealer was to send a top mechanic to Solihull for two weeks' training at the dealer's own expense – *before* receiving delivery of the first vehicle – and another was to install the Dutch-made Stenhoj lift.

The mechanics appreciated this approach. 'I've been working on Mercedes-Benz cars for 17 years, and I'm still looking for my first trip to Stuttgart. I was very impressed with the whole thing.' (Jon Alumbaugh, veteran mechanic with Gengras Motor Cars (Mercedes/BMW/Range Rover) in Hartford Connecticut).

'It's not everyday you get overseas training. It certainly gives you a better appreciation for the product and more pride in your work when you have seen how the product is built.' (John Peterson, mechanic with Prestige Motors, Inc (Mercedes/Range Rover) in Paramus, New Jersey).

Clifford Tidman, service training instructor for Range Rover of North America, and 'chauffeur/scout master' on the UK training courses, said the Americans interacted well with their instructors and the production people. In turn, the Land Rover UK instructors and trainers were impressed with the calibre, skill level and experience of the American mechanics, who asked a lot of tough technical questions.

The course included instruction on the engine and drivetrain components, on the state-of-the-art electronic fuel injection, ignition, emission and electrical systems, and on the V 8 engine, taking it apart, reassembling it and seeing it being built in the ultra-modern Solihull plant. Should a mechanic run into difficulties, a (toll-free) service 'hotline' to the Lanham headquarters is answered by a technical specialist, there solely to assist Range Rover service people. A zone manager who has also had technical training, is assigned to every 10 dealers. For any more serious service problems two field engineers are ready to go wherever necessary. Then there is the highly qualified general manager for service, David Schworm, who tells all mechanics they can call him directly if they need to.

For a fledgling company, another challenge was to organize distribution of parts for delivery across the continent within 24 hours. To meet the challenge an agreement was made with Caterpillar, who have one of the most sophisticated distribution systems in the United States, whereby they agreed to store and distribute Range Rover parts. Their vast distribution centre in Memphis, the air cargo hub of the United States, is computer linked to every Range Rover dealer and to headquarters.

With most of the essentials in place, the Range Rover first went on sale in the United States on 16 March 1987. Demand was immediately strong, based on the numerous reports appearing in the motoring press that 'the Range Rovers are coming' a variation on Paul Revere's cry, 'The British are coming!' Dozens of favourable road tests were reported by newspaper, magazine and TV correspondents, the tests covering rugged wilderness, the Rocky Mountains, the Colorado River, the Nevada desert, winding forest roads and the nation's vast highway system. The media verdict could be summarized as follows:

'It goes everywhere it's supposed to go and it's kind of sexy, too.'

'There can be little doubt that it will be the status car of the year.'

'In suspension, interior, off-road capabilities and character, it offers far more than any American-made vehicle.'

It was also referred to as 'The ultimate Yuppiemobile', 'the car for all seasons' and the 'best bet' among four-wheel drives.

The first year sales goal was 3,000, but in reality 1987 proved a disappointing year for imported cars generally, with economic uncertainties and gyrations in the stock market leading to an unexpected slide in sales of high quality imports. Others in Range Rover's price bracket were reporting declines of up to 30 per cent, then the stock market crash of 19 October exacerbated the trend.

Difficulties encountered as the first vehicles began to arrive included lack of adequate import preparation. Customers had to wait longer, adding to the cancellation risk, and the full colour-range wasn't always available. White, surprisingly, was in great demand, having been out of favour with American luxury car buyers for some years, and the demand for leather interiors far outweighed their availability.

It was a hectic year, a year of uncertainty and of surprises, and one of great pressure for Charles Hughes' team in Lanham as they struggled to ensure an even flow of vehicles, respond to dealers' demands, handle unexpected crises. On 16 March 1988, however, the company was able to announce, 'Range Rover reported today that first-year sales in the United States were nearly 10 per cent ahead of the company's goals, and worldwide sales set new records', and Hughes said 'The Range Rover has clearly succeeded in creating its own niche at the top of the popular four-wheel drive market by virtue of its performance, prestige and price'. He praised their New York advertising agency, Grace and Rothschild, and his colleagues, naming Roger J Ball, director of marketing; John W Horner, vice president sales; Joseph S Gumienny, vice president, parts and systems; David A Schworm, general manager, service; and William E Baker, director of corporate communications.

'No one could have asked for a better team,' he said, commenting that Range Rover was in the top ranking of dealer satisfaction during the year.

Industry experts say Range Rover's American début was among the most successful introductions of any quality import, ever. The 1988 model, codenamed Messenger, reflected further modifications to suit American preferences, including sunroof, new colours and recalibrated transmission to improve in-town responsiveness.

For 1989 the improvements announced for the US model included all the new UK-market refinements together with a new 178 bhp 3.9-litre engine. The increase in engine capacity overcomes the performance penalty that US models hitherto suffered when saddled with emission control equipment.

For the company the introduction has been a stimulating experience, providing new perspectives from this competitive marketplace. There will undoubtedly be further improvements and refinements to help guarantee the Range Rover's continued international leadership in its class.

Sales statistics for Range Rover in North America stood at 3,427 for 1988. December of that year set an all-time record with the sale of 444 American Range Rovers, which was rapidly eclipsed in January 1989 when it totalled 495.

Since the above text was first published, Range Rover of North America Inc

Concours line-up of historic vehicles of the Range Rover Register at Mansell Lacey, Herefordshire in June 1987.

has ceased to exist – and Land Rover North America Inc has been born in its stead. This took place in August 1992, to mark the expansion of their product range, to include the Defender 110 after an eighteen-year time lapse since new Land Rovers were sold in the States. In 1993 the Defender 90 joined the US line-up quickly to be named the 'Four Wheeler of the Year' by *Four Wheeler* magazine. Then by the spring of 1994 the Discovery was also ready to cross the Atlantic (see Chapter 5), and a significantly revised Range Rover for 1995.

LRNA is currently developing a nation-wide network of unique retail outlets called Land Rover Centres, which will not only sell the three Land Rover models, but will also promote awareness and sell off-road equipment and services ('from adventure vacations to safari hats'). President of LRNA Charles Hughes, is again setting precedents in terms of the pursuit of excellence in the 4 x 4 world. His mission: first, take care of the customer; second, make money; and third, grow, because he is all too aware that you don't succeed in a highly competitive market (there are 29 other models of 'sport utility' vehicles to compete with) by standing still. Going on his past track record, even in tough economic times, his vision will doubtless continue to be fulfilled.

Range Rover Register
Some people reckon that the Range Rover has now achieved 'Classic Car' status, and if you define a classic car as a vehicle upon which groups of people

Below left *Discovery was launched in Canada in May 1994, attended by HRH the Princess Royal who presented a refurbished Camel Trophy Discovery to the Cornell Medical Centre for use in field research. Land Rover Canada Inc., whose HQ is in Mississauga, Ontario, is a subsidiary of Land Rover North America Inc. It was founded in 1990 and now has a network of eight independently owned dealers.*

Below right *Since 1991 Land Rover has offered an enhanced facility to its Jungle Track by opening a driver training centre, The Land Rover Driving Experience, where customers can be taught the skills of off-road driving, maximising the potential of their vehicle while protecting the countryside from abuse and damage. The Driving Experience centre comprises a large display area, conference room, waiting area and general offices while the well-known Jungle Track covers over 25 acres, with 4 1/2 miles of tracks and obstacles, including deeply rutted mud, a 2ft depth of natural water, and Log Lane, Articulation Alley, The Mound and The Steps.*

are enthused to spend time, energy and money, then certainly Range Rover has attained that status.

From its launch in 1970, to the present day, it has been polished, fondled, personalised, raced and rallied by its enthusiastic following of 4 x 4 and Land Rover Club members.

In 1985 this enthusiasm went one stage further, when the Range Rover Register was formed on 14 April at an Inaugural Meeting held at Eastnor Castle.

During 1983 and 1984 two 'Velar' owners, Brian Bashall and Geof Miller, had been at work trying to trace the 'H' registered vehicles. This came to the notice of the Association of Rover Clubs committee, and further discussions resulted in the proposal to form a separate Range Rover club.

Twenty people attended that inaugural meeting, in 1985, and the Register now boasts a membership in excess of 600. Regular shows and rallies are held nationally, a club shop sells books, clothing, memorabilia, in fact *anything* to do with Range Rover, and local monthly meetings are held around the centres. Pride of place goes, however, to the annual rally, held as near as possible to June 17, to celebrate the birthday of their pride and joy, the 'Best 4 x 4 x Far' – long may it continue.

Anyone interested should write for further information to the Club Secretary: L. Booth, 667 Lower Rainham Road, Rainham, Kent ME8 7TY.

Inaugural meeting of the Range Rover Register, headed by historic vehicle NXC 240H, with latest 4-door EFI on the horizon.

As a result of a £3 million investment programme, the long-anticipated launch of the all-new Range Rover took place in the autumn of 1994, introducing a luxury flagship model surpassing the previous Range Rover's legendary off-road capability, with greatly improved on-road ride and handling characteristics as well.

Over the years market research has shown that Range Rover customers were reluctant to see major changes in exterior styling. The design team adopted an evolutionary rather than revolutionary approach, retaining such key styling features of the classic model as the command driving position, distinctive bonnet and front end, the large glass areas, and the split tailgate.

It is slightly larger than the original with more headroom, more legroom, a larger rear seat compartment, and 50 per cent more luggage space. Burr walnut and leather are included in the interior.

It is available with three new engines. Diesel versions are powered by a derivative of BMW's 2.5-litre turbocharged and intercooled six-cylinder power unit, specially developed for Range Rover.

Land Rover's V8 was totally redesigned and rebuilt for the new Range Rover in a 4-litre version or 4.6-litre unit giving world-class performance: from 0–60 mph in 9.3 seconds, a top speed of 125 mph and producing 225 bhp and 280 lb/ft torque.

The new Range Rover has a totally new ladder-frame chassis, new front and rear suspension, and new beam axles. Automatic versions feature a

revolutionary new H-gate system for operation of all high-range and low-range functions with one lever.

Standard features include twin airbags, side impact beams, electronic air suspension, advanced anti-lock braking and a remotely controlled anti-theft system.

Exterior styling

The overall approach towards exterior styling was to create a vehicle that would be instantly recognisable as a Range Rover, but more modern-looking. While edges were more rounded, it was vital to retain the elegance of the vehicle to ensure its appeal into the twenty-first century.

4.0 V8 and 2.5 DT standard features

4–door
Side impact door beams
Superlocking and robust immobilisation

Range Rover 4.0 V8

Two remote transmitters
Permanent 4WD with viscous control centre differential
ABS
EAS
Power steering
Driver and passenger airbags
Three-spoke alloy wheels
235 tyres
Transfer box shift button (manual models)
H-gate transfer box shift (automatic models)
Cigar lighter
Anti-theft alarm system
Body electrical control module
Two map lamps
Front door puddle lamps
Radio-cassette system (10 FM pre-sets, 5 LW, 5 MW)
Lockable and illuminated glove box
Burr walnut inserts on fascia and gearchange surround
Cubby box
Side-to-side heater pack with programmed de-mist
Electric heated exterior mirrors
Electric windows with one-touch operation and anti-trap
Message centre in instrument pack
Tilt and reach adjustable steering wheel
Cloth seats with driver's height adjust
Metallic paint

4.0 SE and 2.5 DSE additional features

Heated front screen
Detachable bib spoiler
Cruise control
Five-hole alloy wheels
Trip computer
Mid-line radio-cassette system
Headlamp wash/wipe with wiper arms
Climate control
Leather seats
Heated front seats

4.6 HSE additional features

4.6 litre engine
Automatic transmission

Range Rover 4.6 HSE

Sunroof
Electric front seats with driver's memory
– lazy seat function
– exterior electric heated mirrors
– with reverse gear dipping
– panel dimmer setting
Style fog lamps
ETC
Leather steering wheel
– cruise control switches
– ICE controls
255 tyres
Rear spot lamps
Rear door puddle lamps
Front and rear footwell lamps
High-line radio-cassette CD system and sub-woofer

Burr walnut garnish rail on door casings
Cubby box with reversible lid containing cup holders
Front and rear mudflaps
Auto dimming interior mirror
Illuminated passenger vanity mirror
8 in wheels

TECHNICAL SPECIFICATION

V8 4.0 litre

Model	Range Rover 4.0 and 4.0 SE Automatic/Manual
Engine	4.0 litre V8 petrol
Cylinder head material	Aluminium
Cylinder block material	Aluminium
Number of cylinders	8
Cylinder layout	V
Bore	94.0 mm (3.70 in)
Stroke	71.0 mm (2.79 in)
Capacity	3950 cc
Valve gear	Self-adjusting hydraulic tappets ohv
Compression ratio	9.34:1
Fuel system	Lucas electronic with GEMS-ECU
Maximum power output	190 bhp (140 kW) at 4,750 rpm
Maximum torque	236 lb/ft (320 Nm) at 3,000 rpm

V8 4.6 litre

Model	Range Rover 4.6 HSE
Engine	4.6 litre V8 petrol
Cylinder head material	Aluminium
Cylinder block material	Aluminium
Number of cylinders	8
Cylinder layout	V
Bore	94.0 mm (3.70 in)
Stroke	82.0 mm (3.23 in)
Capacity	4554 cc
Valve gear	Self-adjusting hydraulic tappets ohv
Compression ratio	9.34:1
Fuel system	Lucas electronic with GEMS-ECU
Maximum power output	225 bhp (166 kW) at 4,750 rpm
Maximum torque	277 lb/ft (376.6 Nm) at 3,000 rpm

2.5 litre diesel

Model	Range Rover 2.5 DT and 2.5 DSE

273

Range Rover 4.6 HSE

Engine	2.5-litre six-cylinder turbocharged indirect injection diesel
Cylinder head material	Aluminium
Cylinder block material	Cast iron
Number of cylinders	6
Cylinder layout	In-line
Bore	80.00 mm (3.12 in)
Stroke	82.80 mm (3.26 in)
Capacity	2497 cc
Valve gear	Self-adjusting tappets ohv
Compression ratio	22.0:1
Fuel system	Bosch fully electronic DDE 2.5
Maximum power output	134 bhp (100 kW) at 4,400 rpm
Maximum torque	199 lb/ft (270 Nm) at 2,300 rpm
Turbocharger	Mitsubishi TD04-11G4
	1.2 bar (1.26 kg/cm, 18.0 lb/sq in)

Wheels

Construction	Alloy
Rim width	7J (4.6 HSE 8J)
Tyres	235/70 R16 105H
	255/65 R16 109H

Fuel

Tank capacity	Petrol – 22 gallons (100 litres)
	Diesel – 20 gallons (90 litres)

Fuel consumption

4.6 V8 automatic

	mpg	l/100 km
Urban cycle	12.8	22.1
Constant 56 mph	24.8	11.4
Constant 75 mph	20.1	14.1

	40. V8 automatic		**4.0 V8 manual**	
	mpg	l/100 km	mpg	l/100 km
Urban cycle	14.0	20.2	15.2	18.6
Constant 56 mph	26.8	10.6	27.2	10.4
Constant 75 mph	20.2	14.0	21.0	13.5

2.5 diesel manual

	mpg	l/100 km
Urban cycle	25.8	10.9
Constant 56 mph	37.9	7.5
Constant 75 mph	25.3	11.2

Weights

Gross vehicle weight	2,780 kg
EEC kerb weight	
4.0 V8 auto	2,100 kg
4.0 V8 manual	2,090 kg
4.6 V8	2,220 kg
2.5 diesel	2,115 kg

Towing weight

	On-road	Off-road
Over-run brakes	3,500 kg	1,000 kg
Without brakes	750 kg	500 kg

Performance
4.0 V8

	Manual	Automatic
Maximum speed	118 mph (190 kph)	116 mph (187 kph)

0–60 mph (0–100 kph)	9.9 (10.5) seconds	10.4 (10.9) seconds

4.6 V8
Automatic
Maximum speed — 125 mph (200 kph)
0–60 mph (0–100 kph) — 9.3 (9.9) seconds

2.5 diesel
Manual
Maximum speed — 105 mph (170 kph)
0–60 mph (0–100 kph) — 13.3 (14.3) seconds

Transmission
4.0/4.6 V8
5-speed manual R380

		mph/1,000 rpm	
Gear	*Ratio*	*High*	*Low*
5th	0.730:1	26.70	9.93
4th	1.000:1	19.44	7.23
3rd	1.397:1	13.92	5.18
2nd	2.132:1	9.12	3.39
1st	3.321:1	5.85	2.17
Reverse	3.535:1	5.50	2.04
Final drive ratio	3.540:1		
Transfer box ratio		1.216:1	3.271:1

4.0/4.6 V8
4-speed automatic

		mph/1,000 rpm	
Gear	*Ratio*	*High*	*Low*
4th	0.730:1	26.70	9.93
3rd	1.000:1	19.44	7.23
2nd	1.480:1	13.14	4.89
1st	2.480:1	7.84	2.92
Reverse	2.090:1	9.30	3.45
Final drive ratio	3.540:1		
Transfer box ratio		1.216:1	3.271:1

2.5 diesel
Manual

		mph/1,000 rpm	
Gear	*Ratio*	*High*	*Low*
5th	0.730:1	26.70	9.93
4th	1.000:1	19.44	7.23
3rd	1.397:1	13.92	5.18
2nd	2.132:1	9.12	3.39
1st	3.692:1	5.27	1.96
Reverse	3.535:1	5.50	2.04

Final drive ratio   3.540:1
Transfer box ratio   1.216:1   3.271:1

Dimensions

Overall length   185.6 in (4,713 mm)
Overall width   74.4 in (1,889 mm)
Overall height   71.6 in (1,817 mm) at standard ride height
Wheelbase   108.1 in (2,745 mm)
Track front   60.6 in (1,540 mm)
Track rear   60.2 in (1,530 mm)

Luggage capacity
Rear seat up   18.5 cu ft (0.52 cu m)
Rear seats down   50.0 cu ft (1.64 cu m)
Ground clearance   8.43 in (214 mm)

Approach angle	*No bib spoiler*	*With bib spoiler*
Standard	34	31
High	37	34

Departure angle (to exhaust)	*Petrol*	*Diesel*
Standard	23	24
High	25	26

Ramp angle	
Standard	154
High	151

Wading   20 in (0.5 m)

Suspension

Electronic air suspension
Front
Variable rate air springs   3.7 bar (44–103 lb/sq in)
Anti-roll bar thickness   31 mm

Beam axle located by cranked radius arms and panhard rod

Rear
Variable rate air springs   3.7 bar (44–103 lb/sq in)

Beam axle located by composite trailing link and panhard rod

Steering

Type	Recirculating ball (power assisted)
	Height and reach adjustable standard on all models
Turns lock-to-lock	3.2
Turning circle	38 ft 11 in (11.85 m) kerb to kerb

Brakes

Front	11.7 in dia (297 mm) ventilated discs
Rear	12.0 in dia (304 mm) solid discs
ABS	Four-channel anti-lock system standard on all models
Parking brake	Transmission brake drum on rear output from transfer

Chapter 5
The Discovery Story
by James Taylor

Land Rover changed a great deal during the 1980s; the company that announced the enormously successful Discovery in 1989 was very different from the demoralized organization to have been granted a long overdue injection of investment capital in 1978. Without a shadow of doubt, the responsibility for these very positive changes can be laid at the door of Tony Gilroy, who was the Managing Director of Land Rover Limited from 1982 until 1988.

Gilroy had inherited a company on a downward trend, despite the major investments in new models which had been made over the previous five years. Revitalized Range Rovers in 1979, 4-door models in 1981 and automatics in 1982 had helped maintain sales of the company's flagship model world-wide, but sales of Land Rover utilities were slipping badly. Even the new coil-sprung 110 introduced early in 1983 was not likely to reverse the trend dramatically, because the problem was that Japanese manufacturers had successfully captured the lion's share of the 4 x 4 utility market in Africa from the Land Rover. It was not that the Japanese vehicles were better, on the contrary, but the fact was that they were cheaper and their manufacturers provided a very much better service back-up than Land Rover.

Until this point, Land Rover had relied on the knowledge that their products were the best engineered vehicles of their type. Land Rovers had traditionally sold on their reputation, and customers in underdeveloped countries had been prepared to make allowances for delays in ordering spare parts from Solihull, secure in the knowledge that when the parts eventually arrived, they would be easy enough to fit and that the vehicle would then carry on reliably for several more years. But when the Japanese manufacturers established car dealerships in all the major townships and used these to provide rapid spare parts back-up and cheap servicing for their 4 x 4 products as well, Land Rover simply could not compete. So effective had the Japanese invasion been that Land Rover knew it would take many years to win back their former customers – if indeed they ever could.

It was obvious to Tony Gilroy that the whole focus of the company's operations would have to change if it was to survive. Range Rover sales were already increasing, but they would not offset a dramatic fall in Land Rover sales if that were to occur. So Gilroy set in motion a thorough review of Land Rover's markets all over the world, to see where there was scope for expansion and to determine what the company could do to guarantee its own survival.

The review was completed by the early part of 1986, but some of its recommendations had already become obvious. One of them was that Land Rover should take the Range Rover into the American market, and work had in fact already begun to prepare the vehicle for American customers. But the most exciting of all was that the company should design and build a completely new vehicle to compete in the Personal Transport Sector of the 4 x 4 market. This market sector had emerged only quite recently, and consisted of buyers who used a 4 x 4 estate as everyday transport in preference to a conventional car or two-wheel drive estate. By the mid-1980s, it was almost the exclusive preserve of Japanese manufacturers, who had created it with cheaper Range Rover imitators like the Isuzu Trooper and Mitsubishi Shogun.

If Land Rover were to meet their sales targets and profit margins, they needed this new vehicle on sale during 1989 – just over three years away when the industry norm for designing and developing a new vehicle was five years. To meet that major challenge, the company therefore pioneered a new project team approach, which it hoped would minimise delays during the pre-production phases of the project. In the event, the scheme worked brilliantly.

The beginning

The secret of the new project's existence remained well guarded for around two years. Then snippets of information leaked out to the press. Land Rover was working on a new mini-Range Rover. Land Rover was working on something called Project J. Scoop photographers pictured some prototypes on test, vehicles which looked very much like Range Rovers but which were wearing GRP cladding over their rear bodies to make them look like vans. Pictures of a full-size steering mock-up with a raised rear roof section were leaked to the press by a Solihull employee – and Land Rover called in a leading former policeman to head the search for the culprit.

By the end of 1988, regular readers of the motoring press knew that something new was on the way, but Solihull had successfully confused everyone about exactly what it might be. The truth was that the new vehicle was being developed under the codename of Project Jay, and the Range Rover connection was that it used a Range Rover chassis, less the self-levelling rear strut. It was not 'mini' in size, but it would be on price. And it certainly did have a raised rear roof section, which the GRP cladding of the prototypes spotted on test had been designed to conceal. Production started during the first half of 1989 and a substantial launch stock was ready for the dealers' show-rooms when Project

Jay was introduced to the world as the Land Rover Discovery at the Frankfurt Motor Show in September 1989.

By this stage the turnaround in the Land Rover company's orientation was complete. Whereas the company had always been driven by its engineering division, now it was being led by its marketing division. There was of course a delicate balance to be achieved: the Land Rover reputation had been built upon engineering and so engineering excellence still remained a vital ingredient in the strategy for the new product. But now that engineering excellence was more accurately focused to meet market expectations. The change was an important and fundamental one, and it explains a great deal about why Discovery became the vehicle it did and why it has been so successful.

The market

Land Rover's market analysts had established that the Personal Transport Sector of the 4 x 4 market could be divided into two segments. The first of these favoured 3-door vehicles (ie, with two side doors and one at the rear). Buyers in this market were predominantly young, often without children, and relatively affluent. They viewed their everyday transport as something which promoted their image of themselves to the world, and they preferred to stand out in the crowd. Thus they wanted bright colours, stylish decals, and above all they wanted a wide choice of accessories to personalize their vehicle and to make it different from similar vehicles owned by their colleagues.

In the second segment of the Personal Transport Sector, buyers favoured 5-door vehicles (ie, with four side doors and one at the rear). The extra doors were necessary for practical reasons: these buyers often had children to carry around. Generally affluent, they were nevertheless rather older and more conservative than those buyers who favoured 3-door models. They turned to 4 x 4 vehicles as stylish alternatives to traditional estate cars, but on the whole they were more interested in a vehicle which was smart and functional than one which stood out in a crowd. Yet they, too, liked to be able to personalize their vehicles, often with accessories which made them more versatile and practical.

One further important revelation came out of Land Rover's analyses of the market. This was that buyers in the Personal Transport Sector did not really need four-wheel drive, because they rarely, if ever, took their vehicles into situations where the extra traction was needed. However, what they needed and what they wanted were two separate issues. The younger buyers who preferred 3-door models tended to view the option of using the four-wheel drive in anger off-road as rather glamorous and exciting, even if they never actually got beyond the stage of dreaming about it. The older and more conservative buyers who preferred five doors valued four-wheel drive as an additional safety factor, no doubt partly as a result of the increasing use of four-wheel drive on high performance rally cars and its much publicized benefits for roadholding and handling. In addition, many saw it as of benefit because it improved stability when towing.

Right from the beginning, Land Rover had determined that they should tackle both segments of the market by offering alternative body configurations on the same chassis. All the way through the design and development phase of Discovery, the Project Jay team was constantly being fed with information about the preferences in the Personal Transport Sector in order that the finished vehicle should meet those preferences as closely as possible when it was launched. And the differences in taste between the typical 3-door buyer and the typical 5-door buyer were accurately reflected in the vehicles when they did begin to appear on the market.

The launch

The biggest problem Land Rover faced in bringing the Discovery to market was to differentiate it from the Range Rover. To allow the public to see it as a 'cheaper Range Rover' would undermine sales of the flagship vehicle, and so the company adopted a carefully thought-out market strategy which also had an impact on the Range Rover itself.

For the first year of its existence, Discovery was made available only in 3-door form. This made it look as different as possible from the Range Rover, which by this stage was sold predominantly as a 4-door model. On the mechanical side, Discovery was launched with a 144 bhp carburetted version of the 3.5-litre V8 petrol engine while the Range Rover switched to a 188 bhp injected 3.9-litre type. Discovery also came with the new 111 bhp intercooled turbodiesel engine (200 Tdi) which was not available on the Range Rover, and although the Range Rover could be had with automatic transmission, Discovery could not. Publicity and Marketing did the rest: the image they created for Discovery was designed to appeal to buyers who were younger and less conservative than those who typically bought Range Rovers. And the strategy worked, because most Land Rover customers came to perceive Discovery as a completely separate model from the Range Rover.

Right from the start, most customers ordered their Discoverys with the new 200 Tdi diesel engine. Land Rover's market analysis had predicted that demand would be predominantly for diesels, and for that reason a great deal of effort had gone into the design and development of the engine. On the stocks as early as 1985 – when it had been planned for a completely different vehicle which never went into production – the Gemini engine broke new ground by using direct injection instead of the indirect injection generally favoured for smaller diesel engines.

The advantage of direct injection was that it was more fuel-efficient than indirect injection; its disadvantage was that it was inherently noisier. But the Land Rover engineers reasoned that they should be able to minimize the additional noise by careful design of components such as engine mountings. In truth, the 200 Tdi *was* noisy when it was first introduced, but customers were able to forgive it for its class-leading fuel economy and for the sprightly performance promoted by its turbocharger and intercooler. And as time went on, minor modifications reduced the diesel clatter to more acceptable levels.

Land Rover's market research had highlighted the importance of a strong interior design for the new vehicle, and this was also a factor in distinguishing it from Range Rover. The first Discoverys had a striking Sonar Blue interior with unusual fabrics and a golfball texture for the grab-handles and steering wheel. These elements were the work of Conran design, an industrial design consultancy whom Land Rover called in to offer advice on turning their basic interior specification into reality. That specification had envisaged a single interior design for both 3-door and 5-door models, and one which was both stylish (primarily to suit the younger 3-door buyers), and practical (to suit the older 5-door buyers). The style came from Conran, while the practicality came from Land Rover: Discovery could be ordered with extra seats in the rear to make it a 7-seater, and it had a multitude of handy storage pockets.

Five doors

Discovery was immediately widely acclaimed on its launch in 1989, and sales quickly outstripped those of established Land Rover utilities, although it would be a while before Discovery sold better than Range Rover. During the first quarter of 1990 over 1,500 Discoverys were sold in the UK, about 500 more than its nearest competitor in the Personal Transport Sector of the four-wheel drive market. Equally important, however, was that sales of the new vehicle were not eating into sales of Land Rover's existing products. Most buyers were either turning to Discovery in preference to Japanese 4 x 4s or were completely new to four-wheel drive vehicles.

It was in this latter end of the market where Land Rover hoped to do especially well with the 5-door Discovery, and their expectations were not disappointed. The 5-door models were announced in the autumn of 1990 and immediately awarded a gold medal for design at the British International Motor Show in September. At the same time Land Rover protected the Range Rover market by adding a new refinement which could not be had on the Discovery – anti-roll bars. Five-door Discoverys came with a higher level of standard equipment than 3-door models, and they also came without the garish side decals of the 3-door. For customers who did not like the bright Sonar Blue – the only interior colour for the first year – a more conservative Bahama Beige was introduced. On the mechanical side, all 5-door models and those 3-doors built after autumn 1990 had a 163 bhp injected 3.5-litre V8 petrol engine in place of the early carburetted type, and were now designated V8i models; it was also possible to order this engine in slightly detuned form with an exhaust catalyst. Nevertheless, the Tdi diesel models continued to be very much more popular than the petrol versions, outselling them by around five to one world-wide.

Tough image

Advertising and marketing for the 5-door models reflected their different target audience of more conservative family buyers, but Land Rover had taken great care not to allow Discovery's success as a road vehicle to obscure its very real off-road prowess. It was quite true that most owners were more taken with the image than with the reality of off-road driving, but it was also important in marketing terms to reinforce that image. For this reason, Land Rover entered Discoverys in the Camel Trophy adventure rally held in Siberia in June 1990; and the company has continued to use Discoverys in this annual event ever since.

The buyers welcomed the tough image which came with Discovery's participation in the Camel Trophy, but they also naturally insisted that the showroom Discovery should relate to *their* world and lifestyle. So from August 1991, for its third season on sale, Discovery was given new cosmetic addenda. Five-doors picked up practical side rubbing strips similar to those on the Range Rover, and 3-doors had new side decals with a compass design which were even more garish than the original type! In addition, improved synchromesh arrangements made the original LT77 5-speed gearbox into an LT77S type and gave a much improved change quality to all Discoverys.

In the meantime, Land Rover had been developing Discovery behind its familiar configuration as a passenger-carrying vehicle, to provide the basis of specialist commercial applications. That this should happen was inevitable,

The 36 Land Rover vehicles on parade before being shipped to Dar es Salaam for the 1991 Camel Trophy.

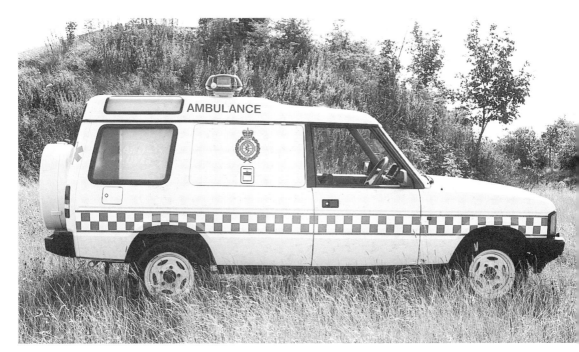

Paramedic Discovery.

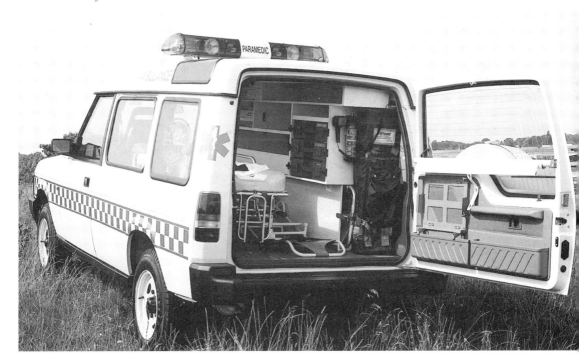

In December 1991 the Queen's Flight took delivery of five standard 200 Tdi 3-door Discoverys.

because the gradually increasing cost of the Range Rover had been pushing it further and further out of the reach of the emergency services who had valued it so highly during the 1970s and 1980s.

The first conversion of the Discovery was for use as a police vehicle, and the first delivery to a police force went to the Dyfed Powys Police in Wales during November 1990. Next came long-wheelbase ambulances: the so-called Paramedic Discovery was first shown at the Ambex 91 exhibition in August 1991. For this Land Rover's Special Vehicles division had extended the wheelbase from 100 to 116 inches and had made full use of the raised roof section to provide working space within the body. It was available in V8 3.5-litre form, or 200 Tdi, and with three or five doors.

Special Vehicles were also responsible a year later for a Discovery equipped as an invalid chair carrier, with an extended high roof and tail lift, and at the same time for a Discovery Commercial. This had blanked-out side windows and no rear seats, and offered a stylish van-type vehicle for users who wanted something out of the ordinary.

More variety
The spring and summer of 1992 saw yet more changes to Discovery. On the home market, changes in company car taxation and a reduction in car tax in the April 1992 budget prompted Land Rover to introduce a special 'tax break' version of the 5-door Tdi model, which lacked some of the previously standard equipment but was priced below the new £20,000 company car tax threshold. As a result, the fully equipped 5-doors were renamed Tdi S (and V8i S), although their badging never reflected the change.

286

Discovery Mpi.

Next on the agenda was an automatic transmission option of the V8i models, and this was announced in the autumn, for Discovery's fourth year in the showrooms. Feedback from customers had shown quite clearly that there was a demand for this, and Land Rover knew that this demand was likely to increase now that Discovery was being moved gradually further up-market. So the V8i was made available with the 4-speed ZF automatic transmission which had been used successfully in Range Rovers since the mid-1980s and the automatic versions rapidly became more popular than the 5-speed manuals. At the same time as the automatic Discovery arrived, exhaust catalysts were standardized for all petrol models, and the Range Rover's anti-roll bars were coupled with stylish alloy wheels and wide-section tyres in a new option called Freestyle Choice. The new wheels and tyres did nothing for the vehicles off-road abilities, but they did make it feel more stable on the road and proved very popular.

Changes came in two stages during 1993 as well, straddling the summer and thus spreading the costs of tooling-up for production and the disruption which production changes always cause. The first novelty was a new version of Discovery known as the Mpi (or, where appropriate the Mpi S). This had been designed primarily to suit some overseas markets where taxation penalized large-capacity engines such as the 3.5-litre V8 and buyers were resistant to diesel power. To sell Discovery in these markets, Land Rover equipped it with a 134 bhp version of the 2-litre T16 petrol engine then available in certain Rover cars. The first examples were shipped to Greece in April 1993, but the Mpi went on sale in Britain and elsewhere during June. There was no doubt it was biased towards road use, as the T16 engine offered little of the bottom-end

Discovery interior.

torque necessary for difficult off-road work, but it filled a gap in the Discovery range and helped to improve sales.

The second stage of the 1993 changes came in the autumn, geared to the start of the new model year. The 1944 model Discoverys were announced at the Frankfurt Motor Show in September, and were distinguished by automatic transmission option for the Tdi models and by the Range Rover's 183 bhp 3.9-litre V8 in place of the 163 bhp 3.5-litre engine in V8i models. Both new features were widely welcomed, but in fact the 1994 Discoverys were to be short lived, because Land Rover introduced what it called the 1995 models just six months later, during March 1994.

Japan and America

Land Rover's objective for Discovery to reclaim the Personal Transport Sector of the 4 x 4 market from Japanese manufacturers had been hugely successful all over the world. Even in Japan, where the relatively small Rover network had begun to sell Discovery towards the end of 1991, the vehicle had aroused great interest. So it was perhaps only natural that the Rover Group's partners, the Japanese Honda company, should have asked to sell a rebadged Discovery in Japan through their own large dealer network.

The agreement was signed in the summer of 1993 and the Honda Crossroad

Discovery is launched in the United States, following the pattern of Camel Trophy events.

– a 3.9-litre V8i automatic Discovery available with either three or five doors – went on sale in November. Although Honda predicted sales of just 1,200 a year in Japan, the vast size of that country's 4 x 4 market suggested that demand would in fact be considerably higher. However, the Honda Crossroad had only been on sale for *three months* when the Rover Group was sold to BMW of Germany, and it was not long before a piqued Honda began unravelling the ties it had established with Rover at the end of the 1970s. While the Crossroad was not among the early casualties, it remains to be seen whether this badge-engineered vehicle has a long-term future.

Meanwhile, Land Rover had bigger fish to fry. It had long been the company's intention to introduce Discovery to the USA in the wake of the extremely successful Range Rover, and a great deal of effort had gone into adapting the vehicles to suit American tastes and preferences. Though by no means a simple or cheap exercise it had the potential to reap enormous rewards because of the size of the American 4 x 4 market.

Discovery was finally introduced to America in March 1994, at the same time as the 'revised' 1995 models went on sale in Europe. Over £50 million was spent on developing the vehicle for the North American market, as part of the comprehensive remake and it was of course based on the very latest specification, but it also incorporated certain unique features: a high-mounted third rear stoplight, and side marker lamps in the front and rear bumper ends. All US Discoverys were 5-door models with the 183 bhp catalyst-equipped 3.9-litre petrol engine, and both 5-speed manual and 4-speed automatic

Discovery 5-door ES.

transmission options were available. Standard equipment levels were high, to suit American expectations.

The revised Discovery

Land Rover introduced their face-lifted Discovery at the Geneva Motor Show in March 1994, and it went on sale shortly after that. This Discovery incorporated the most comprehensive package of changes since its launch, drawing together a number of improvements on which Land Rover had been working for some time. The package focused on refinement and safety, while freshening up the four-year-old design with an exterior and interior face-lift. Greater refinement came from detail redesign to minimize noise transmission within the vehicle, from a thoroughly reworked (although no more powerful) diesel engine, now known as the 300 Tdi, and from a new and much slicker 5-speed gearbox called the R380. Anti-roll bars, optional since autumn 1992, were also made standard.

Greater safety same from fitting side intrusion beams in the front doors, from adding energy-absorbing 'crush cans' behind the front bumper, from offering the Range Rover's ABS as an option, and from the additional option of driver and front passenger airbags. On the cosmetic side, reworked front and rear details and new door mirrors distinguished the 1995 Discovery, while a completely redesigned dashboard and new interior trim removed much of the original Conran concept. Even the Sonar Blue interior colour had gone, to be replaced by a more sober grey.

Discovery on General Wade's road in Scotland.

Features such as airbags and ABS were standard on the new top-model Discovery ES which also came with leather upholstery and a new air conditioning system for the rear passengers as standard. The ES, Discovery's equivalent of the Range Rover Vogue SE, was visually distinguishable from cheaper versions by features including enamelled alloy wheels and 'ES' decals. Inevitably it also cost more, but this enabled Land Rover to push Range Rover prices up even higher in preparation for the launch of the new Range Rover model later in 1994.

Press and public reaction to the revised models was uniformly positive, indicating that Land Rover's continuing programme of market research had once again helped the engineers to come up with a product right on target for its intended market. Naturally, much of the media attention was focused on the most expensive models, but Land Rover had not made the mistake of abandoning the cheaper end of the market. The entry-level 3-door Mpi was still available at a price equating to far less able vehicles, like the Vauxhall Frontera or the Ford Maverick and Nissan Terrano II twins. From there on, prices gradually rose through the 3-door models to the cheapest 5-door (still under the crucial £20,000 company car tax barrier in Britain), and on up to the top-model Discovery ES. A very wide range of options and accessories continued to offer customers the opportunity to personalize their vehicles.

In summary
Discovery has been an outstanding success right from Day One. It quickly

Discoverys fitted by K. & J. Slavin (Quest) Ltd.

became the best selling four-wheel drive vehicle in Britain, and remained so despite the arrival of attractive new competitors from rival manufactures. Looking at the picture world-wide, there is no sign that the competition will be able to make up Discovery's lead in the short term. Discovery represents a rare cause for celebration because it has recaptured for a British manufacturer a market which seemed irretrievably lost to the Japanese. There is also very little doubt it is the cornerstone on which the long-term future of Land Rover is assured.

Discovery facts and figures

Engine	*Tdi*	*V8 and V8i*	*Mpi*
Type	4 cylinder in line	V8 cylinder	4 cylinder in line
Bore/stroke	90.47 x 97 mm	88.9 x 71.12 mm (3.5) 93.98 x 71.12 mm (3.9)	84.45 x 89 mm
Comp Ratio		8.13 : 1 (3.5 V8i 10 : 1 with exhaust catalyst and V8), 9.35 : 1 (3.5 V8i without exhaust catalyst and 3.9V8i)	
Cubic Capacity	2,495 cc	3,528 cc (to 1993) 3,947 cc (1993 on)	1,994 cc
Max Power	111.3 bhp at 4,000 rpm	144.5 bhp at 5,000 rpm (V8) 163.6 bhp at 4,750 rpm (3.5 V8i) 153.41 bhp at 4,750 rpm (3.5 V8i with exhaust catalyst) 183 bhp at 4,750 rpm (3.9 V8i)	134 bhp at 6,000 rpm
Max Torque	195 lb/ft at 1,800 rpm	192 lb/ft at 2,800 rpm (V8) 211.89 lb/ft at 2,600 rpm (3.5 V8i) 192.1 lb/ft at 3,000 rpm	137 lb/ft at 2,500 rpm

Engine	Tdi	V8 and V8i	Mpi
		(3.9 V8i with exhaust catalyst) 230 lb/ft at 3,100 rpm (3.9 V8i)	

Performance

	Tdi	V8 and V8i	Mpi
0–60 mph	17.1 sec (manual) 18.9 sec (auto)	12.8 sec (V8) 11.7 sec (3.5 V8i manual) 8.8 sec (3.9 sec V8i manual) 12.9 sec (3.9 V8i auto)	15.3 sec
Max Speed	92 mph (manual) 90 mph (auto)	95 mph (V8) 105 mph (3.5 V8i and 3.9 auto) 106 mph (3.9 V8i manual)	98 mph

Fuel Consumption

	Tdi	V8 and V8i	Mpi
Manual	33 mpg	16 mpg (V8) 18 mpg (3.5 V8i) 19 mpg (3.9 V8i)	25 mpg
Automatic	30 mpg	17 mpg (3.5 V8i) 18 mpg (3.9 V8i)	

Transmission

	Tdi	V8 and V8i	Mpi
Primary	5-speed manual 4-speed auto (from Aug '93)	5-speed manual 4-speed auto (from Aug '92)	5-speed manual
Transfer box	2-speed High 1.222 : 1 Low 3.32 : 1	2-speed High 1.222 : 1 Low 3.32 : 1	2-speed High 1.41 : 1 Low 3.76 : 1

Dimensions

	Tdi	V8 and V8i	Mpi
Wheelbase	2,540 mm (100 in)		
Length	4,538 mm (178.6 in)		
Width	1,793 mm (70.6 in)		
Height	1,920 mm (75.6 in) without roof bars		
Kerb weight	2,053 kg (5-door Tdi S)	1,919 kg (3-door 3.9) 1,986 kg (5-door 3.9 V8i S)	1,886 kg (3-door Mpi) 1,920 kg (5-door Mpi)

General

Wheels	7J x 16		
Tyres	205 R16		
	235/70 with Freestyle Choice Option		
Fuel Tank	89 litres (19.5 Imperial Gallons)		
Suspension (Front)	Live axle with coil springs, radius arms and Panhard rod; Anti-roll bar (Standard on 1995 model year)		
Suspension (Rear)	Live axle with coil springs, radius arms and A-frame. Anti-Roll Bar (Standard on 1995 model year)		
Dampers	Hydraulic		
Towing Capacity			
(Unbraked)	750 kg		
(Braked)	3,500 kg	3,500 kg	2,750 kg

Chapter 6
The Expedition Workhorse

Britain has always had a strong tradition of exploration – history books abound with tales of intrepid adventurers embarking on devastating journeys, in earlier times by sea, on foot, on elephant-, horse- or camel-back, across deserts, through jungles, up mountains, over glaciers. The challenge was there to be met, and that incorrigible streak of curiosity common to many island-dwellers provoked potential pioneers to seek far-off lands, eventually to build empires. Our more recent attainments have been inescapably linked with technology, for as the undiscovered world was being discovered, science was forging forwards and machines were being developed: sailing ships were fitted with engines, and horse-power was rated in terms of internal combustion. The advent of the Land Rover – with its rugged versatility and robust utilitarian construction – was soon recognized as the passport to new horizons. Designed to withstand the wear and tear of the farmers' demanding off-road tasks, it was the first light-weight vehicle equipped to cope with arduous cross-country driving, and available at the right sort of price. Before it was barely three years old, someone had entered it for the Cape Rally, in 1951, and achieved first placing along with a Jeep and a Delahaye – there were no British entrants apart from Land Rover. It has never looked back. By the 1960s, the overland routes to India, Africa, even Australia, were well-known to Land Rovers which, in various forms, were turning up everywhere. Primitive people, with scarcely a word of English, could readily identify a Land Rover by name – for now amateur adventurers felt that they could indulge their fancies: get a Land Rover, and away we go!

For several years towards the end of the 1960s, we worked for a firm operating foreign tours in Land Rovers, then a rapidly expanding business. Although many of the trekking routes we covered could well have been tackled by regular cars, vans or buses, it was the Land Rovers that sold the tours, for fashions were changing and there was something definitely daring about a holiday 'roughing it' in a Land Rover. At the same time, the vehicle was asking to be put through its paces, and the trekking routes were becoming more adventurous, more remote, and more attractive. Fleets of 'safari prepared' 12-seaters would leave Britain every autumn to spend the winter in the desert, the sites of Morocco by now being far too tame, meeting successive batches of tourists at their airport of arrival and duly depositing them back there again three weeks later. During this era, a lot of expensive lessons were learnt about how to get the best out of a Land Rover in these conditions – or rather how not to abuse it, for the average lifespan of these redoubtable machines was about six months! The reasons were obvious enough: to ensure profits, the vehicles were filled to capacity with passengers, who had luggage, who needed tents, who needed feeding, not to mention the tools, spares, fuel and water that had to be carried to keep the show moving. Some of the drivers had never driven off the road, some had never driven a Land Rover, some had never driven in convoy, and while all these skills were being acquired the vehicle took a pounding. The full-length roof-racks were both ill-designed and over-laden, causing the windscreen to shatter, starting with a crack appearing at the top outer corners, and the same thing occurred with the rear side windows which took the strain of the roof. Cracked chassis frames, split bulkheads, snapped bonnet locks, non-closing doors, tropical roof separating from body, rear wheels sheering off – none of these were uncommon and all were usually attributable to over-loading in one way or another. Since the

Defender 110 used for eco-tourism on St Kitts.

arrival of the Range Rover on the expedition scene, it too has suffered equally from excessive loading.

At one time, Land Rover was able to test the vehicle's expedition-worthiness through the efforts of Colonel Leblanc, who organized a variety of projects using Land Rovers in the Middle East. It was he in fact who first started the Land Rover expedition tradition, by taking his brand new 80-inch model to Abyssinia, as long ago as 1949, when the Land Rover was scarcely one year old and completely untried. The son of a French-Canadian (who was one of the chief engineers involved in the construction of the Paris metro), Colonel Leblanc was a colourful adventurer, whose independent efforts to sell Land Rovers overseas were producing orders for the Rover company even before it had an export department. Leblanc loved expeditions, and he loved deserts: having been a pilot in the Royal Flying Corps in the First World War, he had spent much of the Second World War in North-East Africa with the Sudan Defence Force, and in the Western Desert.

By 1951 he regarded Land Rovers as his old friends, and as production was by then well up, and the company was keen to widen its market, Rover offered him a job as a sort of travelling salesman, demonstrating his Land Rovers wherever he went, for a basic retainer fee. He accepted the job, but turned down the fee: his terms would be no salary, no expenses, but 0.5 per cent of all future sales to the Middle East – a far-sighted policy indeed! At that time such sales were negligible and his terms were met; he received a letter of confirmation from one of the Wilks, and away he went. For his first sales-expedition he planned an impressive manoeuvre all round Africa with half-a-dozen Land Rovers, bi-lingual salesman, specialists and service engineers, Roger McCahey, the retired Manager of UK Government and Military Sales at Solihull, was on that expedition, and takes up the story:

'The Rover company wanted to announce the Rover 75 car that same year, so instead of all that, Leblanc got one Land Rover, one car, and me! We set off on 27 February 1952 and went from Algiers to Nairobi, and back up the other side. We would stop outside the towns to wash the vehicles down, put on clean shorts and clean shirts and polish our shoes, before going in to see the local police chief, army, oil companies, or whoever might be interested, then on we would go. Leblanc drove the car – a P4, or Post-War Model No 4 – and, thanks to his desert driving experience and dogged determination ("I'll get this car back to Solihull even if I have to dismantle it and load it onto a camel!"), the Rover lasted the round trip, faring nothing worse than multiple punctures and broken springs. To my astonishment, Leblanc was a great believer in string, a huge ball of which he carried everywhere; his cure for a broken spring was to bind it copiously with string which as a temporary repair often lasted up to a thousand miles so was hardly to be scoffed at! The tyres were Dunlop "Forts" and when we got home we were still using the original ones we set off with, much patched, of course.

Colonel Leblanc (far right) before setting out on one of his Land Rover expeditions.

Leblanc had filmed the tyres in action, spewing sand all over the place, and from this piece of film Dunlop was able to start developing its first-ever sand-tyre. Travelling around in this way, he gradually formed the basis of a network of local dealers for Land Rovers in the most unlikely places – and Leblanc was tireless: I remember once we were travelling from Beirut to Baghdad in a hurry – this was in 1956 – and we drove without a proper rest for 22 hours. I was dropping with exhaustion but Leblanc only said "Must press on, dear boy!" and it was only the fact that he was in his sixties, and me in my twenties that kept me going! He organized countless expeditions with Land Rovers; another African trip we did together was in 1958-9 from Cairo to Addis Ababa and back again, through Anglo-Egyptian Sudan (the Nubian Desert in those days), taking eight weeks or so. By this time he knew that part of Africa like the palm of his hand ...'

But he also knew the Middle East – he had been sent to Baghdad in the war, where he became a Senior British Officer – and of course his gamble was to pay off. Middle East sales hit the jack pot within a very few years, and Leblanc soon saw the returns on his 'investment'. He died at the age of 78, in 1966, having made a significant contribution both to the Land Rover and to expeditions as a whole.

A Station Wagon with fitted roof tents.

Over the years Land Rovers have carried scientists and explorers through jungle and desert, swamp and snow, demonstrating unparalleled endurance and reliability for vehicles of their class. Other early Land Rover exploits were the Oxford and Cambridge Universities Expeditions to such remote places as Cape Town, Singapore and South America, while a more recent achievement is the British Trans-Globe expedition which is circumnavigating the world through the North and South Poles, using Land Rovers loaned by the company. In 1980 the Royal Geographical Society celebrated its 150th Anniversary, and the occasion was marked by the initiation and sponsorship of an important exploratory and scientific project in the Karakoram range, which embraces Afghanistan, Pakistan, China and India. The international expedition was a tribute to the Society's long history of service to worldwide geographical studies, and to honour the event, Land Rover saw fit to lend three V8 Land-Rovers to the project. Roger Ball, Land Rover's Product Marketing Manager at the time, liaised closely with the expedition in order that the vehicles should render maximum support. In times of such economic restraint, an expedition has to be a bit special to attract that extent of sponsorship, but if the Royal Geographical Society itself does not qualify, what could?

Before the Range Rover was launched in 1970, the Rover Company hired the services of the company we were with to guide two Range Rovers and a 1-ton 109-inch Land Rover, with technical development staff from Solihull, across the Sahara with a 109-inch Station Wagon for support services. Our first sight of the Range Rovers is described in the introduction to this book. The 1-ton Land Rover, soon to become dubbed 'Lulubelle' by the Rover crew, was a test-bed model fitted with the Range Rover V8 engine and transmission. Unlike the V8 Land-Rovers of today, it thus had equivalent power to the Range Rover –and greater payload, which caused us to realize that here was an ideal combination of power and size for many expedition purposes. We were to wait nine years, however, before the V8 became a standard Land Rover engine.

The Range Rover testing trip was an unusual departure from the norm, and none of the Solihull staff knew really what to expect. Early on, Alf was heard to remark to Dennis, as our convoy startled a group of ostriches in the middle of nowhere, 'Bloody big budgies here, mate!' – but it only took the familiar sight of a Land Rover-in-distress to make them feel quite at home. As ambassadors for the company, they could not have worked harder: wherever, whenever a Land Rover of any age or condition was encountered, it was treated to their loving ministrations. One early morning, driving towards the sunrise over empty desert, we met two Land Rovers, one carrying the Governor of the oasis for which we were heading. He was disconsolate at having had to abandon one of the Land Rovers from his fleet a few kilometres back, so imagine his delight at running into a band of Land Rover experts! Naturally, they repaired the offending vehicle's carburettor (diagnosis took place instantly), passing a happy couple of hours with heads bent over engine, while the Governor praised the spanking new Range Rovers with overt envy. His gratitude for the repair to his

Paris Dakar Rally support vehicle (equipped by K. & J. Slavin (Quest) Ltd).

ancient Land Rover was expressed in his invitation to have breakfast with him and his entourage, where one egg (ostrich) made enough omelet to feed everyone! Later that same day we had to check in at an army outpost: well and good, until our party discovered a yard full of Land Rovers at the back of the barracks. Here many hours had to be spent examining, explaining and adjusting – all in the cause of Public Relations and the famous Rover goodwill!

This expedition was something of a milestone for us because it was our first close contact with personnel from Land Rover. During the course of the subsequent 15 years or so, we were to become increasingly involved with the use of Land Rovers on expeditions, finally becoming advisers to Land Rover Limited in the expeditionary field in 1979. The findings from the expedition, as an exercise to see how capable the Range Rover was going to prove, were generally highly favourable. One complaint at the time, though, was that it was impossible to get it stuck in the sand, normally the commonest of desert-driving hazards, without digging it in deliberately – and then it was too easy to get out! But on the Darien Gap expedition, in 1972, it was a different story, where totally different and much worse conditions threw up new obstacles to be overcome.

The Range Rovers reached Panama City from Anchorage, Alaska, having already suffered one major incident when vehicle VXC 765H hit a truck (through no fault of its driver) on a snowbound highway. This provoked a

Ken Slavin and Land Rover team with first ever Range Rover expedition in the Sahara in 1969. V8 powered Land Rover (behind) was used as a load carrier and proved its robust qualities.

Turbo diesel Land Rover on loan to WWF/IUCN in Niger, crossing the southern Sahara in Algeria.

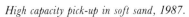

Filming with National Geographic on the occasion of the longest solar eclipse this century in Mauretania, 1973.

High capacity pick-up in soft sand, 1987.

2.00 am phone call from the Ministry of Defence to Geof Miller's house in Warwickshire, requesting urgent dispatch of, 'all the items listed on pages x, y and z of the parts catalogue'.

The next 2.00 am phone call was for differentials, as the later-than-usual rainy season had played havoc with conditions between Canitas (the start of the jungle stretch) and the river Ipeti. It was from here that the third and final 2.00 am phone call was triggered, one weekend in February. Geof Miller reported the bad news to Tom Barton on Monday morning, and they both went to see A B Smith, the then Managing Director, who weighed up the facts, turned to Geof and said 'There's a plane to Panama on Thursday – catch it!' Geof then spent five weeks in Panama, three of them actually driving one of the vehicles, where he was able to log progress at two miles per day doing $3^1/2$ gallons to the mile'.

The main problems that Geof identified (and rectified) were:

(a) The swamp tyres, which were inappropriate for the wet conditions. Changing them to 7.50x16 Super All-Traction tyres made all the difference.

(b) Overload of the vehicles. The back axle was permanently in contact with the bump stops.

(c) The recce party was not equipped with a vehicle, therefore had no way of assessing what a vehicle could cope with, so an 88-inch Land Rover (recently rolled) was purchased in Panama City, prepared under Geof's guidance, and flown out to the advance party by American helicopter.

Conditions at last began to improve, and at one stage the Range Rovers actually caught up with the Advance party. Eventually they all emerged from the jungle into Baranquillito in Columbia on St. George's Day. The Land Rover was rolled away as scrap, while the Range Rovers carried on at 90 mph for another 5000 miles to Tierra del Fuego. They were then shipped back to Solihull from Buenos Aires, straight into a round of PR presentations.

If it was easy to overload a Land Rover, it is even easier to overload a Range Rover, and this factor cannot be overlooked when working on expeditions. If a Range Rover is to be given its full rein and used extensively it needs to be backed-up by a load-carrying vehicle, as we were able to prove on a recent venture. In the first months of 1979, we mounted an expedition in the Western Sahara with the World Wildlife Fund and London Zoo, to research the potential of certain tracts of desert as National Parks, and to ascertain whether or not certain species of antelope still survived in those areas. We were offered the loan of a brand new V8 Land Rover to test on the project, prior to the vehicle being launched (initially on the Export Market only), and so decided to commonize engines and spares on all vehicles taken. We took a Rover 1-tonne V8 101-inch ex-military Land Rover as the principal load-carrier, carrying food, water, fuel reserve, spares and tools, baggage, and one passenger; the V8 109-inch Station Wagon also carried spares and tools, as well as camping equipment and the more delicate scientific and photographic equipment, samples, etc, and one or two passengers; while the Range Rover was lightly loaded, to be used as a reconnaissance vehicle and for path-finding, carrying three or four passengers and extraneous equipment. This combination was the closest to the ideal that we have ever achieved as the line-up for a very hard-pushed expedition, but getting it off the ground was fraught with snags. The prototype V8 Land Rover wasn't ready to leave the factory in time to set off with the 101-inch and the Range Rover,which meant that once the technical development department were finally prepared to release it, our own modifications and equipping had to be effected with alacrity – between tea-time on a Saturday and breakfast-time the next day. The following preparation was carried out during the night:

> Roof rack – full length, clamped to roof gutters
> Side jerry can holders
> Internal tie bars, behind rear seat
> External reinforcing bars, over rear side windows
> Internal storage boxes, behind rear seat
> Extra windscreen mounting brackets
> Extra pop rivets into body side panels and rear door post
> Rear side-facing seats and internal trim removed
> Mud flaps removed (these cause obstruction in sand)
> Pop rivets added to various known weak points of body

Prototype V8 Land Rover being driven by Ken Slavin in Africa.

The channel crossing, the drive across France, the Mediterranean crossing to Algiers, and the drive down through Algeria and Niger can take upwards of a fortnight – given delays at border crossings, and officialdom generally – but thanks to the increased mobility, power and comfort of the V8 (not to mention the interest it stimulated wherever we took it, which helped to persuade officials to 'make an exception'), we arrived at Zinder, our first destination, two days earlier than the other two vehicles, within nine days of leaving home. The fuel consumption was better than anticipated, at 18 mpg, and the constant 4-wheel-drive made light of the usually treacherous tracts of soft sand to be crossed, while the passengers could enjoy a far more comfortable ride than would ever have been possible in the 4-cylinder over such terrain. At one point it had looked as if we might be marooned in Southern Algeria for two days, but the V8 stepped in (indirectly) to speed us on our way. While parked on the outskirts of an oasis, to do routine maintenance to the vehicle before heading south, a chap wandered over to have a look under the bonnet, and ask questions. We gave him a demonstration, and were invited back to his office to meet a friend of his: it turned out that he was the Governor of the oasis, while his friend was the Military Commander for the area. We talked about V8s in particular and Land Rovers in general for an hour (their greatest requirement was for Land Rover buses and Range Rover ambulances), then made our exit, impatient to get back on the road. Outside the town, at the Customs Post, we found we were forbidden to leave. They had run out of documents and by the time replacement stocks were due, the Customs Office would be closed – for two days! This, we gathered, was 'final', so we went quickly back to the Town Hall, where the Governor told his secretary to type out new documents for the Customs then and there, and go with us to ensure that we had no further delays. Subsequently, we heard that the Algerian Army had a V8 Land Rover for assessment, so perhaps the precedent set by Colonel Leblanc back in 1949 still holds good: Land Rovers will sell themselves if you can get them to where the need is.

Once established at a base camp, the Land Rover and the Range Rover were stripped down to minimal weight and used daily for local exploration and research. Because of the improvement in fuel consumption and in speed, it was possible to cover greater areas each day than predicted, and to devote more time to working in the field, completing that stage of the survey sooner than it would otherwise have been feasible to contemplate. The Range Rover had had to have its wheel arches cut back to allow Michelin XS tyres to be fitted (more commoni-zation between the fleet) and was light enough to glide over the dunes like a ski champion on the snow, faltering at nothing. The V8 Land Rover still lacks the sheer smoothness of the Range Rover's suspension, and the view from the front seats certainly does not equal that of the Range Rover since like all Land Rovers, it lacks the windscreen height that makes Range Rover driving such a pleasure. Because it is relatively dependent on another vehicle for carrying weight, the Range Rover will never be able to match the Land Rover's suitability as an expedition workhorse, however; and what the Land Rover used to lack in terms of performance has now been recitified by the introduction of the Stage I V8, from which departure only exciting improvements can emerge.

(Since this was written, we have of course had the 110-inch Land Rover enter the scene, with its superior coil suspension, and increased windscreen height, answering the above criticisms of the V8.

1988. Ever since the BBC film revealed the plight of drought-sufferers in Ethiopia in 1984, awareness of all such victims has heightened in the Western World, giving a whole new dimension to the word AID, the famous Band Aid concert starting the ball rolling. Four wheel drive vehicles have a vital part to play as transport in undeveloped regions and the competition has hotted up, the relative merits constantly under discussion: 'Land Cruisers are so much cheaper'; 'Land Rovers are far more durable'; 'Toyota parts are more generally available'; 'Land Rovers are more robust'; 'But what about the door locks?'; 'There are many more Land Rover options, and the quality goes up and up, but you just can't get the parts in a hurry'. So the manufacturers have been addressing the problems. Our own Company (Quest 80's) has become increasingly involved with supplying and backing-up Land Rovers shipped to Africa for literally dozens of aid-related agencies, delivering convoys of new

British aid to the Gambia. Jimmy Whitworth, a doctor from Britain, checking on the progress of a patient who suffered a head fracture and broken arm in the Gambia, Africa's smallest mainland country.

British aid to Zimbabwe. A reconditioning scheme for derelict Land Rovers, run by Leyland Zimbabwe Ltd, has been funded by Britain and has provided over £500,000 of foreign exchange for the purchase of essential spares and equipment. This photo shows a reconditioned Land Rover being checked before delivery to a customer.

One Tens across the Sahara and setting up Land Rover workshops in desert countries like Mali (for Norwegian Church Aid) and Niger (for World Wide Fund for Nature). The range of projects we have supplied covers orphanages, mobile vaccination units, anti-locust, anti-poaching, preservation of rhinos and gorillas, park reconnaissance, food distribution, water drilling, mobile workshops; the list is endless. Impressive funds have been raised to donate to charities but there were some hard lessons to learn. An instance in the early days of Band Aid was when a supplier (since gone out of business) sent a petrol Land Rover to Ethiopia accompanied by nothing but diesel spare parts! Buyers from even the major aid organizations have also had a lot of homework to do on 4 x 4 vehicles, and we have learnt that the supplier's role can be one of great responsibility: the more trust the buyer is able to have in the supplier, the better prepared the vehicle will be for the job in hand, which entails close

Band Aid Land Rovers in Addis Ababa.

Frankfurt Zoological Society Land Rover during anti-poaching control in Serengeti National Park.

Frankfurt Zoological Society workshop Land Rover in background, with Land Rover transporting water tank to ranger post.

High capacity pick-up – a very underrated Land Rover product.

Norwegian Church Aid Land Rover in southern Sudan.

involvement with the end-user, and regular feedback. Agencies like CAFOD, who send Land Rovers to the most desperate regions, are tireless in reporting back to us, and such communication means they get better service from the vehicles.

Land Rover's Export Service department, which has built up an excellent reputation, is always glad to offer the benefit of its collective knowledge to sort out any unusual or sticky problems, but their task is made doubly difficult by Land Rover's diminishing in-field presence in Africa, for instance, where it is simply uneconomic to maintain a comprehensive parts network. That the African market will eventually build up again to justify such a network, makes the current dilemma worse for Land Rover because it has to keep a foot firmly in the door, to stop it closing.

Supporting aid projects with Land Rovers is like mounting expeditions with Land Rovers, in that the vehicles must be as self-sufficient as possible – unlike the much publicised rally vehicles that have massive back-up from the manufacturer for the ensuing kudos.

*   *   *

Some years ago, Land Rover Limited asked us to amend and revise the *Guide to Land-Rover Expeditions* that they had found necessary to compile in answer to the quantity of enquiries and requests for information – and, inevitably, sponsorship – regarding the use of Land Rovers on expeditions. As it contains a great many points of general interest, we have seen fit to include this Guide here.

A GUIDE TO LAND ROVER EXPEDITIONS:

The number of overland journeys and expeditions using Land Rovers, and now Range Rovers, increases every year, and the scope of projects tackled in difficult terrain is ever-widening, but to successfully achieve their objectives these projects require meticulous preparation and planning: the more knowledge that is gathered beforehand, the greater the economy will be in expense, time and effort, not to mention the safety factor. The purpose of this Guide is to help expedition-planners to avoid some of the pitfalls and to protect their vehicle investment.

Body Style: Now that car tax has been abolished, it gives the expeditioneer a better opportunity to buy the vehicle that suits his budget and his plans for the trip. For example, you no longer have to buy a 12-seater, you can have a cubby box in the middle, or you can buy a Hard Top with side windows. For full information on any problems you have regarding this, contact HM Customs and Excise at VAT Office, Northgate House, 1 Remnant Street, Lincoln's Inn Fields, London WC2A 3JH.

General: There is always a tendency to take too much equipment, thereby over-loading the vehicle. The recommended maximum axle loading, as specified in the Land Rover Manual, should be taken seriously: it is important to remember that the lighter the vehicle is, the faster and more economical it will be to run, and the longer it will last. It is not recommended that a trailer be taken but, if considered necessary and cross-country driving is anticipated, the trailer should be fitted with wheels as large as possible to reduce rolling resistance. It is a good idea to use the same size wheels and tyres as fitted to the vehicle. If consideration is given to a roof rack, it should only be used for carrying light-weight, bulky items, evenly dispersed, the normal maximum loading for a Land Rover being 150 lb (inclusive of the roof rack). A Land Rover Station Wagon can be modified to take a heavy-duty roof rack by strengthening the bulkhead and windscreen, and fitting internal tie-bars at top and bottom of rear seats; external reinforcing bars should be fitted from roof rack to side body panels or side jerry can holders. Here we would like to stress there is a tendency for expeditions, government bodies, even Aid people to fit extra fuel tanks inside the rear of the vehicle. If this is done, please check that it has been approved and, more importantly, tested, because if you do have problems with a tank like this, Land Rover is not liable for any Warranty work or damage or loss caused whatsoever. For extra storage inside, rear seats can be removed, and a plastic mesh partition can be fitted behind second-row seats to prevent the load in the rear from being thrown forward over uneven ground.

If the expedition is to a hot climate with a hard-top Land Rover, a tropical roof is highly recommended to shield the vehicle roof from direct sunlight in daytime, and retain heat during cold nights. Alternatively, a complete Station Wagon roof assembly comprising roof (with Alpine lights and ventilators), tropical roof panel, trim and interior light can be fitted to hard-top models. There is no cost difference between left-hand and right-hand steering if purchased in Britain, so if the vehicle is returning to Britain it is advisable to purchase a right-hand drive model, while if the vehicle is to remain overseas it is advisable to purchase a vehicle with steering on the appropriate side.

It is recommended that two, or possibly three, people should travel in a short-wheelbase, and four, or possibly five (if baggage is not excessive,) in a long-wheelbase Land Rover. The more people per vehicle the less comfort, and with the numbers advised the payload should be near maximum including the personal baggage. These considerations, however, will be governed by the itinerary of the expedition and the distances to be covered on it.

Engines:

Land Rover engines in standard form can operate over an extremely wide temperature range, and for most expeditions modifications need not be considered. Contrary to popular belief, oil coolers are not required on 4-cylinder Land Rover models, unless the vehicle is to be used to drive ancillary equipment whilst stationary. The following ambient temperatures at which the standard Land Rover can normally be started and operated are given for guidance:

> Minimum: Petrol models: —30°C (—22°F)
>
> Diesel models: —30°C (—22°F) (subject to low temperature
> fuel availability)
>
> Maximum: 2.25 litre petrol engine: 48°C (118°F)
>
> 2.6 litre petrol engine: 45°C (113°F)
>
> 2.25 litre diesel engine: 40°C (104°F)

Note: These maximum temperatures are for a vehicle operating continuously at peak torque second gear high transfer (ie representative of a vehicle working in soft sand or towing a heavy trailer up a hill). Under lighter load conditions the Land Rover can operate in ambients of about 50+°C (122+°F).

When driving in high ambients the driver must always keep a close watch on engine temperature and coolant levels, and if the vehicle is to be used for driving ancillary equipment the 4 x 4 Special Projects Department, at Solihull, should be consulted.

In areas which have higher ambient temperatures than Europe, oil coolers should be considered for 6-cylinder and diesel Land Rovers.

A heavy-duty cooling specification is available ex-works for 2.25 litre petrol engined Land Rovers for use in ambient temperatures above 48°C (118°F), comprised of fan, radiator cowl and shroud as fitted to 2.25 litre diesel units. It is essential to use only high grade fan belts with this feature.

Advantages of the Petrol Engine Versus the Diesel Engine

1. Higher power and torque output
2. Higher maximum speed
3. Quieter (can be relevant when travelling in areas such as wildlife parks to reduce disturbance of wildlife)
4. Lighter
5. Generally more easily understood
6. Less expensive to purchase

7.　As a fuel, petrol is cleaner and less pungent to handle
8.　Petrol is usually easier to obtain

Advantages of the Diesel Engine Versus the Petrol Engine
1.　No ignition system (beneficial when wading or when fire risk exists)
2.　Fuel generally less expensive
3.　Fuel consumption considerably better
4.　Better low-speed torque, good in soft sand

Government Tourist Offices and Embassies can usually supply a list of petrol and oil prices appertaining to most parts of the world, and also indicate where fuel is difficult to obtain. In some countries fuel coupons are available.

Preparation
Expeditions and long-distance journeys are best undertaken in new Land Rovers or Range Rovers, but if a second-hand vehicle is used it is essential that it be thoroughly overhauled and serviced by reliable mechanics before the outset: time and money is well spent on thorough pre-expedition servicing. Although there are Rover Distributors and Dealers throughout the world (see Appendices) it cannot be over-emphasized that the more remote the location the more difficult and expensive it is to obtain spares, and therefore a comprehensive spares kit should be taken.

Particular attention should be given to suspension and engine performance. Faulty suspension may, in the course of time, and depending on the nature of the terrain traversed, cause structural and mechanical damage. Reduced engine performance and poor compression may lead to other defects besides loss of power. Tell-tale oil leaks should be examined and rectified and all nuts and bolts securely tightened at the earliest opportunity.

It is most desirable that drivers should possess sufficient mechanical aptitude and knowledge of their vehicle to perform servicing and repairs, often to be carried out in adverse conditions. A vehicle handbook and workshop manual are *essential* and can be obtained from Rover Dealers and Distributors.

Vehicle Extras: When preparing a vehicle for an expedition the following items are desirable (those items marked * are required only for arduous off-road conditions):

9½-inch diaphragm spring clutch (standard on current models)*
Door locks
Bonnet lock
Locks for spare wheel on bonnet
Lock for fuel filler
De-luxe seats
Spare wheel carrier on bonnet
Deluxe trim for doors and floors

Capstan winch with 50ft of rope (preferably manilla, but keep it dry so that it does not rot)*
Covers for propeller shaft universal joints (for use in grassland)
Fire extinguisher
Reverse lamp kit
Seat belts
Sun visors
Wire mesh guards for all lights
Laminated windscreens
Extra fuel tanks (available on special order only)

Bo Slavin drives NAS 90 in Mexico, 1993.

Extra containers for petrol and water may be carried. Metal or plastic jerry cans containing water can be fitted in the radiator recess (not on V8 model) although this may interfere with the fitting of other equipment (chaff guards etc). (Front-mounted jerry cans should not be used to carry fuel due to fire hazard in the event of front-end collisions.) Jerry cans cause a restriction in air flow to the radiator which may result in overheating in very hot climates; drivers must watch the engine temperature closely, particularly with diesel and 6-cylinder petrol models. Jerry cans carried inside the vehicle should be properly secured, care being taken with regard to fire hazard. In some countries it is illegal to carry fuel inside the vehicle. Plastic cans should never be used for carrying fuel. (The usual place for carrying extra fuel is either in roof-mounted jerry cans or in side-mounted jerry cans, but it should be noted that each jerry can full of petrol weighs approximately 50 lb.) Provision should also be made for carrying adequate supplies of oils, distilled water, brake fluid, etc.

Non-Rover Equipment:
> Roof rack
> Side jerry can holders
> Front jerry can holders
> Sand ladders for desert use
> Internal load nets
> Reinforcement of chassis, windscreen frame and bulkhead*
> Internal reinforcing bars*
> External reinforcing bars*

When extensive cross-country usage is contemplated with permanent pay-loads in excess of 500 lb (88-inch models) or 1,500 lb (109-inch models) heavy duty suspension is advisable. Under normal circumstances, with a high proportion of light-load duty on metalled roads, heavy duty suspension gives a harsh ride, so on the return of the expedition it may be considered more suitable to refit standard springs.

A hydraulic steering damper is available to reduce 'steering kick' and is advisable for long distances on rough roads. A propeller shaft universal joint cover should be fitted for use in long grass. After wading in mud or muddy water, cleaning out the brake-drums will prolong brake-lining life.

Chaff-guards restrict air flow to the radiator, so should only be fitted where essential, eg for operating in long grass where seeds may clog the radiator.

All vehicles should be fitted with safety harnesses, though for cross-country driving the lap-and-diagonal type harness may be uncomfortable; using just a lap-strap type gives greater mobility and comfort.

A loud and penetrating horn is necessary in many countries.

Flyscreens on dash vents are essential in tropical climates, and come as standard on Series III and V8 models.

Locks on doors, spare wheels, petrol cap, jerry can holders and bonnet deter pilfering.

External mirrors, of the 'springback' boomerang type, are advisable when visibility through rear view mirror is obscured by baggage inside.

De-luxe seats greatly increase comfort, improve support for the driver, and are strongly recommended for long journeys.

2¼ petrol-engined vehicles have alternative carburetter jets available for prolonged use above altitudes of 5,000 ft, while for low altitudes it is essential to refit the standard jet to prevent engine damage due to the weak fuel/air mixture.

Painting the bonnet and top of the wings matt black reduces dazzle in bright sunlight, but also increases absorbtion of solar radiation thus increasing under-bonnet temperature.

Tyres: As an all-purpose tyre does not exist, the tyres must be selected for the predominant terrain. Information regarding some Land Rover approved tyres is given below:

Standard tyres,	Suitable for all road and track
Dunlop RK3 or	usage and cross country terrain
Avon Ranger:	in favourable conditions.
Michelin XZY:	Road and track use together with rough terrain.
Dunlop T28 or	Rugged rough terrain, mud and
T29A (Trakgrip):	other difficult conditions.
Michelin XS:	Desert of all types – soft sand, scrub or rock. (Grip on wet tarmac not outstanding.)
Michelin XL:	Available in 6.50 x 16-inch size, for mud conditions.

On 88-inch models, fitting the 109-inch type 7.50 x 16 inch tyres and wheels can be advantageous, giving higher overall gearing and increased ground clearance (subject to Rover approval).

A spare wheel – weight approx 75 lbs – can be carried on the bonnet, or on a roof rack, but for rough cross-country driving a spare wheel mounted on the rear door is not recommended as its weight damages the efficiency of the door catch and lock and distributes weight unevenly.

An extra inner tube and self-vulcanizing puncture repair outfit with a clamp is recommended. For emergencies, sleeve patches are useful for making temporary repairs in case cracks develop in the tyre wall. Always use metal dust caps as, unlike the plastic type, these will form an air seal. Other useful items available from Schrader Ltd are:

5-in-1 valve repair tool
Valve core kit
Electric pump (essential for diesel models)

The latter two are extremely useful, as manually inflating large tyres in hot conditions can be very exhausting.

If driving in conditions where night temperatures are low and midday temperatures are high, correct tyre pressures should be set before starting in the morning, and not bled during the day, as damage could result. Pressures return to normal when the temperature drops at night.

Lowering tyre pressures to 75 per cent of normal can give superior traction and flotation in soft sand or mud, but it is essential that only very slow speeds are used in these conditions, that great care is taken around obstacles, and that tyres are re-inflated after the soft patch is past. Failure to re-inflate will result in tyre overheating and blow out. A 20 per cent overload can reduce tyre life by as much as one-third!

General: A tow rope (tested to at least 2 tons) and shovel are recommended. The rope should be at least 100 ft long so that the towing vehicle can maintain a reasonable distance between it and the vehicle to be recovered. An extra fold-up trenching tool is light and takes up little room. Military-type shovels are recommended for serious recovery work. Towing points on the front and rear of the vehicle can be useful.

Some expeditions have found a hand throttle useful, which at one time was standard on diesel Land Rovers.

A winch is most useful in an emergency. Some form of anchorage, such as trees or rocks, is of course a necessary adjunct in winching. The front Capstan winch, with 3,000 lb pull, is generally satisfactory for self-recovery, obstacle removal, etc. The winch is protected by a sheer pin to prevent damage through overload, and several should be taken. A drum winch is easier to use, but dearer and heavier than the Capstan winch, and usually has limited cable length. When fitting a winch it is also advisable to fit diesel front springs because of the extra front end load.

A fire extinguisher of at least 1 kg capacity, preferably larger, is essential and should be stowed in an easily accessible place.

For improved ventilation the top half of each front door can be removed on older models by undoing two nuts.

For long distances on good road surfaces free-wheeling hubs may be considered. The function of these is to reduce the rolling resistance of the vehicle when 4-wheel drive is not required. They isolate the front wheels from their drive shafts and transmissions both in forward and reverse directions.

If severe sand storms are encountered the radiator grille should be covered when stationary to prevent blockage by sand. The windscreen should also be covered to avoid sand abrasion which could render it opaque and the vehicle should be positioned with its back to the wind, also to protect the screen.

For travelling 'off the beaten track' the following extra equipment is worth taking:

    Set of socket spanners
    Electrical screwdriver
    Valve lifter or spring compressor
    Pin punch

Feeler gauges, 0.0015-inch to 0.025-inch
Hammer, 1 lb
Large mole grips
Chisel
Small magnet with bar
Hand drill with bits
Brake bleeding kit
Inspection lamp and extension lead
Steel tape (metric and imperial)
Hacksaw and spare blades
Flat file, smooth and rough
Round file
Box spanner, 1⅛-inch x 1¼-inch Whitworth
Oil can
Box of assorted nuts and bolts, screws and hose clips
Length of electrical wire and electrical connecters
Large flat metal drip tray for mechanical repairs
Long nose pliers
Roll of electrical insulation tape
Roll of masking tape
Tyre levers
Puncture repair outfit and spare inner tubes
Radiator sealer (emergency use only)
Fibreglass repair kit and filler for repairing tanks, sumps etc
Assorted strands of welding wire
A hydraulic jack may be substituted for the standard jack
Flat plates to support jack on soft ground
An axe
Length of flexible petrol pipe
Penknife

For touring, the following may be of assistance:

Petrol Touring Pack

Description:	Quantity:
Decarbonizing gasket set	1
Spark plugs	1 set
Spark plug covers	2
Spark plug cover seals	2
Distributor contact set	1
Distributor cover	1
Rotor arm	1
Condenser	1
Coil	1

Petrol pump (electrical or mechanical)	1
Fan belt	1
Flexible petrol pipe	1
Brake fluid	1 can
Bulbs	1 set
Wiper blade	1
Exhaust valve	1
Puncture outfit	1
Schrader valves	1
Fuses	1 set
Set of water hoses	1
Oil filter and joint washer	1
Front and rear main spring leaves	1 of each
Spring bushes	3

Diesel Touring Pack

Description:	Quantity:
Decarbonizing gasket set	1
Fuel lift pump	1
Fan belt	1
Flexible fuel pipe	1
Brake fluid	1 can
Wiper blade	1
Bulbs	1 set
Exhaust valve	1
Puncture outfit	1
Schrader valves	2
Fuses	1 set
Set of water hoses	1
Oil filter and joint washer	1
Injector	1
Heater plugs	2
Fuel filter element	1

Tyres: It is essential to start the expedition with good quality tyres – and to exercise great care in traversing rocky ground (see also remarks on tyre pressure). With this proviso it is not necessary to burden the vehicle with more than one spare wheel and cover. An extra spare inner tube, a comprehensive tube and cover repair kit and a set of long tyre levers is essential. If the vehicle is old, it is worth having the covers removed before departure (to break the grip of a rusty rim) and put back using tyre lubricant: the benefit will be felt the first time you have to repair a puncture in the field.

Maintenance

Routine inspection of the vehicle should be carried out right from the start.

Daily checks are imperative: a few minutes spent checking for oil leaks and the tightness of nuts and bolts can prevent a major break-down later. It is advisable to stop for the evening early enough to complete the end-of-day inspection before dusk.

The Handbook for the appropriate model of Land Rover indicates the full scope of routine checks and lubrication to be carried out and these should be adhered to. More frequent inspection of sparking plugs is recommended in countries where only inferior grade fuel is available. In such countries it may be necessary to retard the ignition in accordance with the details given in the Instruction or Workshop Manuals. Lubrication checks must be scrupulously observed – failure to do this may cause irreparable damage. In sandy conditions more frequent oil changes are recommended. Fuel obtained in these areas is frequently dirty; extra filtering may be necessary when filling the tank.

Garage and service facilities in most under-developed countries usually fall short of British standards. Although mechanics are often quite good, it is advisable to supervise all repairs. In many countries the village blacksmith is the only person who can undertake structural repairs, but it is surprising how effective they can be. Since spare parts may be hard to come by, improvisation is often necessary.

Hints on cross-country driving
When a Land Rover is used cross-country, regular inspection and maintenance is vital. Wear and tear is greater than on normal roads, and although the increase can be kept to a minimum by a good driver, special attention must be paid to ensure that the vehicle is operating correctly.

The following notes are intended as guidance on some of the more important aspects of driving technique which in the end, of course, only experience can perfect.
1. Adopt a relaxed, upright sitting position ensuring that the safety belts are correctly adjusted. Maintain a firm grip on the steering-wheel but do not attempt to 'fight' violent steering-wheel movements: allow the wheel to slip through your fingers.
2. Never wrap your thumbs around the steering-wheel rim. If the vehicle hits an obstacle the steering-wheel could be jerked so hard that the spokes could catch and break your thumbs. This lesson has often been learnt the hard way!
3. It is generally desirable to use 4-wheel drive in conditions of poor adhesion. When on rocky corrugated surfaces, 4-wheel drive can sometimes be useful even in high range. It will halve the shock-loading on the rear half shafts and also give surer grip. It should be borne in mind that transmission 'wind-up' can occur between front and rear axles resulting in excessive tyre-wear. When the low range of gears is selected, 4-wheel drive is automatically engaged. Contact between the right foot and the adjacent body (side) panel will improve accelerator pedal control.

4. Where the conditions are soft, ie marsh or sand, reduced tyre pressure will increase the contact area of the tyres with the ground, which helps to improve traction and to reduce the tendency to sink. Tyre pressures should, of course, be brought back to standard when such situations have passed.

5. Where conditions appear particularly difficult, the shape of the ground surface with possible obstacles should be determined by a preliminary survey on foot, and a path selected, thus reducing risk of damage, or 'bogging-down'.

6. Before attempting a difficult section, select a suitable gear and remain in it whilst crossing. For most purposes second gear, low range, is very practicable.

7. Keep the application of the clutch and brake pedals to a minimum. For descending steep and slippery slopes select the same gear as you would use to go up; allow the engine to provide the braking retardation, which it will do easily without the assistance of the brakes. Braking on slopes, or selecting too low a gear, can induce sliding and loss of control.

8. Apply the accelerator pedal cautiously as sudden power surges may induce wheel spin.

9. The momentum of a fast moving vehicle will overcome drag and reduce the traction needed from the wheels. When it is clear that no obstacle is in the way to cause damage, a fast approach to steep slopes, soft sand, waterlogged sections etc is often the most effective, but even a Land-Rover will break if grossly overstressed.

10. Bearing in mind the action of differentials, select a path so that the condition under each wheel of the same axle is similar. The same applies in determining the correct angle of approach to an obstacle to avoid wheels being lifted off the ground.

11. Be aware of the need to maintain ground clearance under the chassis, and a clear approach and departure angle. Avoid existing deep wheel ruts, sudden changes in slope, obstacles etc, which may interfere with the chassis and/or differentials. If there is any danger of under-vehicle damage in severe sections, have your passengers get out and marshall you through; they can see all parts of the vehicle and clear you over rocks.

12. The maximum advisable fording depth is 1½ feet (0.45 metres). Before fording make sure the clutch housing drain plug is in position and, if the water is deep, remove the fan belt and avoid overspeeding of the engine to prevent saturation of the electrical system, although if the exhaust pipe is submerged engine speed should be high enough to prevent stalling. Sometimes a sack over the engine (well clear of the fan belt) will keep it dry enough to survive bad spray. There are many water repellent agents on the market which are extremely effective in protecting the ignition system.

13. After being in water, make sure the brakes are dried out immediately, so that they are fully effective when needed again. This can be accomplished by driving a short distance with the foot brake applied. Also remove the clutch housing drain plug. If the ford has been unexpectedly deep, check the air cleaner for water ingress. Bear in mind that deep or prolonged fording in cold

water can cool the air space above the axle oil enough to suck in water through the breather. A subsequent check of the oil condition is worthwhile.

14. Should it be found that the vehicle is immobile due to loss of wheel grip, careful thought and practical experience will usually provide the solution to this problem, but improved driving technique will in itself ensure that such instances are kept to a minimum or avoided completely. Driving practice in 'impossible' conditions is highly desirable before leaving on a journey.

The following hints will be useful:

Where the vehicle is fitted with a winch, recovery becomes relatively straightforward. Avoid prolonged wheel spin as it only makes matters worse. Additional resistance to the spinning wheels must be provided by some means. Attempt the removal of any obstacles, ie rocks, parts of trees, etc, which may also involve the clearing of earth piled in front of the wheels, bumper or chassis. Resist the temptation to skimp the digging in a recovery situation! A few minutes extra work will ensure a 'first time' recovery. Part or complete removal of the payload, or the equalizing of front and rear axle loads, can improve traction.

If the ground condition is very soft, reduced tyre pressures will give an improvement in adhesion.

Clogged tyre treads should be cleared.

Reverse as far as possible; the momentum gained in going forward again

A bogged-down Land Rover on the beach where the Sahara meets the Atlantic. Shovels have been judiciously placed to denote the position of sand-ladders beneath the surface.

may get the vehicle over the obstacle.

Brushwood, sacking, or any similar 'mat' material placed in front of the tyres will help in procuring tyre grip. If necessary, jack up the vehicle to place material under the wheels. Avoid the exhaust when placing brushwood, as heat can start up a fire.

15. In soft sand or marsh conditions avoid following the tracks of the preceding vehicle; the crust of extra load bearing ground will have been broken.

16. When sand-ladders are required for traction to free a vehicle from being bogged down in soft sand, the following should be borne in mind: (a) with Series II Land Rovers, care should be taken not to damage the exhaust system with the ladder; (b) removing the sills from the sides of the Land Rover facilitates use of sand-ladders; (c) note where the ladders are placed in the sand, as once the vehicle is clear they can be well submerged and time can be wasted in searching for them.

17. In sand dunes always recce on foot if in doubt. Dangerous surface angles can be obscured from view when the sun is overhead. Steep slopes should be avoided.

18. When negotiating difficult terrain two vehicles are better than one, as they can assist each other, particularly if one or both are fitted with winches. Always get one vehicle across an obstacle before attempting it with the second.

19. Land Rover's own book, *The Land Rover Experience* written by Tom Sheppard is worth taking with one on an expedition. (Land Rover Part Number STC.8545.AA, £15.99.)

General Information

Visas: In some countries travel and visas are restricted. If you have doubts you should check with the Embassy concerned *well in advance* of your departure date. Vehicle customs carnets are required before entry is permitted to some countries. Up to 100 per cent of the value of the vehicle may have to be guaranteed by the carnet issuing agency. This is payable as customs duty in the event of the vehicle being sold or otherwise disposed of in the territory. Carnets are obtainable through the RAC or AA or your local Chamber of Commerce. Also make enquiries regarding unusual local entry regulations.

Information concerning visas, health and currency regulations, customs and climates, etc, can be obtained from a booklet entitled *Guide To International Travel* available from: ABC Travel Guides Ltd,
                    33-40 Bowling Green Lane,
                    London EC1.

Routes: Transcontinental routes are many and varied. Seasonal weather changes will influence which route to choose, eg some roads are impassable during the rainy season. Delays due to predictable weather conditions are most frustrating. A compass is a useful item to carry.

International road information can be obtained from:

The Royal Automobile Club,   The Automobile Association,
Touring Services,   Overseas Touring,
PO Box 92,   Fanum House,
Croydon,   Basingstoke,
Surrey CR9 6HN.   Hants.

Local permission is occasionally required to follow certain routes, variable according to season, eg the north-south route across the Sahara.

All expedition drivers should learn the basic motoring laws of the host countries, otherwise an offence can be unwittingly committed, for which the penalties are sometimes very severe.

Maps etc: The RAC and AA can also advise on appropriate maps, but the following are especially recommended:

Bartholomew's World Series, scale 1:4,000,000
GSGS Map, scale 1:1,000,000
Carte Michelin

Embassies, Consulates and High Commissions often issue tourist maps and supplementary useful information.

Photography: Most expeditions take at least one good camera. A photographic dealer can advise on equipment, but the following tips may be helpful.

1. Be fully conversant with all your equipment and correct any faults before you leave. Read the instruction book before you leave (not when you come back!).

2. Insure your equipment adequately.

3. For 35mm users, a 36 exposure cassette is no larger than a 20 exposure cassette.

4. Excessive heat, sand, dust, and water (particularly sea-water) can quickly damage your camera and films. A polythene bag offers general protection, but remember that changes in temperature may cause moisture to condense on the inside of the bag. This danger may be eliminated by use of silicagel crystal

Sand ladders facilitate progress up soft dunes.

sachets which absorb the moisture, but the best precaution is meticulous care with blower and brush every night, as well as the use of polythene bags.

5. Have exposed film processed as soon as possible to prevent deterioration, particularly in humid conditions. Films purchased abroad can be of a different process rating to that supplied in Great Britain, so before developing, ensure that the correct rating is used for development.

6. When exposing a large amount of film without being able to have it processed on your travels, it is advisable to see the results of one early reel to confirm that the camera is working properly and the exposure is being judged correctly.

7. Keep sensitized materials in the manufacturer's containers as long as possible. Some customs checks use infra-red/X-ray detectors, and these can damage film negatives, so care must be taken.

8. Films and cameras must be kept cool; do not store in the footwells, parcel shelf nor leave on the seats in sunlight.

9. Particular care should be taken of lenses, since they are more likely to be contaminated with airborne grit in tropical conditions. A lens cap should be used when not filming. Plain glass in a filter mount is a permanent lens protector.

10. To get the best use out of your camera, take plenty of pictures. The more you take the more proficient you become, and you may never be there again.

11. Remember, in some countries even the most innocent of buildings or structures can be classed as 'of strategic importance', and respect the fact that some people object to having their photographs taken.

12. It may be cheaper to purchase photographic supplies in some foreign countries rather than in the United Kingdom. They can however sometimes be delivered free to ports of exit.

Domestic: Land Rover travellers are usually campers, and adequate equipment is therefore necessary, but as the equipment will naturally depend upon both the size of the party and its field of operation, to suggest an exhaustive inventory for all possible contingencies here would involve too long a list. However, weight and space are the most important factors – especially weight – so if in doubt, don't take it.

Care should be taken when loading the Land Rover to ensure correct balance, aiming for an even weight distribution. Stowage should be carefully planned to avoid rattles and clanks, unnecessary wear and tear on equipment and extra work involved in looking for mislaid items. A well packed rattle-free vehicle tends to encourage better driving.

Some suggestions are as follows:

A gas cooker of adequate size is probably the best type to use. A large gas reservoir will last for weeks with normal use. Petrol stoves are almost as convenient and fuel is readily available if commonized with the vehicle supply, but safety precautions must be scrupulously observed – accidents happen all too easily with petrol stoves. Unbreakable, light plastic containers with screw top lids and polythene utensils should be carried, avoiding glassware and breakable crockery. Mugs and bowls that stack into each other save space when packed.

An inflatable or Dunlopillo mattress, and a light camp (Safari) bed are comfortable and demand little storage space. Beware of sharp thorns with inflatable mattresses and pillows. Polythene closed-cell foam mats, such as Kampamats, are extremely light and surprisingly effective if weight is a problem. The better the quality of a sleeping bag, the greater the comfort – but select with a view to climate. Avoid sleeping bags with zips in deserts (ie sandy or dusty conditions). Washable bags are available, but cotton sleeping bag liners are recommended for reasons of hygiene. 'Space blankets' are efficient: light yet warm. Sleeping bags should be checked for spiders, scorpions, etc, before each use, as should shoes and boots.

A canvas groundsheet is very useful: for repairs under the vehicle in adverse ground conditions; as a sunshade or windbreak; to lash down stores on the roof; and to provide a clean floor for sorting out equipment, etc. A mosquito net that tucks under the sleeping mat keeps mosquitoes as well as other unwelcome insects at bay, and allows less covering up in warm temperatures.

Creaseless and non-iron clothes are a great boon, but they must be tough enough to withstand really hard wear and be appropriate to all climatic conditions expected.

Paper towels are more disposable and more hygienic than cloth towels where laundry facilities are limited. They have a hundred uses, from washing-up, to face flannels and washing cloths. Take plenty. Don't forget toilet paper, preferably flat-pack tissues.

A length of clothes line and pegs should be carried, and elastic straps for lashing down equipment inside the vehicle. A ball of strong string is also very useful.

Large Thermos containers for hot or cold food and drinks are most useful, but secure them properly.

A lockable container bolted securely to the inside of the vehicle can be used to carry valuables and documents.

A convenient way of washing clothes whilst travelling is to put them in a waterproof, sealed container in the back of the vehicle with a suitable amount of water and washing powder. After 100 miles they should be clean! Water for rinsing must of course then be available.

Food and Health: The following information is for the guidance only, and more specific details should be obtained from your own doctor, or from one of the Schools of Tropical Medicine, or specialized units in the country.

Foresight in equipping your medical chest sensibly can allay anxiety about health whilst you are abroad, and thereby add appreciably to your enjoyment of the trip.

Any left-over food at the end of the expedition is always gratefully accepted by local people. Spare medical supplies can be handed to any doctor or hospital.

Water: As a guide to the quantity to take, well-organized expeditions in hot desert areas allow approximately 2 gallons of water per person per day. Ambient temperatures above 105°F and/or prolonged exertion such as digging or climbing can cause consumption to rise alarmingly to 3 or 4 gallons per head. Cut usage in any other way but do drink all you need; the human body just will not work without enough water. Halazone, Aqua Clene, Sterotabs, or other water purifying tablets should be used if there is any doubt abut purity. Metal jerry cans should be treated before carrying water.

Food: There is no need to be unduly squeamish about eating strange dishes as they are usually prepared from the staple food of vast populations and can be eaten with enjoyment and benefit, provided certain precautions are observed. Generally all hot, well-cooked food is harmless; on the other hand cold food should be viewed with suspicion in hot countries, especially such things as shellfish, salads, and ice cream. Make sure that all food is fresh when purchased and cleaned before being eaten. In hot climates take additional salt.

Only a limited quantity of tinned food should be carried as an emergency supply because of the weight involved. There is an increasingly wide range of AFD (accelerated freeze dried), and dehydrated foods on the market these days; ready meals, vegetables, fruit, milk, desserts, etc. Provided adequate water is available en route, dried food is strongly recommended for weight-economy. Dried fruit should be included regardless of water supply as it can be eaten without re-hydration and contains vital vitamins.

An insulated box can be used to carry some foods or keep drinks cool, and portable 12-volt refrigerators are available for those who like 'Scotch on the Rocks'!

Health: Bowel upset: however much care is taken, this remains one of the commonest hazards of foreign travel. If in doubt, water should be boiled before drinking and the same applies to milk. One tablet of Streptotriad taken twice a day is a useful precaution, increasing the dose to three tablets three times a day if trouble arises.

Immunization: As soon as your travel plans are definite, you should consider your state of immunization in relation to the countries that you plan to visit. Try not to leave it to the last minute, thereby avoiding the risk of a strong reaction to a vaccine occuring during the early stages of the expedition. Time should also be allowed for a course of vaccinations prior to departure, eg a second cholera vaccination may need to follow the first after a two-week interval. Consult your doctor, the RAC, the AA, shipping companies, airlines, or the Embassy of the country concerned for information on compulsory immunization. If you are likely to travel overseas unexpectedly, it is worth adhering to a regular schedule to keep your immunization levels at a peak, and avoid last minute panic. Immunizations may generally be divided into the compulsory and the optional, but the latter may be regarded as a good investment, especially for the seasoned traveller. Your International Certificates should be presented to the doctor for signature, and should be countersigned by the local Medical Officer of Health.

Sunburn: Beware of the sun, particularly if you have a fair skin, until you have had time to acquire a protective tan. Reflected sunlight from water, sand or snow can burn the skin, and even if one is beneath an awning the sun's rays can penetrate.

There are many skin preparations on the market for the prevention and treatment of sunburn, and of these Skol or Sol Tan cream for application before exposure, and After-Sun lotion later, are probably as good as any. Considerable work has been done in recent years on the use of oral preparations to combat sunburn and for anyone who is especially susceptible, Sylvasun (a vitamin A compound) can be taken in a dose of two tablets at night for prevention, increasing if necessary to two tablets hourly until relief is obtained. For the highly sensitive, a barrier cream such as Uvistat is indicated. A good pair of polarized sun glasses, or well-fitting skiing goggles are advisable for driving in desert zones or in any bright or dazzling atmosphere. It is worth taking a spare pair.

Malaria: This disease is still epidemic in many parts of the world and if your journey is to involve even a transient stay in a malarial zone you should take a tablet of Paludrine 24 hours before you are due to arrive and then continue with one daily for a month after leaving the area. The usual anti-malarial precautions such as mosquito-proofing and the use of insect repellent should be observed at night.

Snake Bite: The danger of snake bite tends to be exaggerated. First aid treatment consists of reassurance and aspirin, while covering the bite with a cloth. It should be neither cut nor sucked, as there is a risk of infection and incisions may produce bleeding and damage to important tissues. The amount of venom injected can be judged by the swelling 10 minutes after the bite. If local swelling has appeared and medical treatment cannot be started within the hour, a firm but not tight (repeat not tight) ligature should be applied a few centimetres above the swelling using a cloth or handkerchief, and left on until the victim reaches the nearest hospital. The affected limb should be moved as little as possible to inhibit the spread of venom. Try to identify the snake to help the doctor find the appropriate antidote. Do not give the patient alcohol.

Heat Exhaustion: See 'water'. Thirst, headache, vomiting, cessation of sweating, increasing body temperature and, eventually, unconsciousness, mark the progression of heat exhaustion. Be alert to the symptoms. Regular and copious drinking of water will avert more serious problems. If body temperature rises, soak the patient's clothes to benefit from evaporative cooling. If vomiting precludes absorbtion of water, a saline drip and/or hospital treatment –quickly – will be necessary. Avoidance by drinking plenty is far better than the cure.

First Aid Kit: Take a small but adequate kit including a supply of sealed sterile dressings of various sizes, eye pads, Micropore Tape, several tins of 3-inch Elastoplast (which should be kept in as cool a place as possible), triangular bandages for use as slings, and an antibiotic preparation such as Fucidin ointment. A book on First Aid should be kept handy.
NB: It is generally advisable to take an extra supply of Aspirins to meet local demand.

General Comments: When travelling in remote areas where good medical care is unlikely to be near at hand, if you are prone to any particular ailment that responds to a specific drug, make sure that you take an adequate supply as it may be difficult to obtain, or sold in an unrecognizable form. If any illness develops after returning from abroad tell your doctor where you have been, as this may give a clue to the diagnosis.

Finance: Adequate currency should, obviously, be carried. American Express or Cook's cheques are commonly recognized by most foreign banks, and sterling bank notes or dollar bills command ready acceptance. Always make a note of travel cheque serial numbers and keep this separately, revising it as cheques are used, so that if cheques are lost the appropriate company can be notified immediately. In a few remote areas, only hard cash is acceptable. The overseas department of your bank will be able to offer advice on finance generally. The free market rate of exchange in some countries often differs appreciably from the official bank rate. Although profit can be made through dealing in this market, it is illegal and can lead to serious consequences. You should always find out the official bank rate of countries to be visited as it is often more advantageous to buy foreign currency in some countries than others.

For costing purposes it can be taken that the fuel consumption of the 4-cylinder and 6-cylinder petrol Land Rover should be about 12 mpg, of the V8 about 18 mpg, and of the diesel about 20 mpg. These figures include an allowance for any arduous conditions the expedition might encounter. Oil consumption for an engine in good condition should be at least 250 miles per pint.

Embassies and Consulates: While British representatives abroad will always assist in an emergency, this does NOT extend to lending money to disorganized travellers who cannot afford the return fare to the UK. Adequate funds must always be reserved to get you home from wherever you are in case you have to return in a hurry.

Documents: Particulars of insurance and documentation of the vehicle can be supplied by the AA or the RAC who can also advise concerning visas. Having all papers in order before starting the journey is highly recommended to avoid subsequent inconveniences and delays.

Where any doubt exists concerning visas, the appropriate Consular Authorities should be consulted.

Passport Photographs: Take some spare passport photographs since various countries, eg Afghanistan, require travellers to fill in supplementary forms on arrival for circulation and route permits, and possession of photographs of the right size will forestall possible delays.

Insurance: Arranging Land Rover insurance outside Europe is a complicated business. It is advisable to consult an insurance broker, as few insurance companies offer cover.

Comprehensive cover, if obtainable, would be exorbitant but third party excluding passenger liability need not prove too expensive. Passengers and valuables can be covered under separate policies.

Sponsorship: The Land Rover has been associated with expeditions for many years and the publicity to be gained from these and similar ventures is now minimal. Consequently, as a rule, any request for monetary or material assistance will not be considered.

Chapter 7
As It Is Now

So much for the Wilks brothers' stop-gap agricultural Rover for the farmer, intended only to tide the company over until more favourable conditions prevailed and they could look again to the serious and lucrative business of manufacturing their prestigious motor cars ... The intervening years have shown that, from the beginning, the Land Rover was here to stay. Having existed as a mere off-shoot of Rover cars for so long, Land Rover and Range Rover finally became a company in their own right in 1978, as Land Rover Limited. Under the umbrella of BL, it has its own sales and marketing team, a workforce of over 12,500 and an annual turnover of £380 million. To run the company, Sir Michael Edwardes – the then BL Chairman – chose Mike Hodgkinson as Managing Director, whose 5 year era saw dramatic improvements. In 1983 when Hodgkinson left he was replaced by Tony Gilroy, and man known to have a sharp concern for quality, especially in engineering, whereas his predecessor had been more of a finance man.

Ever since the late 1960s, Land Rovers had been losing ground through lack of capital, at a time when the value of the pound was low and the demand for 4 x 4s was rising fast. Mike Hodgkinson has said since that, 'if we hadn't had a 10 year sabbatical on product development, the overall picture of Land Rover might be looking altogether different.' But during these years, Land Rover and Range Rover production was fluctuating at between 50,000 and 60,000, and although a major investment was proposed in 1975 by Lord Ryder and his team, it was not to be implemented until 1978 after the massive shake-up of the management, when Mike Hodgkinson arrived on the scene. With his background of industrial economics and his enthusiasm for the product, he took the bull by the horns and started to make changes, recognizing at once that Land Rover was going to have to make up for lost time and step into the world of aggressive marketing, to counter the increasing threat of competition from overseas manufacturers. He managed to get final approval of the

The Land Rover 110 assembly line.

investment programme within a few months. The facilities available were largely directed towards product development, manifest in such strides forward as the 110-inch, the 2.5 litre diesel engine, the brand new 90-inch, not to mention the 4-door, automatic Range Rover, but productivity was also undergoing a shake-up. Since moving into the stream-lined, up-to-date North Works Plant productivity has doubled. The stream-lining hasn't stopped there either, as further 'centralisation' has since taken place with the re-opening of the former Rover Saloon car plant at Solihull, built in 1976 at a cost of 30 million pounds, at the time the most modern car assembly plant in Europe. Land Rover's management reckon that by getting the whole of its manufacturing operation on one site, closing down satellite sites in Cardiff and Birmingham (with an eventual loss of over 1500 jobs), the cost savings will amount to about 14 million pounds a year, while also radically improving

334

efficiency. Current MD Tony Gilroy says, "it is a once-in-a-lifetime opportunity... to replace a series of mainly very old, small, uneconomic plants with a single, integrated modern facility. It will improve our competitiveness significantly...".

It is reckoned that if Land Rover Limited had to stand alone it could not only survive but could finance its own development on normal commercial terms, since – apart from Unipart – it is the only self-contained business within BL to make a profit. Instead however, the Land Rover management has constantly to look over its shoulder to the parent company. Recent speculation has even suggested the possibility of the Land Rover company being sold separately, which indicates that whatever the destiny of BL proves to be, Land Rover Limited is destined to survive and grow, come what may.

Since the formation of Land Rover as a separate entity from BL, the workforce has seemed to identify more strongly with their product, and the old Land Rover loyalty is apparent throughout every department. Younger men now hold some of the key positions, but Mike Hodgkinson maintains that they have achieved the right blend of experience and youth, with a strong emphasis on teamwork, to which he attributes Land Rover's survival through the 1970s. This enthusiasm is reflected far less, unfortunately, in some of the larger Land Rover franchise holders in Britain. The under-developed countries benefit by

The ex-military Series II 88-inch Land Rover belonging to Norman Barrett (secretary of the Association of Rover Clubs), on a competitive safari course at Leighton Buzzard in 1978.

The aims of the Association of Rover Clubs include development of interest in all new Rover products, whether vehicles or optional extras, together with the organization of caravan rallies and 4-wheel-drive motor sport, ranging from gymkhanas and family vehicle trials through to full cross-country trials and speed events.

having Land Rover personnel on the spot to manage the sales for their specific region, bringing with them the commitment to the vehicle that the firm generates, but the off-hand and often ill-informed approach of many local agents does little to boost sales at home. In some cases their hands are tied, by having to handle diverse models of which Land Rover and Range Rover are but two, but as Land Rover Ltd, forges forward with new products, staying always in the front line of the 4 x 4 market, there is – in truth – no reason to make excuses for our home market agents. If 9 out of 10 blokes that you meet at Lode Lane can express so much interest in, enthusiasm for, and knowledge of the product, surely there is something sadly lacking in the method of distributing dealerships in the United Kingdom. In our experience, those franchise-holders entitled solely to sell Land Rovers and Range Rovers are a completely different breed from the run-of-the-mill dealers/distributors: their involvement with the product equals that seen at Solihull, and is, without question, reflected in their order books. It is a constant disappointment to us that a company with such high standards in almost all areas, should apparently care so little how it is represented on the home market. 1988: Since the above was written, Land Rover has made significant improvements in the quality of distributors in the UK. As we write the same process has begun to streamline their export houses, but sales have dropped dramatically in Africa and these houses will have to take on a wider responsibility. It is to be hoped that Land Rover uses the opportunity to have a fresh look at the export market projecting itself towards the future when the Third World market ripens again. Within Land Rover's structure, in-depth knowledge of the problems facing end-users in the Third World is still not a strong point but a crucial department here is now Export Service, who have striven to build up a liaison with the Sales people, in response to the criticism that Land Rover Sales personnel are unable to help with technical problems. Export houses ought to be specialised, each respective organisation having not only knowledge but first-hand involvement in the territories so that they can maximise the after-sales back-up. Clear policy on this now will ensure that Land Rover is geared to cope when Africa comes back on stream as a market.

Of all the 4-wheel-drive vehicles that have evolved in competition to the Land Rover, Toyota poses the biggest threat. Once the Japanese began producing 4 x 4s, it was only a matter of time before they started exporting to the developing countries where the importance of built-up cars was prohibited, but not of utility vehicles. Their network grew so fast that they are now the world's most prolific 4 x 4 manufacturers, with Toyota well in the lead. The trend towards increasing sales was helped immeasurably by the fact that the yen/sterling balance permitted Toyota to sell the Land Cruiser at between 10 and 60% per cent less than Land Rover could afford to sell their own vehicle for – but even this did not daunt Mike Hodgkinson. He commented at the time that as Land Cruisers are built with steel bodies that rust, and Land Rovers are built with aluminium bodies that don't rust, the Land Rover's life is at least one-third, if not two-thirds longer, and a lot of Land Cruiser buyers are now returning to Land Rovers.

Defenders and Discoverys in Cambodia. (Enterprise Oil)

337

Body frame assembly of the 4-door Range Rover in the new North Works.

Body assembly in the more spacious new assembly plant.

The new Land Rover engine building and assembly line.

Land Rover engine storage is now controlled by computer.

Every Land Rover engine is tested on a TV visual display unit.

Pallets are moved by robot stackers and conveyors.

Range Rover bulk stores.

Final assembly and inspection of the Range Rover.

The Jeep, the forefather of them all, and other American 4 x 4s, such as General Motors' Chevrolet 'Blazer', and Ford's 'Bronco', have all been suffering from a heavy drop in demand in the United States, particularly in the 'leisure sector', caused by major fuel price rises which have inhibited the use of thirsty 4-wheel-drive vehicles just for fun. Sales of all-wheel-drive vehicles in the United States fell dramatically in the early 1980s, including the traditional

Jeep. The prospects for the Jeep are encouraging, however, since it is virtually managed by the French firm of Renault, now joint-owners of the company with American Motors Corporation, and the new management's plans could spell closer-to-home competition for Land Rover. Nissan's 'Patrol' vehicle, and the Daimler-Benz 'Galaendewagen' (produced with Steyr-Daimler-Puch in Austria) are two of the more serious attempts to compete with Land Rover, but our opinion of the latter is that, considering all the enginering expertise that went into the mechanical functioning of the vehicle, it ought to have been dressed accordingly: the body-style leaves much to be desired, and the end product is in the Range Rover price bracket, while offering less than Land Rover comfort.

Whatever the competition comes up with, there are those sectors of the Land Rover's market that are fairly safe – six out of every ten Land Rovers are sold to military customers, for example – and as a workhorse it has the advantage of a long-established reputation. During the 1970s it became obvious that regular customers were not enough, and at the end of that decade the then MD, Mike Hodgkinson, stated that 'although our vehicles are arguably the best in their particular market sector, we are planning further developments on all fronts and I can promise a constant and steady development plan taking us right through the 1980s. Believing in progress by evolution, we are working hard on the next generation of vehicles, which will provide more comfort by advanced suspension, with increased wheel travel and better seating, together with improvements to visibility, braking and quietness – so the Land Rover will still be the best of the 4 x 4 worldwide workhorse range.' So far, so good. Even though he is no longer with the

A 110 on the new rolling road test cell at the factory.

company, his promise is holding good. Since he made that statement there have been a series of new developments emerging from the (very streamlined) Solihull premises, as detailed in the latter pages of Chapter 1, and in Chapter 4 regarding the progress on the Range Rover. In fact, a study of the entire Land Rover organisation as it is today would undoubtedly reveal that it is ready for anything: ready to tackle whatever competition might arise with their own advanced products, ready to manufacture at whatever rate the market demands with the technologically modernised and compact, efficiency-orientated factory, and ready to maintain their exceptionally high standards under the watchful eye of the quality-conscious Mr. Gilroy, and ready even to be denationalized as events demonstrated in the first weeks of 1988!

History has revealed that Land Rover's fortunes went through an exacting few years during the 1970s. The Third World recession hit here as hard as elsewhere, and radical measures were essential for there to be any way out of the doldrums, and any prospects for competitiveness in the 4-wheel drive world. When Tony Gilroy, a soft-spoken Irishman from Cork, became Managing Director following Mike Hodgkinson, his first target was to get the production operation streamlined by 1985, which included the closure of satellite factories and complete centralisation at Solihull, encompassing the ex-Rover Car works there, and modernising every aspect of the organisation. The success with which the company was steered out of its prolonged 'hibernation' can perhaps best be shown here as it was shown to us, at the long-awaited launch of the new "Ninety" in May 1984.

Eastnor Castle is an imposing nineteenth century baronial mansion imitating the fortified tradition, in sombre grey stone. It sits at the end of a close-cropped green valley, 'master of all it surveys'; the uplands are densely wooded ancient forest, and it is this delightful pocket of the West Country that Land Rover has the honour to use, by long-standing arrangement with the resident owners. We were ushered to a car park at the side then, somewhat circuitously, up stone steps inside a turret, along a parapet, and into the castle's Reception Room... through a window! At the presentation, in a darkened room guarded by gleaming suits of armour, it was announced that the purpose of the occasion was three-fold, but not until we were eventually herded down to the hall and out through the main entrance to the courtyard did the reason for our rather furtive initial welcome become really clear. The wide gravelled square, with the castle's keep beyond, was bedecked with spanking new shiny Land Rovers and Range Rovers, in the new colour range – dozens of them. Predominant was the 90-inch in all its forms, from basic soft-top pick-up to the pert and streamlined 'County' station wagon, and this was the first time any of us present had seen the machine close up. 110s were represented to show off all their new features, also for the first time, and Range Rovers to demonstrate that "luxury need not stop where adventure begins". We were invited to pick a vehicle and drive off, following the route as detailed in our brief, which was 35 miles or so of road and motorway; we found

342

ourselves in a 90-inch 'County' station wagon, with power steering, fitted carpets, unfamiliar windows, new dashboard, upholstered seats – and so on. Our destination was a hillside venue where we all changed vehicles. We hopped into a 90-inch hard-top diesel pick-up and were told to follow the route indicated by white dots, which led into the forest along an unmade lane which degenerated – by degrees – into crude track strewn with obstacles. There were four separate routes marked out to follow, weaving and writhing through the tangled undergrowth, each taking half an hour to an hour; white dots were the 'nursery slopes', through red and blue to black dots, which could only be tackled by those who knew just what they were doing as the course ploughed across flooded gulleys, up and down impressive inclines, through swirling mud like thick grey custard up to the door sills, and pivoting round hairpin bends at fearful angles.

Land Rover had marshalls discreetly posted at judicious points in case of dire distress, and at the end of each course we selected a different vehicle, getting a chance to test all the new models as well as the new features of existing models. At about midday all vehicles converged on a woodland clearing, fragrant with bluebells, baked potatoes and barbecued meat, for a restorative lunch, before chugging back into the wilderness to search (in vain) for terrain terrible enough to flummox these workhorses. Whatever we were driving, however, was unstoppable in the face of every hazard. We were particularly impressed by the ride and handling of the 2.5 diesel 90-inch, but also by the dramatic improvement in comfort, on all models, with the superb suspension. In such severe off-road conditions you expect to incur a few bumps and bruises to the body, but we couldn't have had a safer, smoother and better-supported ride, which was inconceivable in a 4-wheel drive vehicle only a few years ago. Throughout the day Land Rover's management team were on hand to chat over all aspects of their new products, and again we were struck by the guileless enthusiasm they all radiate. One of the ingredients contributing to the vehicles' success from its inception has been the camaraderie and product involvement of the work force at all levels, and this is as evident now, under the management projected by Tony Gilroy, as ever it was. He is a firm but quiet and agreeable man whose attitudes and high standards make him exactly the right person, leading Land Rover from the front, to steer it on to further strengths and an even brighter future towards the year 2000.

Since publication of the above we have been back across the Sahara with Land Rover aid convoys, in 1986 and 1987 sampling a cross-section of Land Rover vehicles. It was immediately obvious that Land Rover has surmounted one of its worst problems, quality control. Though irritating faults still exist, it has been interesting to see how quickly the company now acts to rectify the problems compared to the seventies and early eighties. The economically disastrous over-stocking of vehicles in the factory has also ceased, which had led to severe difficulties due to a great number of vehicles standing idle in the open, not for months but years in many cases.

As far as the future is concerned, we still say that from now to the end of the century the progress of Land Rover and Range Rover should be as interesting as it is exciting, and all the indications are that when we are all long gone, there will still be Range Rover and Land Rover derivatives doing a grand job in most of the countries of the world.

1994

Early in 1994 John Russell was appointed MD of Rover International, Chris Woodwark having left the Rover Group during the previous August. John Russell, who joined the company from Peugeot Talbot in 1986 as Land Rover's Marketing Director, had been Commercial Director for Land Rover prior to his move across to lead the Rover International team. Below, he explains how Rover International came to be structured:

> 'The Single European Market was a prime factor in shaping the organization of the Rover Group for the 1990s. The challenge, both within the European Community and the international arena, demanded a structure that capitalized on the needs of customers today and in the future.
>
> 'To meet that challenge, in the latter stages of 1991 a major restructuring of the commercial divisions within Rover was undertaken, resulting in the amalgamation of five separate organizations into just two very focused areas:
>
> • Rover Europe – responsible for developing the Rover Cars and Land

Armoured Defenders for EC monitoring in Bosnia.

Defender 110 fitted with hydraulic wheelchair lift for Cambodia Trust.

Rover franchises within the European Community and EFTA; and
• Rover International – responsible for Rover Group activities elsewhere in the world.

'Rover International consists of three separate but interlinked business units headed by Rover Group Chief Executive John Towers. These are:
• National Sales Companies of which there are three, based in North America, Japan and Australia.
• Business Development which has responsibility for technology and know-how transfer of both current and past product lines into overseas markets, and
• International Operations, with responsibility for the sale of built-up, semi knock-down and complete knock-down products into 20 markets world-wide, through a network of Partly Owned Distributors, Independent Distributors and Specialist Export Distributors.

'International Operations, while recognising the individuality of every market, focuses on five major geographical areas:
• Middle East and North Africa
• Central and Eastern Europe
• Central and South America

345

- Asia and Pacific Rim
- Sub-Sahara Africa

Each one is headed by a Regional Sales Director with a dedicated team of Area Sales Managers, based either in the UK or at regional offices at key centres around the world.

'This team travels over two and a half million miles a year to bring a hands-on approach to international markets. Throughout the world, Rover's global outlook, coupled with a local focus, is reaping huge dividends in the terms of enhanced image with the customer.

'The new structure has given a focus to the international markets that has allowed policies to be formulated and implemented on a world-wide basis. Programmes that in the past might only have been developed for the domestic market are now conceptualized for global application.

'This directly impacts upon performance and in 1993, in a world steeped in economic depression and civil unrest, sales were a staggering 90 per cent higher than in 1992 and immediate benefits are being reaped at a time when a medium to long-term platform is being established.

'Conquest programmes were developed in 1992 to penetrate competitive product fleets. International Operations emphasized product benefits, lifetime costings, tailored customer usage and finance packages linked to strong after-sales support, all of which has been rewarded with major orders for the Land Rover range. Contracts as far and wide as Poland, Bangladesh, Botswana, Russia, Qatar and Mauritius have been secured, and such international purchasing organizations as the United

K. & J. Slavin (Quest) Ltd Aid Convoy crosses the Sahara.

Crown Agents' Defenders on a road construction project in the West Indies.

Nations have acknowledged Land Rover as the preferred supplier in many markets around the world.

'In 1993, 30 new markets were opened or reactivated by Rover International and its aims now are to build upon success to date, but also to develop and implement longer-term programmes which meet the needs of the customer.'

In 1992 we attended a major International Distributor Conference in Morocco when Rover International set the tone and the pace for the remaining years of this century. The next such conference took place in Scotland at Gleneagles during February 1994, when the news that British Aerospace was selling off the Rover Group to BMW was still very hot.

The specialization that BMW favours will surely enhance the Rover Marque across the board in the years to come, improving the all-important sales figures and customer satisfaction at the same time.

The unswerving course that John Towers, Group Managing Director since the end of 1991 and now Chief Executive, has set for the company leaves no room for complacency. From a background of engineering he joined Land Rover in 1988 and as MD has brought a realistic, hands-on approach to the

British High Commission Defender station wagon outside the British Trade Library in St Lucia for the reintroduction of Land Rover to the Caribbean after 20 years.

business while setting high targets for the future. As long as John Towers is at the helm, the persistent weakness within British industry of middle management will continue to be challenged, and the product can only go from strength to strength. As their slogan goes, 'The Best 4 x 4 By far' – to which could be added, 'The 4 x 4 For Good – And All'.

Appendices

ROVER INTERNATIONAL DISTRIBUTORS

Abu Dhabi
Al Otaiba Group of Establishments
PO Box 467
Abu Dhabi
United Arab Emirates

Angola
Uniao Commercial Automovies
c/o Hull Blyth Angola
Avenida 4 Fevreiro No 23-R-C
Luanda
Angola

Argentina
Canley SA
Juan B. Palaa 369
(1870) Avellaneda
Pcia De Buenos Aires
Argentina

Bahrain
A A Zayani & Sons
PO Box 26332
Zinj Garage
Bahrain

Bangladesh
Multidrive Ltd
HR Bhaban
Kakrail
Dhaka 1000
Bangladesh

Barbados
Detco Motors Ltd
Bay Street
Bridgetown
St Michael
Barbados

Bolivia
British Motors Bolivia SRL
AV Arce 2798
Casilla 13529
La Paz
Bolivia

Brazil
Land Rover Do Brazil Ltd
Av Salim Antonio Curiati, 136
04690-050 Sao Paulo SP
Brazil

Brunei
Champion Motors (Brunei) Sdn Bld
Km 3 1/4 Jalan Gadong
PO Box 1702
Bandar Seri Begawan 1917
Brunei Darussalam
Brunei

Bulgaria
Car Trade Ltd
Blvd Tzar Boris III
No 126 Sofia 168
Bulgaria

Burundi
Old East SARL
BP 330
Bujumbura
Burundi

Chile
Commercial Explorer SA
Los Conquistadores 1700
Piso 23 Providencia
Santiago
Chile

British Cars SA
Los Conquistadores 2464
Providencia Santiago
Chile

Colombia
British Motors Colombia
Av 13 No 114-82
PO Box 25 12 07
Santafe De Bogota
Colombia

Costa Rica
Motores Britanicos – Costa Rica
Aptd 722-1150
La Uruca
San Jose
Costa Rica

Croatia
Anglo Croation Cars Ltd
11 Knowl Road
Mirfield
West Yorkshire
England
WF14 8DQ

Dominican Republic
Empire Motors
Ave John F Kennedy
Apartado 973
Santo Domingo
Dominican Republic

Dubai
Al Tayer Motors PVT Ltd
Al Garhoud Road
PO Box 7310
Dubai
United Arab Emirates

Ecuador
Autocom Ltd
PO Box 17-01-0069
Av Los Shyris Ygasper De Villarroel
Quito
Ecuador

Egypt
Technotrade SAE
10 Access Road
To Mokattam City
Cairo
Egypt

Ethiopia
Mitchell Cotts Ethiopia Ltd
Cotts House
PO Box 527
Addis Ababa
Ethiopia

Falkland Islands
The Falkland Islands Co Ltd
Port Stanley
Falkland Islands

Ghana
Rover Ghana Ltd
PO Box 2969
Accra
Ghana

Guadeloupe
Guadauto SA
Morne Vergain
Abymes 97110
BP 148, 97154 Point a Pitre
Guadeloupe

Guatemala
Britauto SA
Calzada Roosevelt 13-66
Zona 7
Guatemala City
Guatemala

Transequipos SA
10A Avenida 20-43
Zona 1
Guatemala City
Guatemala

Guyana
Guyana Stores Ltd
PO Box 372
Garage Division
13–15 Water Street
Georgetown
Guyana

Hong Kong
Dodwell Motors
15th Floor
Mita Centre
552–566 Castle Peak Road
Kwai Chung
NT
Hong Kong

Hungary
Landimex Trading & Marketing Ltd
Baross U110
H-1082
Budapest
Hungary

Valent British Motors Kft
PO Box 550
H1538
Budapest
Hungary

Indonesia
P T Java Motors
17 JL Kramat Raya
Jakarta - 10450
Indonesia
10002

Israel
Eastern Automobile Marketing Ltd
PO Box 20063
76 Petah Tikva Road
Tel Aviv 61200
Israel

Jamaica
John Crook Ltd
PO Box 21
5–13 Hanover Street
Kingston
Jamaica

Jordan
Said A Malhas & Sons Ltd
PO Box 177
Station Road
Amman 11118
Jordan

Jordan Automobile Company
PO Box 175
78 King Abdullah Street
Amman 11118
Jordan

Kenya
Land Rover Kenya
PO Box 30135
Nairobi
Kenya

Korea
Inchcape Korea Ltd
277-10 Seongsudong 2-Ka
Seongdong Ku
Seoul 133-120
Korea

Sam Song Industries Ltd
Joung Woo Building 1005/6/7
13–25 Youido-Dong
Seoul
Korea

Kuwait
Al Khalid Car Company WLL
PO Box 3777
Shuwaikh Industrial Estate
Safat
Kuwait
13038

Baharah Trading Co
PO Box 5869
Safat
Kuwait
13059

Lebanon
Avianco SAL
DR KH Chebli Building
Independence Avenue
PO Box 166171
Beirut
Lebanon

Macau
King's Motors Ltd
Avenida Venceslau de Morais
s/n/r/c 'BF' 'BG' e 'BH'
Centro Commercial 'Fat Tat'
Macau
GPO Box 1320

Madagascar
Jos Hansen & Soehne
Aussenhandelsgesellschaft MBH
PO Box 10 26 40
D 20018 Hamburg
Germany

Malawi
Halls Land Rover
Corner of Glynn Jones
& Livingstone Road
PO Box 368
Blantyre
Malawi

Malaysia
Land Rover Malaysia Sdn Bhd (HO)
8th Floor
West Wing
Wisma Tractors, No 7 Jalan SS 16/1
Subang Jaya
47500 Petaling Jaya
Malaysia

Edaran Oto Indah Sendirian Berhad
5 Jaian PJS 7/13
Bandar Sunway
46150 Petaling
Jaya
Malaysia

Martinique
Crocquet SA
BP 579 Kerlys
97207 Fort de France Cedex
Martinique

Garage Guitteaud
129 Avenue Abbe Lavigne
Terres-Sainville
97200 Fort de France
Martinique

Mauritius
Automotive Sales & Service Ltd
PO Box 1117
Edith Cavell St
Port Louis
Mauritius

Morocco
Smeia
47 Boulevard Ba Hamad
Casablanca
Morocco
203000

Mozambique
Tecnauto
Av da Olla 121
Caixa Postal 2510
Maputo
Mozambique

Nepal
Tara Impex
GA1-133 New Road
PO Box 596
Kathmandu 3
Nepal

New Caledonia
Nouvelle Compagnie SATMA
Routes des Portes de Fer
RT 13 Boite Postale 91
Noumea
New Caledonia

New Zealand
Motorcorp Holdings Ltd
550 Great South Road
Green Lane
PO Box 17-019
Auckland
New Zealand

Nigeria
Eurafric Trading Co
Cunard Building
Liverpool
England
L3 1HR

Allens
25 Creek Road
Apapa
Nigeria

Oman
Mohsin Haider Darwish LLC
PO Box 3880
Ruwi Muscat
Oman

Pakistan
Mansons Corporation
Nelson Chambers
1.1 Chundrigar Road
Karachi 1
Pakistan

Panama
British Motors
Edifico BMW Calle 50
Apartado 6-3597
El Dorado
Panama City
Panama

Papua New Guinea
Steamships Trading Company Ltd
PO Box 1070
Hubert Murray Highway
Boroko, Port Moresby
Papua New Guinea

Paraguay
Motores Britanicos ACE SAL
Lugano 452
Asuncion
Paraguay

Peru
Intermotors & Trading SA
AV Republic De Panama 2349
Santa Catalina Lima
Lima 13
Peru

Poland
Ascot Auto Co Ltd
Rydygiera 8
01-793 Warszawa
Poland

Qatar
Middle East Traders
PO Box 273
Doha
Qatar

Russia
J Hohermuth AG
PO Box EBNI 18
CW 9053 Teufen
Switzerland

EMH Automotive Ltd
Wold House
58 Easton Road
Bridlington
North Humberside
England
YO16 4DB

Rushen Trading
18/24 Westbourne Grove
London
England
W2 5RH

Rwanda
ETS Rwandais
BP 109
Kigali
Rwanda

Saudi Arabia
Saudi Rover
c/o Saudi Max Group
PO Box 4959
Riyadh
Saudi Arabia
11412

Arabian Automotive Company
PO Box 5111
Dammam
Saudi Arabia
31422

Singapore
Regent Motors Ltd
475 Tanglin Halt Road
Singapore
0315

Intra-Motors (S) PTE LTD
Alexandra
PO Box 20
Singapore
9115

Slovenia
Automotiv (Ljubliana)
SLO - 61000 Ljubliana
Robbova 2
Republic of Slovenia

South Africa
Associated Automotive Distributors
Corner Old Pretoria Road
Jek Park 1459
PO Box 6226
Johannesburg
South Africa 2000

Sri Lanka
Colonial Motors Ltd
297 Union Place
PO Box 349
Colombo 2
Sri Lanka

Taiwan
Sampo Automobile Corporation
7F 215 Sec 3
Nanking East Road
Taipei
Taiwan

Tanzania
CMC Motors Ltd
PO Box 1852
Azikiwe Street
Dar Es Salaam
Tanzania

Thailand
Thai Ultimate Car Co Ltd
371 Vibhavadee Rangsit Road
Phayathai
Bangkok
Thailand
10400

Trinidad & Tobago
Plentipart Ltd
Claire Street
Eastern Main Road
Laventille
Trinidad & Tobago

Tunisia
Société Le Moteur SA
Zone Industrielle
La Charguia
Tunis
Tunisia
2035

Turkey
Boronkay AS
Barbaros Bulvari No 81
Besiktas
Istanbul
Turkey

Otobus Karoseri Sanayi AS
Eski Londra Asfalti 20
34590 Bahcelievler
Istanbul
Turkey

Uganda
Cooper Motor Corporation Ltd
PO Box 2169
Kampala
Uganda

Uruguay
British Cars SA
La Paz 2052
11800 Montevideo
Uruguay

Vanuatu
Motor Traders Ltd
Box 1010
Port Villa
Vanuatu

Yemen
Al Rowaishan Invest and
    Development
Ali Abdulmoghni Street
Sana's
Yemen

Zaire
Land Rover Zaire
56B Avenue Du Flawbeau
Kinshasa
Zaire

Zambia
Motors Holdings Zambia Ltd
PO Box 30672
Cairo Road
South End
Lusaka
Zambia

Zimbabwe
Quest Motors Co Ltd
Simon Mazorodze Road
PO Box ST 395
Southerton
Harare
Zimbabwe

*MANAGING DIRECTORS OF THE
ROVER COMPANY*

The position of Managing Director of the Rover Company has been held by the following men since 1933:

1933 – 1956   Spencer B Wilks.
1956 – 1957   Spencer B Wilks and Maurice Wilks.
(Spencer Wilks was Chairman from 1957 until 1962, when he retired from the Chairmanship to become the company's President, which title he retained until his death in 1971.)
1957 – 1960   Maurice Wilks and George Farmer.
1960 – 1962   Maurice Wilks.
1962 – 1969   William Martin-Hurst.
1969 – 1973   A B Smith.
1973 – 1975   Bernard Jackman.
1975: Partial nationalisation of British Leyland, abolition of Rover as separate entity.
1978 – 1982   Mike Hodgkinson.
1983 – 1988   Tony Gilroy.
1989 – 1991   G Simpson.
1991 to date   John Towers.

Index

Terry Davey